Gendered Practices in Working Life

Edited by

Liisa Rantalaiho

Professor, School of Public Health
University of Tampere
Finland

and

Tuula Heiskanen

Research Director, Work Research Centre
Research Institute for Social Sciences
University of Tampere
Finland

Consultant Editor: Jo Campling

First published 1997 by
MACMILLAN PRESS LTD
Houndmills, Basingstoke, Hampshire RG21 6XS
and London
Companies and representatives
throughout the world

ISBN 0–333–61853–X hardcover
ISBN 0–333–61854–8 paperback

A catalogue record for this book is available
from the British Library.

This book is printed on paper suitable for recycling and
made from fully managed and sustained forest sources.

10   9   8   7   6   5   4   3   2   1
06   05   04   03   02   01   00   99   98   97

Printed in Great Britain by
The Ipswich Book Company Ltd
Ipswich, Suffolk

Published in the United States of America by
ST. MARTIN'S PRESS, INC.,
Scholarly and Reference Division
175 Fifth Avenue, New York, N.Y. 10010

ISBN 0–312–16367–3 (cloth)
ISBN 0–312–16368–1 (paperback)

Contents

v

Acknowledgements

We are grateful to a number of people and organisations for their support. This book is an outcome of a cooperative effort. That the research group had the opportunity to work together for several years was due to the grant given by the Finnish Academy. We want to express our gratitude to the Academy's Social Sciences Commission, and also to two departments of the University of Tampere, the Work Research Centre of the Research Institute for Social Sciences and the Tampere School of Public Health, for providing the necessary resources for our work. We are also indebted to Ms Laura Tohka, who translated a major part of the text into English (Chapters 3–8, 10–11), and to Ms Mary McDonald-Rissanen whom, as a native English speaker, we consulted in our language problems. We would also like to express our appreciation of the expert advice given by our consultant editor, Ms Jo Campling.

Foreword
Joan Acker

This book explores gendered practices in Finnish working life. I think of the concept 'gendered practices' as an intellectual tool useful in elucidating the processes through which social structure is reproduced. 'Practices', as used here, are the ordinary things that people do as they go about their daily activities. Complexly coordinated practices constitute the structures within which we live. Many practices are 'gendered'. That is, they are consonant with assumptions about differences between women and men and often, in their repetition, contribute to the reproduction of those differences. The notion of gendered practices, whether in paid work or in other activities, has emerged in feminist social science as part of the effort to understand how women's relative (within class and racial divisions) subordination is so often recreated even as it is changing.

This idea has, for me, roots in dissatisfactions, beginning in the 1970s, with the inadequacy of sociological theories, as well as of many feminist alternatives, for comprehending continuing gender subordination. For example, structural theories of sex segregation and the gender wage gap argued that these patterns result from interactions between many variables. Variables, however, are sociological constructs that interact only in a statistical sense. These statistical associations do not reveal how what we see as structures are actually produced, how these processes work. For that, we must look at concrete actions and activities, at the everyday practices of constructing labour forces and wage systems. Moreover, sex segregation should fade away and gender-based wage differences should decline, particularly in countries such as Finland, where a very high proportion of women are full-time wage-workers and where day-care and other family support services are available. Although the position of women has improved in such societies, gender inequalities still survive, often emerging in new forms even as social policies to reduce inequality are implemented. This historical tenacity of gender inequality indicated, I thought, a need for a better understanding of the concrete ways in which gender differentiations are produced.

An additional reason to rethink was the increasing recognition among feminists that there is no unitary 'woman' existing in a single set of patriarchal relations. Women live in different historical times, in different cultures, in different racial, class and ethnic contexts. A major question was, and still is, how should we conceptualise the intersections of these diverse phenomena?

One answer is that the intersections of structural processes can be found in concrete, everyday experiences of different women, in the gendered, racialised, class-influenced practices that constitute the material of their daily lives.

I began to think about gendered practices in my own work on comparable worth, the wage system of the State of Oregon, and efforts to change that system (Acker, 1989a). To interpret my material, I tried to identify characteristics of gendered practices in work organisations. A first characteristic is that difference in gendered practices is widespread in organisations. Although not everything that people do at work is imbued with gender implications, it is a reasonable assumption that such implications exist.

A second characteristic is that gender is embedded in practices and procedures. 'Embeddedness' implies deeply connected, almost submerged. Gendered assumptions may inform the classification of jobs, the level of wages or even the design of workplaces, tools and machinery. Gendered expectations affect the content of work. Work content is understood, and allocated, through images of gender, although what constitutes women's and men's work sometimes changes. Gender is embedded in hierarchy in several ways: men are almost always at the top and women are disproportionately at the bottom, while images of those who lead and manage represent a particular masculinity.

Gendered practices may be highly visible or substantially invisible. Visibility is relative and historically variable. Some gendered practices are invisible because they are so embedded in abstract, often written, procedures that they cannot be seen without close examination. For instance, the reasons for the gendered results of job classification and pay-grade systems only become visible as classification and wage-setting practices are examined in detail.

Invisibility is increased by the belief that organisational policies and practices are gender neutral. Organisations make rules, explicit or implicit, about such things as attendance on the job, behaviour at work and commitment to the organisation. These apply to everyone; they are apparently gender neutral. Often, however, such rules and the actual practices through which they are enforced assume a male worker who has minimal commitments outside the workplace. Those who cannot, or who are assumed to be unable to, abide by the rules are seen as less suitable for certain jobs and responsibilities. Of course, the less suitable are almost always women.

Gendered practices are always local in the sense that they take place in specific local places, but they are often shaped extra-locally and, thus, are part of the extended social relations of any society (see Smith, 1987). For example, in many countries national or centralised wage negotiations take place. The gendered practices of these negotiations shape local results, often lower wage gains for women than for men. Everywhere there are processes that maintain sex segregation, devalue women's work and define masculinity and femininity in work-appropriate ways. Gendered practices extend over national boundaries, particularly those of the Northern Euro-American countries. Extensive cross-national contacts produce similarities. For example, international firms sell management techniques which often contain gendered assumptions and content. One example is Hay Associates, an international consulting firm with a well-known job evaluation system, widely used as well as criticised for its gender bias (Steinberg, 1992). As this and other systems are adopted, the gendered practices embedded within them are instituted in new locations.

The globalisation of the world economy also stimulates new gendered practices based on local cultures. Many recent ethnographic studies of women's work provide a picture of diverse gendered procedures for organising work in the new world economy (for example, Rowbotham and Mitter, 1994). Women everywhere are relatively low-wage workers, but different practices maintain their status as a separate and cheap labour force, contributing to profits for local and transnational capital. Gendered practices do not fade away with competition in rapidly changing market economies, but persist and are reorganised, as these studies of Finland also demonstrate.

To think about these changes, we can fruitfully use the idea of structure as process – as multitudinous activities through which people produce, distribute, coordinate, regulate, organise and generally carry out the tasks of constructing social life. The idea of gendered practices helps us to see how this works.

Notes on the Contributors

Tuula Heiskanen is the research director of the Work Research Centre, a unit of multidisciplinary working life studies in the University of Tampere, Research Institute for Social Sciences. She is a doctor in psychology and has studied work organisations in both public and private sectors, in both male and female dominated branches. She has a long-term interest in international scientific cooperation. Her current interests focus on potentials of scientific research and knowledge in enhancing daily problem-solving in work organisations and professional practice.

Merja Kinnunen is a researcher in the Department of Sociology, University of Tampere. She has studied white-collar work and the social construction of statistical information, and works actively in feminist social science publishing in Finland.

Riikka Kivimäki is a researcher in the Work Research Centre in the University of Tampere. Her guiding research interest has been to study the relationship of the spheres of work and family, in close cooperation with Nordic colleagues.

Päivi Korvajärvi is a researcher in the Work Research Centre in the University of Tampere. She has extensive experience on follow-up studies in clerical and white-collar work, and through her studies she has contributed to the public discussion on working life transformations.

Riitta Martikainen is a researcher in the Finnish Ministry of Labour, where her activity has served to promote gender sensitivity. Her research interests focus on gendered processes in collective bargaining systems.

Liisa Rantalaiho is a professor of sociology and psychology of work in the School of Public Health, University of Tampere. She has studied gender in working life from the aspects of technological change, class position and welfare state systems. She has been involved in feminist research, networking and politics both in Finland and in international contexts. She is presently interested in the relationships of gender, citizenship and national identity.

Leila Räsänen is the general secretary of the Finnish Council of Equality. She has been active in the Finnish women's movement since the 1960s and participated in the campaigns for day care, abortion law and parenthood leaves. She has close Nordic contacts both in research and equality policy.

Minna Salmi is a senior researcher in the Finnish National Research and Development Centre for Welfare and Health. She is a doctor in sociology, has studied domestic work and home-based work, and functions presently as expert on family policy at both national and European level.

Hannele Varsa is a senior researcher in the Finnish National Research and Development Centre for Welfare and Health. Her studies have focused on problems of sexuality, and she has worked as an active organiser of international events combining feminist research and policy-making.

Marja Vehviläinen is a researcher in the Department of Computer Science, University of Tampere. She combines in feminist research a background of both computer science and social psychology. She has extensive international contacts and experience in the field of women and technology.

Part One
Introduction

1 Studying Gendered Practices

Liisa Rantalaiho, Tuula Heiskanen, Päivi Korvajärvi and Marja Vehviläinen

Weight on her chest. Weight so heavy that Little Red
Riding Hood cannot really breathe, night and day the same
weight, constricting, straining.
The walls around the house where she lives with Wolf and
the cubs feel unscalably high, over them you can not see,
not climb. You are enclosed, unless you yourself take
care of getting out in time.
Wolf thinks it's good to be here inside, the world is
excluded, here is everything they might need, warmth,
closeness, safety. Little Red Riding Hood and Wolf and no
one else except the cubs, who are part of themselves,
nothing else exists.
Little Red Riding Hood cannot breathe, the weight on her
chest pulls her down.
When the constriction becomes too much she has suddenly
climbed over, stands on the other side without knowing
how she came to be there and what made her climb
she is outside, she gets herself a key and a front door
where she can come and go, she can do as she pleases, she
can smile and talk, meet other people, there is air and
possibilities
and only now is the house behind the walls a shelter, not
a prison to Little Red Riding Hood.

(Tikkanen, 1986: 279)

The author is a Finnish woman writer, who from the shadow of her famous artist-cum-author husband has won herself a place in the Nordic cultural scene and international acknowledgement. Her text reflects the pressure
of expectations she has felt while seeking room for herself and trying to
fit family responsibilities with literary work. It sets up the exciting question of the dynamics of gender relations, the question of change and permanence, which is also the central tension of our book. Little Red Riding

3

Hood meets the system of gender relations through Wolf, her husband. In our book we look at that in another perspective through the processes and structures of working life, including the interrelations of work and family. The context of a Nordic welfare state gives a background to the questions. That context is in many ways favourable to gender equality: in addition to the formal equal rights – which nowhere guarantee equality in practice – Nordic women and men have about the same educational level and rate of participation in working life, and it is considered a social right of the citizens that the society provides full day-care for children, school meals and other services that help people combine work and family responsibilities. The index of United Nations' world-wide gender equality survey (Human Development Report, 1995) ranked the Nordic countries Sweden, Finland, Norway and Denmark in the four top places. Close behind came the USA, Australia, France, Japan, Canada and Austria, and last on the list came some African countries (Burkina Faso, Niger, Mali, Sierra Leone) and Afghanistan. The index counts such indicators as gross income per capita, life expectation, educational level and women's income level compared with men's – and therefore favours industrialised rich countries and penalises poor developing countries. For example, in Afghanistan, women could be expected to live on the average to 44 years; in Niger less than 6 per cent of women were literate. In almost half of the world's countries, women were completely lacking from the parliaments or had a share of less than 5 per cent, whereas in all the Nordic countries more than a third of parliament members were women. In a global perspective, the Nordic countries seem relative oases in a desert of inequality.

However, from the point of view of women living in such oases, equality seems a mirage: when you get there, it has fled. We have not escaped the gender wage gap, the gendered segregation in work and education, the hierarchic difference of the valued masculine and devalued feminine, or sexual violence and indignity. Does this mean that in talking about equality we are chasing a deceitful image? Certainly it points out that equality is no simple problem for either politics or research.

WHAT ABOUT PATRIARCHY?

A feminist author who has consistently tried to understand the dilemma of gendered inequality in working life is Cynthia Cockburn (1983; 1985; 1991). Her book *In the Way of Women* (1991) looks at just how and why attempts to promote gender equality in working life may run aground. The book's subtitle is 'Men's resistance to sex equality in organizations', but

Cockburn is not proposing a straightout male-conspiracy theory. The resistance she studies is systemic: 'not casual but structured, not local but extensive, not transitory but stable, with a tendency to self-reproduction' (Cockburn, 1991: 6). Therefore Cockburn decides to use the conceptual tool of patriarchy for the systemic subordination of women.

The concept of patriarchy had its heyday in feminist research by the late 1970s and early 1980s, when the debates about the nature of patriarchy mostly concerned its origin and scope – since behind the common term there were actually very different understandings (see, for example, Sargent, 1981). The whole concept of patriarchy was also strongly criticised, mainly for being universalistic and ahistorical (Barret, 1980). But such a use of the concept is not necessary, according to Cockburn (1991: 7), since patriarchy can change historically. And indeed, feminist research has brought up how, for instance, the old father-right has changed to a modern generalised male sex-right of fraternal patriarchy (Pateman, 1988), or how the Nordic welfare states have substituted private patriarchy with a public patriarchy (Hernes, 1984). Cockburn's book also proves that another common point of the criticism is mistaken: the patriarchy concept is not limited to questions of 'The Origin' of gender inequality, but can also be used in a study of concrete social mechanisms of resistance to equality.

For the purposes of our book, some interesting aspects of the patriarchy concept come up where feminist researchers have studied working life. Heidi Hartman's classic article of job segregation by sex (1976) in a male-dominated branch emphasises the centrality of hierarchy and solidarity between men as the basis of their control over women. Sylvia Walby started from men's exclusion of women from the labour market and trade unions (1986), and later generalised her concept of patriarchy to a multiple system of social structures that result in women's subordination and exploitation by men (1990).

Patriarchy is useful as a research concept because it is concerned with power relations and can be used in a systemic way. But is it useful enough? Cynthia Cockburn uses it as 'a popular shorthand term' (1991: 8), even if she also hints that a different term might be needed and briefly mentions Gayle Rubin's concept 'the sex/gender system' (Rubin, 1975). The patriarchy concept is also encumbered with futile disputes. Cockburn refers to the heated debates of the relative importance of gender and class (and race); whether patriarchy or capitalism is the basic system of subordination, or two separate and equally basic systems, or just one systemic unity (Eisenstein, 1979; Acker, 1989b). She concludes that the question is unnecessary since from one empirical perspective it will be gender, from another class, or race, that is relevant, and the important thing is to study the articulation of these sets of relations. She also makes a very interesting comment: our view of the dilemma depends more on what interpretation we give to the concept of 'system' than what interpretation we give patriarchy or capitalism (or racism) (Cockburn, 1991: 8).

THE CONCEPT OF A GENDER SYSTEM

In this book we will use the concept of a gender system just because we wish to emphasise the systemic character. But first some points should be clarified, both about gender and about system.

We do not agree with a sex/gender distinction that posits a sexed 'natural' body as the ground and material on which gender is socially constructed (for an early critique, see Gatens, 1983). In our thinking, sex, sexuality and the body are also constructed culturally. We will use just the term gender; it has also the advantage of yielding verb forms (to gender, gendering, gendered) which connects it to what people are doing.

A system should be differentiated from a structure. Both are complex wholes where the whole is more than the sum of its parts. To speak of structure means to picture a set of relations as in a cross section, whereas a system is a set of processes happening. A schematic presentation of your car motor is a structure, but gas flowing in, a spark igniting it and kinetic energy transferring to the wheels form a system. Social systems differ much from mechanical ones: any system is a functioning whole, but social systems are not necessarily consistent and well ordered like wellfunctioning machines; instead they may have many inner contradictions, gaps and ruptures. They also have histories, they are in a state of constant potential change and yet tend to reproduce themselves, or at least their inner logic.

A gender system is both a methodological and a theoretical concept. The methodological aspect is concerned with the concept's multilevel nature: that gender is organised simultaneously in social structures, cultural meanings and personal identities, according to Sandra Harding's presentation (Harding, 1986) – and we would add social interaction, bodies and desires to the list. It is simply a reminder that research on gender needs to take into account many interlocking levels of our lived world of action and meaning.

To speak of a system means that its constitutive elements must be connected according to certain rules, that the system has its own overall logic. The theoretical aspect concerns questions about this logic. Only on a very general level of abstraction can we speak about 'the' gender system, otherwise it is better to think about gender systems, plural, limited by social and cultural space-time.

Whatever the disputes, feminist research is quite unanimous about the overall logic of present gender systems: it is male domination. The basic rules of the present male-dominated gender system – or to use the shorthand term, patriarchy – seem to be amazingly similar. The Swedish historian Yvonne Hirdman calls them the two principles of 'difference' and 'hierarchy' (Hirdman, 1990). In practice these are intertwined in multiple ways but conceptually it is also useful to examine them separately. Since they are general rules of the gender system their manifestations may change historically, even several times over, although the basic logic itself remains unchanged.

'The difference' means that woman, female or feminine should be clearly distinct from man, male or masculine, in both ideas and practices. There are many alternative ways to achieve this – for instance, structurally by creating a public sphere for men and a private sphere for women, or segregating women and men to each their 'own' jobs and tasks in working life. In this process both genders may develop their own special skills which then seem to be part of their 'nature'. The structural gender segregation of social positions is reinforced by the process of constructing individual gender identities on the difference of femininity and masculinity, sometimes quite consciously and intentionally. The differences will be normatively controlled with ideas of deviance and proper conduct. Islamic fundamentalism may require physical separation and visual obstacles, while European cultures mostly tolerate a lot of physical contact and superficial similarity of men and women. Women usually have more freedom to enter male arenas and behave like men, while the maintenance of difference from women is socially and psychologically more important to men. That is connected to the other principle of the gender system.

The principle of 'hierarchy' – or as Hirdman puts it, 'the primacy of the male norm' (1990: 79) – means that in every instance man, male or masculine should take precedence or rate higher than woman, female or feminine, especially with reference to power and prestige. The gender figure of Man is the basic norm of abstract humanity, and compared with it woman or feminine are incomplete or deviant. Male and masculinity carry cultural prestige whereas woman and feminine lack significance, cultural 'glamour', regardless of the concrete individual women and men in question. Let's take an actual example: women may for decades busy themselves with their pretty little knittings and it is of no importance, but a man as a designer of knitting patterns is an international cultural figure. Hirdman even talks about 'the iron law of gender', the well-known phenomenon that when women enter a formerly male area of work its wages and status start to sink – whereas when men enter female areas they quickly rise to top positions, 'like cream' (Hirdman, 1990: 79).

Hierarchy and difference certainly seem to be central dimensions in numerous studies of the gender system in working life (or patriarchy, see above the references to Hartman and Walby). A criticism of Hirdman's theory would not deny the importance of those two. Instead, it is reasonable to ask whether there might be other very basic rules in addition to the two. We would suggest that one such rule could well be 'compulsory heterosexuality', as Adrienne Rich calls it (Rich, 1980). That would actually reflect back to the concept of gender and its taken-for-granted categories: why do we see just two genders or two sexes, men and women? why not more? This is not the place to go further into the matter, and for the purpose of studying modern working life the two rules of hierarchy and difference will suffice in most cases. But the principle of theoretical openness is important. Here the concept of a gender system has an advantage to the concept of patriarchy. Patriarchy is organised by power relations, dominance and subordination. A gender system may include theoretical aspects that are analytically (not empirically) separate from dominance and subordination: for instance, qualitatively different cultural constructions of women's and men's bodies and bodily experiences, including sexuality – but not restricted to that either.

FROM A GENDER SYSTEM TO GENDERED PRACTICES

We start from the point that a relatively persistent system organises gender relations both in working life and other areas of human life. Our interest is focused on the processes that reproduce and change a gender system. Research on the interrelations of social structures and human action, the recurring central problem of sociology, is therefore a core idea of this book.

Our thinking about the relationship of structures and actions has also been influenced by the work of Anthony Giddens and Dorothy Smith. The central idea Giddens (1984) uses to analyse the structuration of social relations accross time and space is 'duality of structure'. He defines structure as the medium and outcome of the conduct it recursively organises. According to him the structural properties of social systems do not exist outside of action but are chronically implicated in its production and reproduction (1984: 374). This theoretical frame has led him to emphasise the study of day-to-day life in the analysis of the reproduction of institutionalised practices (1984: 282).

Dorothy Smith approaches the relationship of structures and actions through the concept of 'social relations' (1987: 183). She wants to study how actual practices form or articulate social relations. Like Giddens, she takes people's everyday activity as the starting point. Smith searches for social relations through the accounts and activities of concrete people, seeing social reality not as fixed, but rather as an ongoing production, 'always in the making' (1987: 126). This orientation is in line with her view that a social relation is only created while active subjects shape it through their own practices, sequences of action; on the other hand social relations have power over the active subjects, they reach beyond specific individuals and are reproduced independently of individual objectives.

Some feminist sociologists have conceptualised the ongoing production of gender in working life as 'gendering processes'. Joan Acker (1987; 1992) has studied both public and private organisations and outlined four sets of processes that reproduce gendered social structures: the production of gender divisions, the creation of symbols and forms of consciousness that deal with those divisions, the patterned social interactions enacting gendered relations, and what she calls the internal mental work of individuals in their construction of gendered understandings of their world of action (1992: 252–4). Building on Acker's work, Barbara Reskin and Irene Padavic (1994: 6–12) start with a list of three gendering processes in working life: the sexual division of labour, the devaluation of women's work and the construction of gender on the job. They are able to show how these processes mould gender relations and women's position relative to men all over the world.

Both Acker's and Reskin and Padavic's list display a multilevelled understanding of gendering – it is not just one thing or one process, but many simultaneous processes. Both take up first the division of labour (whether the term is 'gendered' or 'sexual') as a process, something that has an evident structural result. Acker's processes seem to have a more methodological orientation, telling us on what level of sociological abstraction we ought to look, where something important might be happening: on the structural level, in interactions, in symbols, in thoughts. Reskin and Padavic get closer to the theoretical content and location of gendering: what is taking place is devaluation, and it happens on the job. Interestingly, though, the basic difference between the two lists lies in the concept of gender. Although both talk about social construction of gender, Reskin and Padavic see gender as construction of exaggerated differences between natural biological categories of sex (1994: 2–4), while Acker is very conscious also of the social construction of the body, sex and sexuality (1992: 251).

The weakness of a system concept is that while it necessarily includes processes, it may neglect the human (individual or collective) actors in the system. Her studies have led Joan Acker to think that systems should be studied through practices, through the ordinary things that people do as they go about their daily activities. Many such concrete activities are gendered in that they are consonant with assumptions about differences between women and men – as Acker suggests in the Foreword – and often, in their repetition, contribute to the reproduction of those differences. We shall use the concept of gendered practices in a roughly similar way in the book.

The important step from a concept of processes to a concept of practices is the necessity of looking for concrete social actors. Process is a concept related to the reproduction and change of a system. It just takes place, requiring no subject, imputing no intentions, no responsibility, offering no lever for change. Practice is what people do, again and again. With practices we can ask about who is doing, and how, where, when, in what circumstances. The concept of gendered practices as a methodological tool has helped us to start our study from everyday concrete practices, from the actions and voices of living people. Practices are local, situational – and alterable.

There are by now several studies of concrete practices that maintain inequality or either improve or impair women's position in workplaces, organisations and on the labour market. The experience of equality policies has shown that there are huge gaps between legislation or programmatic declarations and practical measures, and that these gaps cannot be bridged without serious consideration of the forms of cultural resistance that appear in concrete practices, such as those local recruitment and career advancement practices that restrict women's input in organisations (Cockburn, 1991; Buswell and Jenkins, 1994 – to mention a few examples from many studies). This has meant an emphasis on local knowledge also in working life research (Cockburn, 1991: 239–41). Methodologically important has been the aim to deconstruct and reconceptualise: neither women nor men should be treated as dichotomous and internally homogeneous groups, and many different kinds of masculinities and femininities in working life need to be considered (Cockburn and Ormrod, 1993). That is an aim we also want to share.

Peta Tancred (1995) discusses the contribution of feminist writings on women's work to the sociology of work. She argues that the basic categories of analysis were originally adopted without due consideration of gender, and this still hampers their use both for the understanding of women's work and the changes that are taking place in men's work. She lists three key areas: the definition of work, the nature of the firm or organisation, and the conception of skill. Our book will relate to all three problem areas. We shall include both explicitly gendered and such seemingly gender-neutral practices that have implications to the gender system. We do not limit work to a separate sphere, we try to analyse the gendered and gendering logic of organisations, and the profound importance of gender in the social construction of skills.

The methodological metaphor of our approach has been a house of several floors with windows facing in many directions. Depending on from which floor and to which direction you look, you get a different view. From one window you can see wide panoramas, from another window you can zoom in on details.

An idea of the place and terrain of the house emerges when the viewer takes the trouble to go around inside it. We have been able to show each other the view from our respective locations. We have come to understand that there is not one master scene but different takes of manifold scenes. Together they tell of the multiple processes where gender is overtly or covertly involved. This insight has led us to accept a basis of theoretical and methodological pluralism, not in the sense of arbitrary eclecticism, but as a principle that obeys the logic of the gendering processes. Institution-alised structures, textual practices, symbols and face-to-face interaction can all express and maintain gendered practices. Each of them requires a research approach relevant to the particular object of study.

Part One gives a background for the other parts of the book, describing the locality where the house stands. It outlines how the structures of working life are related to the gender system. The present outcome of gendered divisions and hierarchies is connected to the historically formed gender contract which defines the social rights and duties of women and men. In our Nordic welfare state women's right to participate in wage work is also their duty, a matter of course in social life. The chapter tells about the problems and solutions that people have to reconcile the often conflicting demands of social production and social reproduction in the context of the welfare state, and about the intrinsic tensions the solutions imply in the gender system.

Part Two looks at those practices which continually reproduce hierarchic differences between men and women and between the masculine and the feminine in wage work. When we learn how concrete actors meet and modify cultural understandings and textual interpretations about men and women and their position in working life, we obtain a deeper insight into those understandings.

The analyses introduce us to the circular relations that prevail between the workers' own evaluations and ideas, cultural conceptions and the texts that report on and regulate working life. Merja Kinnunen studies the power of textual definitions to control the material world. Searching for the cultural basis of categorisations, she parallels the labour force categories of official statistics, the interpretations that social scientists give to work contents, occupations, hierarchical positions and to gender, and people's own definitions of their work. Riitta Martikainen examines the construction of a seemingly gender-neutral text that takes part in the production and reproduction of the gendered working life reality. She focuses on the bargaining practices where the text of collective agreements is negotiated and formulated. Päivi Korvajärvi takes us to the workplace level, to the everyday processes of doing gender. She is especially interested in how fixed or transformable the boundaries are between spaces defined as masculine or feminine.

While Part Two uses the example of the white-collar worker and her work, looking at it on several levels, or from different floors of the methodological house, Part Three opens a window to the wider scenery where work appears as one – partial – area of human life activity.

In research as well as in organisational practice work is often seen apart from the rest of life. An abstract worker has no body, no gender and no personal goals outside work. If a link is seen between work and the life outside work, it is seen in a negative light and particularly connected with women: women's family obligations and orientation towards the family restrict their full involvement in working life. Part Three repudiates such rigid division into life spheres. The authors take the concept of everyday life as their guideline when they examine women's and men's ways to combine work and family. Their special focus is use of time. Riikka Kivimäki studies the relations between work and family responsibilities in different types of workplaces. She tries to show how certain types of workplace present typical possibilities and limiting conditions to combining work and family. Minna Salmi asks how a homeworker's daily time use differs from the everyday time of the average wage worker. She also wants to know how women's and men's typical way of doing home-based work reflects the structural constraints of their everyday life.

Part Four follows two accounts of threatening or challenging gendered processes in working life. Here the women come to realise that they face practices which may seriously undermine their activity as autonomous individuals. In the process of sexual harassment described by Hannele

Varsa the gendered practices are penetratingly oppressive, and much more subtle in Marja Vehviläinen's case of information technology use in a bureacratic organisation. In both cases the women concerned have to actively orient themselves to the situation and to find their own words to account for it to themselves. The authors are interested in the processes where women strive to order the situational elements in a language which is familiar to their thinking, and from their own standpoint. They examine what happens during this process of definition to the women as individuals and subjectivities.

Parts One to Four take up persistent practices that maintain inequality between men and women in the working life, but also breaking points where new ways of thinking and new practices may emerge. Part Five specifically focuses on strategies that have been intentionally used to improve women's position in working life. These strategies are a subject of contention in the international feminist movement. The adherents of each strategy have differing theoretical and practical arguments to support their way of thinking. The cases in Part Five represent different strategies and are based on somewhat differing discursive traditions. Leila Räsänen tells about an experiment to break up gender segregation, Tuula Heiskanen about an application of comparable worth ideas. Instead of gauging the power of arguments for each strategy, the authors focus on the basic social processes which come into test in the work for change. Part Five leads us to see what requirements of recognition, learning and social problem-solving are involved in trying to change gendered practices.

The empirical cases of the book provide a view of the mutual play of such gendering processes Joan Acker describes – production of divisions and symbols, interactions between people and constructions of personal understanding (1992: 252–4). The cases reach from workplace level to the level of institutions regulating working life, and from individuals to collective actors. The common organising theme that runs through the cases is the logic of the gender system: difference and hierarchy. Together the cases try to characterise the principles according to which concrete practices maintain gendered divisions, distinctions and differences in working life, and – as a contingent but non-obligatory result – inequality between women and men. The role of the empirical cases is both to illustrate the principles and to show how they function.

The definition of gendered practices points out that it is a situational, local matter. That does not contradict the fact that practices may be very similar from one country or culture to another or that a practice may originate extra-locally. In any case, however, to speak about gendered practices requires knowledge about the specific context where they take place.

In addition to the international discussion above, the approach of our book has definitely been formed by the local context of the Nordic feminist research and equality discourse where the writers themselves have participated. The Nordic feminist research on working life is strongly connected to concrete research and search and support for new practices. It emphasises the material context of the action of women and women's groups, and their shared cultural community. That kind of approach has widened working life research from the boundaries of the employment relationship to the study of women's everyday life-totality (Strandell, 1984; Davies, 1989; Salmi, 1991). Studies of women's work, whether care work in public organisations or work in offices and street-level bureaucracies, have stressed the importance of the logic of action women share in their workplace communities. An implicit frame of technical and/or bureaucratic rationality in sociology of work has proven both grossly insufficient and in itself gendered masculine. Instead, these studies of women's work have produced concepts such as rationality of responsibility (Sørensen, 1982; Korvajärvi, 1990) and rationality of care (Boman, 1983; Waerness, 1984; for a review see Ungerson, 1990) or reproductive work orientation (Rantalaiho, 1985, 1986), which take into account the context of social relations in women's work. In the main(male)stream traditions of sociology, the study of social structures and the study of cultural dynamics from a structural perspective have a solid position, but they are rather indifferent to the problem of subject or agency (Alapuro, 1995). In contrast to that, studies of women's work have emphasised an actor perspective (Rantalaiho, 1986; Korvajärvi, 1990; Simonen, 1991; Silius, 1992).

Also as researchers we are located in a specific context. The authors of this book have had the opportunity to work together as a group for several years: we have shared the house of our research. Twelve resident women, with different life events and ideas, tend to have a variegated life. During the research process we have shared both harmony, controversy, sulking and the joy of working together. The most important research method maintaining the house turned out to be our shared discussions. Around the same table theoretical debates and concrete diaper changes overlapped into a continuity, instead of separate levels or spheres. Economically, sharing this house was possible by employment relationships to the Finnish state as well as state benefits for maternity or unemployment. As researchers, we lived in the very world we studied.

We are aware that based on their life experience the social actors of this book – the researchers as well as the people who have supplied their experiences for the writers to interpret – all share a collective gendered understanding that acknowledges women's public and professional competence. It is not possible for us to see full-time commitment to the labour market as a 'male characteristic' (cf. Witz and Savage, 1992: 12) or to agree with a clear-cut division of public and private spheres. The stage-set of the book's case studies is a society where women have a substantial role in public life – although not quite as substantial as that of men. Little Red Riding Hood has acquired a key that has opened doors to political life and public administration, to decision-making about social issues together with men. She has found new possibilities, but she also encounters new pressures and constraints. This book tries to bring out the gender conflicts that may emerge when women widen their room of action.

2 Contextualising Gender
Liisa Rantalaiho

'My wife would hardly have died of cancer if she had not had to pine at home but could have gone to work like other people,' says a recently widowed Finnish man whose late wife had decided to stay at home to take care of their severely handicapped child (*Aamulehti*, 10 January 1993). All parties of the human interest story: the widower, the journalist and the readers, take for granted that normal people go to work and that women are normal people.

What produces this understanding of women's normal place? What does that mean in working life? Does such an idea guarantee equality, or do gender hierarchies coexist with women's labour market integration? Gendered practices take place in particular circumstances in particular times and places. To understand the gender that is constructed in the practices, you must be able to place it in its local and temporal context. Our case studies of gendered practices are located in their particular cultural context, and in this chapter I will give you a brief overview of that using the concepts of gender system and gender contract.

THE FRAMEWORK OF GENDERED STRUCTURES

Women's increasing labour force participation has been the silent revolution of the late twentieth century in all Western industrialised countries. In most of the countries it had changed only marginally until the 1950s, and sometimes even in opposite directions (Therborn, 1995: 61). The change in women's participation took off in the 1960s and accelerated in the 1980s when in Western Europe employment growth was actually due to women's employment (Allén, 1989).

The common feature in all industrialised countries is a gender gap between men's and women's labour market participation. The size of this gender gap varies greatly from one country to another, and national differences have even tended to increase in the last twenty years. In Europe the gender gap is smallest in Sweden and Finland (5 and 8 per cent), and largest in Ireland (47 per cent). Women's employment is indeed both practically and ideologically normal in the Nordic countries. The majority, 70–80 per cent, of Scandinavian women of working age participate in the labour market, compared to the 40–60 per cent of women in Central and Southern Europe, especially Ireland and Spain (*OECD Employment Outlook*, 1991; *Women and Men*, 1994; Rantalaiho and Julkunen, 1994). Particularly dramatic has been the increase in labour force participation for working mothers. Again we find large national differences in the statistics. The typical Scandinavian pattern is that having a family and children no longer breaks up a woman's working career. Actually, in all Nordic countries a greater proportion of mothers with children under three years are employed (over 80 per cent) than of all women of working age. In most other European Union countries motherhood still tends to shut women outside labour markets (*OECD Employment Outlook*, 1991; Sorrentino, 1990; *Women and Men*, 1994; Rantalaiho and Julkunen, 1994). From the USA, too, Reskin and Padavic (1994: 143–4) report a clear decline of the stay-at-home wife and mother, and the interesting feature of the long-term development is that women's participation rates tend to converge regardless of race and ethnic origin, whereas racial and ethnic differences in men's participation rates have increased.

The growth in women's labour force participation has also taken place in Finland, but here the starting level had already been comparatively high (36–40 per cent) from the early decades of the century (Pohls, 1990: 56). Since then, Finnish women have kept up their traditionally active participation in working life. Nowadays they make up half of the country's total labour force – a little over half when we consider just wage employment, but less when we also include private entrepreneurs because only a third of them are women. What distinguishes Finnish women from the other working women in Scandinavia and most other industrialised countries is that Finnish women ordinarily work full-time – in the early 1990s only 10 per cent of them worked part-time compared, for example, with 40–50 per cent of employed women in other Nordic countries, the Netherlands and Britain (*OECD Employment Outlook*, 1991; Rantalaiho and Julkunen, 1994).

Some other aspects of Finnish women's position in working life seem very favourable to them: women have a high educational level, and in the age cohorts under 40 years, women's level of education is already higher than men's (*Women and Men*, 1994). Belonging to a labour union is the normal case, so that the whole Finnish labour force is very highly unionised (varying by branch between 70–80 per cent) – but, again, women's rate of unionisation is even higher than men's (Kauppinen and Köykkä, 1991).

I have not taken up all these aspects arbitrarily. It is a common experience that formal democratic rights in a modern society have not been enough to abolish the hierarchic gender division and women's subordination. Why should it be so? Some political arguments are repeatedly used as explanations, and many of them are connected to working life, the major provider of social status and rewards in modern societies:

- Women's involvement in working life is quantitatively lower than men's, far fewer women are employed than men, and they do not work full-time: therefore women cannot achieve the positions and rewards that men do.

- Women's involvement in working life is also qualitatively lower than men's, they take career breaks and leave their jobs because of family responsibilities, because women are not really committed to their jobs: therefore they cannot achieve the positions and rewards that men do.

- Women's labour power is objectively cheaper than men's, since women are less educated than men: therefore it is to be expected that women get lower wages and inferior jobs on the labour market.

- Women do not organise to protect their interests, they do not join labour unions: therefore it is to be expected that they get lower wages and inferior jobs on the labour market.

Each of these factors has been blamed for the subordinated position of women: 'if only women . . .' (had an equal employment rate with men, were working full-time, worked without career breaks, had better education, were unionised), then certainly women would be paid as well as men, women would reach the same positions, and their work and life sphere would not be devalued in society. Now none of these arguments is valid in the case of Finnish women. If these explanations were enough, then Finnish women ought to be in an enviable position of full gender equality. But that is not the case.

Instead, in all branches men have the upper and decision-making positions; almost all, or 90–99 per cent, of the leading positions of economic life and administration are held by men (Ruostetsaari, 1992). Women work on the lower steps of the organisational hierarchies. Organisations tend to support men's careers and to forget women under 'the glass ceiling' (Luokkaprojekti, 1984; Lehto, 1988; Aitta, 1988). Similar disadvantages are quite familiar to women in the USA, Japan, Australia or many other countries (for a recent overview see, for example, Reskin and Padavic, 1994). It is the same with the famous gender wage gap. Also the Finnish women's wages stay systematically under the wage level of men, even when several explaining factors are held constant. Women's wages and salaries in full-time work are on the average about 75 per cent of those of men, and the wage differences emerge already in the starting period of the work career. Not even a good education closes the gender wage gap, although it certainly improves a woman's position compared to other women

(Allen et al., 1990; Keinänen, 1994). During the 1980s the gender wage gap slowly but promisingly started to narrow. The promise of optimism was false, however, since the gap is widening again in the 1990s – a development that seems to happen also in other countries (Jackson, 1990). We can speak about the above hierarchical gender differences as vertical segregation. The term gender segregation of the labour market is often used just to refer to the horizontal gender segregation. That is also well known in all industrialised countries: branches, occupations and jobs are usually branded either male or female. Equality of labour market participation and lack of gender segregation do not hang together, however. For instance, in Japan, Greece, Italy and Portugal occupations are relatively little segregated by gender; in Norway, Austria and Britain they are relatively highly segregated. On the whole, the Nordic countries, including Finland, show a greater degree of occupational gender segregation than the continental European countries (Therborn, 1995: 61–2).

Less than one Finnish person in ten works in an occupation which is gender balanced (a fifty–fifty, or even forty–sixty gender composition) and correspondingly over nine-tenths work in occupations which have a more or less clearly gendered character. This segregation has remained quite stable for several decades, and may actually have increased when structural change from agriculture to industry and services is taken into account (Kolehmainen, 1995). All branches are distinctly male or female dominated, women working in care giving, nursing, services, offices, teaching, men in technical design and operation, maintenance and repair, construction, transport and traffic. Also within occupations the work tasks of men and women differ clearly, and that happens even when the group in the aggregate looks gender balanced – a journalist, for instance, is a gender balanced occupation where men and women are recruited in equal numbers, and yet male and female journalists get different tasks (Anttalainen, 1986; Naiset ja miehet, 1994; Kolehmainen, 1995).

The theories of 'the dual labour market' treat women as an example of 'a secondary labour force', the part that is discriminated against and disadvantaged, has short-term employment, low pay, bad working conditions and few career possibilities (Doeringer and Piore, 1971; Baron and Bielby, 1984). Feminist critique has certainly pointed out the inherent masculinine bias of the theories, which construct the secondary labour force as a negation to the stable primary (male) labour force (Kenrick, 1981; Beechey and Perkins, 1987). Finnish women do not fill the central criterion of being in stable employment, and in other respects also do not fit the label of 'secondary' labour force (Lehto, 1992). Around 40 per cent of the country's income taxes come from women's work. And yet, in each stratum of the labour force women have a secondary labour market position compared with that of men (Nätti, 1989). In contrast to the feminisation of poverty in most countries, in Finland poverty and marginalisation are masculine phenomena (Allén, 1989). Also contrary to the general European situation where women are unemployed more often than men, unemployment has hit the Finnish men earlier and harder than women (Naiset ja miehet, 1994: 88–9). But the long-term results of individual unemployment are gendered: women more often than men end up in a situation of 'permanent temporariness', as the follow-up studies show in both Finland (Koistinen and Suikkanen, 1990) and Sweden (Gonäs, 1989).

Does all this lead to the general conclusion that it is no use for women to enter the labour market, to get education and to organise? That is not the idea. At the very least women do acquire economic independence and wider room for action. But it does mean that there is no single key to abolish gender inequality. Inequality is systemic. As a system, it reproduces itself like a mythical monster: when you hack off its head, it grows two others.

GENDER INTEGRATION AND STATE FEMINISM:
PATTERNS AND ROOTS OF A GENDER SYSTEM

It is obvious from the above that with all its features of gender equality, the Finnish gender system still exhibits the common general logics of hierarchy and difference (which were presented in the Introduction). However, it is not theoretically very interesting that a local gender system illustrates general principles. More important is the how: to analyse how the particular features are connected with each other to form a whole, and when possible, to do this on several analytical levels simultaneously. Many of these features are common Nordic patterns, but some are specifically Finnish.

That the gender system puts relatively less emphasis on difference than on hierarchy is a common feature of all Nordic societies. Practically it means that 'women can do anything, as long as they do it in relative subordination to (their) men' (Haavind, 1984: 147). In the Finnish gender system a clear male dominance in the socioeconomic power structures is connected to a labour market citizenship that is shared by both men and women, but in a gender segregated labour market structure. The women are also traditionally involved in public institutions that have been branded male in many other countries, such as trade unions or politics. So, for instance, Finnish women were never excluded from trade unions as they were in Great Britain (see Walby, 1986).

The logics of hierarchy and difference are not enough to deal with the cultural meanings, identities, bodies and interaction patterns. We need to include the logic of 'compulsory heterosexuality', or heterosexism for short, to get the feeling of the gender system's articulation. Compared to many other countries, the Nordic scene typically combines a heterosexist culture with a rather uneroticised working life. Women and men meet as subordinates and bosses, or as colleagues or work mates, but there is a relative lack of 'femininity' and erotic signals. The desirability of 'an erotic peace' in working life is a Swedish feminist idea which is heartily supported in Scandinavia (Liljeström, 1983).

Altogether the culture is imbued with a strong work ethic. Motherhood defines women's social identity much more than wifehood, and what is important, motherhood is not something sacred but a matter of work and everyday chores and responsibilities – typically, for instance, the term 'housewife' is not translated in Finnish as '-wife' but as 'house-mother'. The logic of difference certainly figures in psychological gender identity construction, and the logic of hierarchy shows, for instance, in the taken-for-granted importance of male cultural voices.

The roots of this gender system go deep. A special aspect that tends to relieve the intensity of the logic of difference is the structure of the Finnish language. It is rather weak in gendering: there is neither 'she' nor 'he', just one and the same non-gendered personal pronoun ('hän') for all humans (and nouns have no gender either). Neither does the language separate the terms sex and gender. The one word for both ('sukupuoli') can be literally translated as 'kin-half', which I would interpret as an indication of deep heterosexist logic in the gender system.

The socioeconomic history of the Nordic countries gives a common basis to their gender systems. For centuries they all were poor, sparsely populated countries with smallholding agricultural (or fishing) subsistence economies. The poverty of free peasants in an arctic climate implies that everybody must work all the time for survival. All were relatively poor, and social class differences in the Nordic pre-industrial estate societies never grew to the scale of Central or Southern Europe. The official state and the Lutheran church were patriarchal, and the division of labour in agricultural tasks clearly gendered. Still, the demands of survival created a work-oriented partnership between men and women. They needed each other's contribution, and that was evident to all. Women and men did not live in idyllic harmony, for sure, but within the bounds of common necessity.

The sparse settlement pattern in the cold climate also emphasised the importance of the shared daily life. The scene of sociability in the countryside was inside the farm house, women and men together – not men

gathering separately on open village streets or street cafés, clubs or pubs
which in the South contributed to the differentiation of the gendered 'public' and 'private' worlds. The necessity of mutual dependence contributed
to a lasting cultural avoidance of presenting gender as conflictual. Poverty
and necessity gave an uneroticised character to the heterosexual partnership. A strict work ethic made a combination of work, care and motherhood the prime attributes of Nordic femininity.

Industrialisation took the Scandinavian countries from poverty to afflu-
ence; it also increased class conflicts. The development, however, took
place later and faster than in such earlier industrialised countries of Europe
as Great Britain, France or Germany. Especially the Finnish pattern of
socioeconomic development is noticeable for its rapid and radical changes.
Here the final movement of the economically active population from agriculture to industry and services took place as a massive wave only after
the Second World War in some 15–20 years, while the same social change
in the other Nordic countries took at least three times longer, and took
centuries instead of decades in the large European countries. The rapid
Finnish modernisation once started has been very thorough, especially in
the field of information technology – in today's Finland ATMs and mobile
telephones are used by all age and social groups.

These are no empty figures for the gender system. The picture of hard-
working farm family life is of course familiar from many countries in pre-
industrial times. Industrialisation meant the spreading dominance of market
economy and money over subsistence economy. It meant that most of
women's traditional productive work was incorporated into the market and
the middle-class home became an ideological ground for the 'cult of do-
mesticity'. The late start and fast rate of industrial development meant that
some typical institutions and ways of life of an industrial society with its
urban bourgeoisie did not have enough time to get firmly established –
such as the division into male breadwinner and female housewife. That
predisposes the society towards a higher degree of gender integration.

Finland went almost directly from an agricultural to a modern service
society. One result is that the housewife institution never became a dominant practice in people's everyday life. It certainly had ideological strength
(Saarikangas, 1993), but for the majority of the population it remained an
ideal more than reality. First, there could be no separate breadwinnership
and housewifery on a farm, second, working-class women's factory work
was traditional in the small cities, and third, the gentry was a very thin
layer. No wonder that the women who 'had always worked' took to full-
time employment as a matter of course – and that even the employers
never thought about offering part-time jobs to women.

All the Nordic countries are nation states with small and culturally very homogeneous populations. They differ from each other in many respects, but in the present context I am more interested in analysing their commonalities. Modern democracy has produced in Scandinavia a specific type of citizens' relationship to the state: the state and the civil society merge into a close network of social relations. The interest representation of both capital and labour within the state is institutionalised into tripartite corporatist structures, and all professions, too, get their legitimation from the state. People are used to organising but their idea is to act on behalf of their issues through the state, to pressure 'the state to do something'. As the growing ground for the welfare state institutions, this creates an idea of the 'People's Home', as the Swedes put it. At the same time, all the Nordic states have multiparty political systems, which means an ingrained practice of negotiation for compromises instead of rulers versus opposition.

Again, the picture is relevant for the gender systems. Women's political citizenship has been strong for almost a century, since the first wave of feminism: Finnish women achieved the vote in 1906, and got 18 women to the parliament in the first elections. Nowadays women form almost 40 per cent of the MPs, and their insider positions – and the problems they face – in the state administration are comparable to the phenomenon of the Australian 'femocrats' (see, for example, Eisenstein, 1991). The Nordic term for this involvement is 'state feminism' (Hernes, 1984). Also the gender equality movement has seen the state not as an oppressor, but as an ally and defender. The state rather became a benevolent instrument for turning against private patriarchy (Holli, 1990). This is quite different from countries where women's movements work outside the state apparatus, or parts of the women's movement even have an oppositional stand towards 'The State' as the patriarchal oppressor, as in Germany and the USA. The difference may also have something to do with the Nordic countries being unitary states, which gives them a very different type of political system from large federal states, such as the USA, Canada, Australia or Germany, and therefore an easier field structure for political action (Tyyskä, 1995). That cannot be the whole explanation, however, since the Australian feminists have developed their 'femocracy' in a federal context.

Nordic women have also been active agents in the construction of the welfare state. Many social and health services, maternity benefits, child care, school meals, etc. are 'women's reforms', for which they have fought as political citizens (Saarinen, 1987; Sinkkonen and Haavio-Mannila, 1980; Hirdman, 1991). We might say that women have long had some democratic political power in Finland – in their 'own' issues, and provided they do not disturb men's positions. The corporative power structures of the labour market, however, have been a bastion of male power. Until the 1980s women in trade unions used to be the rank and file members, which men led and represented, in public statements as in cabinet negotiations (Haavio-Mannila et al., 1985; Mikkonen, 1987). The Finnish gender system actually has a special articulation with politics because of the country's struggle for survival. Finland formed a part of Sweden until it was incorporated into Czarist Russia during the Napoleonic wars, and achieved its independence only after the First World War. Especially the Russian dominance during the nineteenth century taught the importance of national culture, language and legislature. The state became 'our own' state since its laws guaranteed protection from Czarist repression, and the nationalist project emphasised the creation of a national identity through enlightenment, education and cultural life. This political identity, the Finnish citizenship, was from the beginning a gendered project. Women's contribution was seen as necessary to it because women were the bearers of national culture and language from one generation to another. The national enlightenment project has since then been realised in women's action in many ways: education has from the start been both an important part of the programme of women's movements and women's organisations, and an individual and collective strategy for women. Today the results show themselves in the Finnish women's visible part in the country's politics, in their high level of education and their strong commitment to state feminism.

CHANGING GENDER CONTRACTS

In this brief overview the level of abstraction is necessarily high, meaning that a lot of concrete details and distinctions must be ignored. The concept of a gender system may be useful for describing the complex pattern of gender relations in a whole society, but it has limitations (see Introduction). The concept of gendered practices is better suited to studies with concrete identifiable social actors in their local context. But to include also the role of collective social actors in changing a gender system I wish to introduce the concept of a gender contract.

Carole Pateman introduced the concept of 'a sexual contract' (1988) to criticise the Enlightenment philosophers' idea of 'a social contract' being gender blind. Pateman argues that the social contract between male individuals is just a contract between 'brothers' to free each other from 'the father', from political autocracy. But the fraternal contract presupposes another implicit one. This hidden contract is 'the sexual contract' of the male right to use women's bodies. Women belong to Nature, not to Culture, and thus they are not autonomous individuals. Women cannot be direct citizens in a society as themselves, but only through the mediation of some man. The abstract individual of Western political thought is therefore implicitly male. To Pateman the concept of 'a sexual contract' is an instrument for feminist philosophical critique.

Nordic feminist researchers have used the concept of 'a gender contract' somewhat differently, to analyse the historical structuration of social institutions and cultural practices (Hirdman, 1990b; Silius, 1992; Rantalaiho, 1994; Rantalaiho and Julkunen, 1994). A gender contract tells about the unspoken rules, mutual obligations and rights which define the relations between women and men, between genders and generations, and finally between the areas of production and reproduction. It is 'a simple concept to describe the complex reality of interdependence between men and women', says Yvonne Hirdman (1990b: 78). She herself has studied the history of the successive gender contracts in Swedish society from 'the housewife contract' of the 1930s, via 'the equality contract' of the 1950s to 'the equal-worth contract' of the 1980s, and the processes of public debate that transformed them (Hirdman, 1990a).

Gender contracts are transformed through discursive shifts in the prevailing understanding of gender relations. The shifts are constructed to solve social and economic tensions and they produce institutional consequences and new cultural practices. Structural changes do not automatically transform gender contracts, instead a new contract has to be created in 'negotiations' between collective social actors. Using the concept of contract in this context aims to draw attention to these discursive struggles and the parties involved in the solutions (Rantalaiho, 1994).

The transitions of the gender contract in Finnish society have been characterised by a redefinition of women's citizenship. There are two clear phases of transition. At the turn of the century Finnish women became political citizens in a process that produced the first modern gender contract of 'women's social motherhood' (see also Sulkunen, 1990). The principle of a special feminine citizenship was also a common line elsewhere in the international feminist movement at the time (Bock and Thane, 1991). Women themselves wanted to maintain the gender difference and to shape it into men's and women's separate arenas of social action. Finnish women, however, had a special chance to realise the feminine citizenship because of the country's political situation. They were important as mothers of the whole nation. The central idea was that women's motherhood should not be restricted within a particular home; instead women had to take the responsibility of making the society a home for the people. This gender contract was negotiated between women and men as collective groups, adapting the logic of difference for women's purposes, but leaving the logic of hierarchy untouched. With relatively minor changes, it lasted for several decades.

Women were in the first instance members of the political parties of their own class. Still, they could cooperate over party boundaries just on 'women's issues'. And since the logics of the gender system separate male and female arenas of action and set the men's arenas hierarchically higher, this maintained gendered divisions into the 'general' party organisations and women's separate organisations inside the parties. Paradoxically, the secondariness made women unquestioned experts on their 'own' areas, and representatives of their own female constituencies. Women could not be politically bypassed. In the earlier generations, women cabinet ministers achieved their top positions very much through the influence of women's separate political organisations (Kuusipalo, 1990). Women also used the strategy of education to acquire knowledge and competence on their 'own' professional areas (Henriksson, 1994).

As a society changes, its gender contract may become outdated so that it has to be 'renegotiated'. The new form of women's citizenship that was institutionalised together with the construction of the Nordic welfare state model can in Finland best be characterised as 'wage-worker motherhood'. Its basic tenet is the normalisation of women's paid employment.

During the war times – the Finnish-Soviet 'Winter War' and the Second World War – women's civic activity was strongly based on their social motherhood. Over the same period, their position on the war economy labour market improved. In many other countries this was a temporary phenomenon, but Finnish women were not 'restored home' after the war. Instead the economy started growing, and women's labour force was much demanded in the rapid structural change. Many women, and many mothers, chose individually to become wage workers, in spite of the daily practical difficulties their choice entailed. It took almost a generation before the new gender contract of wage-worker motherhood was negotiated to provide the social rights to combine work and family, in the radical cycle of the late 1960s when the modern Finnish welfare state was rapidly created (Julkunen, 1994). This differentiates us from Sweden, where equality policies were intentionally used to construct the Swedish welfare state (Hirdman, 1990a).

The gender contract of wage-worker motherhood has anyway many parallel features across all Nordic countries. The Nordic welfare state is heavily involved in the contract. On the one hand, the welfare state is an instrument for equality and social rights. It acknowledges parenthood as part of the worker citizen's responsibilities and provides social rights and services (such as parenthood leave, child care, elderly care, school meals, health care and education) for the organisation of everyday life. On the other hand, it is women's paid and unpaid labour that handles the daily contradiction between production and reproduction. Women have the right and the duty to paid employment and the economic and social independence this entails. They are in principle individuals on the labour market like men. But in practice they have a secondary position: they accept the male dominated hierarchies in working life, 'women's wages' and rules-of-the-game formulated by men. Occupations and jobs in paid employment are gender segregated. Women take the responsibility for social reproduction, both in their private lives and on the labour market. Joan Acker has called this a tacit 'gender compromise' (Acker, 1989b).

Scandinavia is not the only place with a typical configuration of welfare state and labour market patterns. There is a comparative typology of 'welfare state regimes' started by Esping-Andersen (1990) which differentiates the Nordic 'social democratic', the Anglo-Saxon 'liberal' and the Continental European 'conservative' regimes – and which feminist scholars have criticised for gender blindness (Langan and Ostner, 1991; Schunter-Kleeman, 1992). Combining the above feminist critique we could characterise the 'liberal regimes' of the UK, USA and Canada as 'market patriarchy'. Here the state is expected to remain in the background except for selective poor-relief programmes. The regimes favour those who have full labour market individuality, i.e. no restrictions of their time or place, which means for women that they are on the labour market on the condition of trying to function like men. A great majority of women work in a secondary labour market, and social rights or publicly funded services related to parenthood are weak. This is a policy of equality shaped by the primacy of the male norm.

The middle European 'conservative regime' emphasises either 'marriage patriarchy' as in Germany, Austria, Switzerland, the Netherlands and Luxembourg, or 'family patriarchy' as in France, Italy and Belgium (Schunter-Kleeman, 1992: 145). Both subtypes rely on the traditional notions of the family (read: women) providing personal services and stability, and realise that largely through extensive rights to money transfer programmes instead of social services. Women have good social security through their status as dependents, wives and mothers, not as individuals. This type of regime is characterised by a policy of difference instead of equality: men and women are set apart as different, neither the same nor equal.

The Nordic regime is also not simply a 'social-democratic regime' or a 'partly egalitarian patriarchy' (Schunter-Kleeman, 1992: 145), because it contains an inner gender division. In a way we could speak of two parallel welfare states: a men's welfare state which guarantees the rights of the wage workers and social security benefits in case of disturbances in the employment relationship, and a women's welfare state, which offers services and help in organising everyday life (Anttonen, 1994). This also maintains two separate discourses, the hierarchically more important masculine discourse on economy, class and power which is carried on in the arenas of corporatist power, and the hierarchically secondary feminine discourse on care, family and equality by women and the state administrative bureacracies (Acker, 1989b; Hirdman, 1990b).

The gender contract of wage-worker motherhood was indeed negotiated between women and the welfare state. That was possible since women already had an established political and professional position within the state. But the men as a collective group were left in peace, their potential duties were not discussed – they allowed the contract to take place but did not actively participate in the negotiations. The logics of hierarchy and difference were made to bend a little to give women more room, but were basically never questioned.

EMERGING TENSIONS

None of the above regimes has solved the strains that arise from their gender contracts – the contradictions between difference and equity, parenthood and equal labour market citizenship. The gender contract of wage-worker motherhood also has its inner tensions. A basic cause of tension is the fact that the labour market individualises women and motivates the individual development of abilities and qualifications, but women's individuality still has to be reconciled with social ties and responsibilities in daily life. The further women get on the road to individualisation the less they are satisfied with meagre rewards, blocked opportunities, cultural invisibility and exclusion. These contradictions do not only concern women as concrete individuals who demand justice, they expand to concern the question whether production and reproduction, monetarily accountable market activity and sustaining human life, are equal in value.

During the last decades the traditional class-based conflicts of Finnish society have changed to a climate of consensus. Still the old social divisions are rather clear as far as men are concerned. In factories men work on the shop floor and behind the largest managerial desks, men go to Europe, some loading and driving transport trucks, some flying to negotiate on economic policy in Brussels. Women's reality has become much more uniform, because their everyday life is constructed on similar conditions, time constraints and responsibilities. A paradox is evident: the farther women become individualised as wage workers, the more they share similar everyday life conditions as women. This has created a basis for common identities, political gender mobilisation, and social pressure to change the society's gender system.

Yvonne Hirdman (1990b) examines these contradictions starting from the tensions between the processes of gender segregation and gender integration. 'The conflict of equality' arises every time women enter areas which used to be exclusively male. The further gender integration proceeds, the more women and men can be found in the same positions doing the same jobs, and 'the male norm' cannot remain hidden as it did in the segregated situation but is encountered more often, and its revelation looks increasingly glaring. 'The conflict of difference' exacerbates when it becomes obvious that gender integration is only possible in practice on male terms, and the institutions of society are revealed as male constructions for men. The situation forces women to an unsolvable problem of self-definition: what are they in the first instance, women or human beings? On the other hand, from the point of view of the society it is women as a gender group that begin to look like a social problem, not the society's gender contract.

Wage-worker motherhood includes both types of gender conflict. Indeed the discussion nowadays is more conflict-oriented than before. Women are no longer content with their own protected areas in society; they are more and more challenging men directly. The gender contract should not concern just women any more. Women need a society which recognises both equality and difference – but so do men. When women change it is necessarily reflected in men's positions and modes of living and it presupposes that these also change.

Altogether the 1980s saw a change in several aspects of the gender system. Numerically female-dominated trade unions started to elect women to leading positions. Their high degree of unionisation gives women an organised power basis which they have started to use. A women's wage movement got well under way in the 1980s, women demanded both rises in the low 'women's wages' and systems of re-evaluation in the gendered criteria for rewards: equal pay for work of equal value. Politics seems to be an arena where Finnish women nowadays can appear as women, not as quasi-men with a gender handicap. Political action can be a part of positive feminine identity. Women's organisations across the political spectrum have formed a common organ of cooperation, and women are organising cultural efforts collectively as women. Some of the male elite have inadvertently contributed to the process: the notorious incident of a pornographic postcard sent by the core group of male labour market leaders to a well-known feminist politician had the effect of mobilising women to protest more than any long-felt structural inequality had done (Holli, 1993).

European society is currently experiencing the threat of a fast increasing mass unemployment. That necessitates a search for new structures. Also the Finnish welfare state faces financial and political threats, but even during a deep recession public opinion gives higher priority to the welfare functions and social services of the state over its other functions (Sihvo and Uusitalo, 1995). But if the welfare state changes, it will mean change also for the gender system. And indeed the public discourse is presently filled with themes of gender conflicts. Some themes are the same that appear in the women's movements and the backlash attacks (Faludi, 1992) all over the world, and some of course are specific to the Finnish scene.

There are certainly backlash signs in the air, but on the other hand, women's voices are also getting stronger. Some suggest that 'women should stay home' and others tell them that the gender segregated labour market makes even the idea ridiculous: an unemployed construction worker cannot replace a trained nurse. Mothers whose children are not using kindergartens demand that the state should pay them a wage for their work because they are saving public money. New norms praise everyday fatherhood. Sexual violence is openly discussed. Some men have started publicly analysing the dark side of cultural masculinity: men's inability to express feelings and the consequences in alcoholism, coronary disease and suicide. Other men complain that Finnish women's equality demands cause men to import properly submissive wives from South East Asia, and some of those wives tell the media that they are organising to counter their exploitation. The social differences between employed and unemployed women are ominously increasing. Feminist debates are diversifying. Public opinion supports making gay and lesbian marriages official. The negotiations for a new gender contract have started.

Part Two
(De)constructing Gendered Hierarchies

Introduction

Merja Kinnunen, Päivi Korvajärvi and Riitta Martikainen

In working life men are more often than women in top positions, do higher esteemed tasks and get better wages. Our aim in this part is to deconstruct the practices which in waged labour reproduce again and again the hierarchical difference between women and men and between the feminine and the masculine. We examine doing gender in the practices of the statistical classification of social positions, collective bargaining, agreement texts and in the concrete work processes in workplaces. How are the cultural conceptions and textual interpretations of men and women and their positions in working life formed in these practices, and what are the limitations and scope of women's and men's actions?

Let us take as an example the wages clerks in a modern metal factory.[1] The six women working in the open-plan office all have a commercial college education. The outcome of their work can be seen in the contents of the pay packets of the factory's 2000 metal workers and 300 white-collar workers. Wages clerks are on the lowest rungs in the workplace hierarchy, and this is shown by their own meagre pay cheques although a really large sum of money passes through their hands. A picture of the contents of their work can be constructed from many different standpoints, from several texts and from what people say, and this we attempt to do.

The wages clerks themselves emphasised the physical demands of their work. They told us that their work requires a good memory, alertness and accuracy. They are always busy and have to cooperate with many different kinds of people. One of the wages clerks said that at work '[. . .] you have to have a mother hen nature. You have to see to it that all goes well. I suppose this is the traditional role of women.'

The wages clerks' male superiors also emphasised attributes that are very hard to define when they were asked about the women's work requirements: experience learned through working in the field, flexibility, the ability to cope with stressful working conditions, as well as helpfulness and consideration with colleagues. The key issue is to know the contents of collective agreements and the ability to interpret them. The wages clerks have acquired a considerable amount of knowledge and skills during their years in the job. According to the supervisor '[. . .] women can cope with

34   *M.K., P.K. and R.M.*

the work load much better than men in this job. They are devoted and take the work to heart.'

The written job description, which the wages clerks and their managers draw up together in the company, lists twelve different tasks, those with whom they seek cooperation, and as a special requirement knowledge of collective agreements and labour legislation. Nevertheless, work requirements are then summarised as basic knowledge of computers and accuracy. The wage bracket is defined on the basis of the job description which makes no mention of sex.

In the metal industry the white-collar workers' collective agreement does not define wages according to the occupational title, such as a wages clerk. According to the agreement, wages are mainly fixed on the basis of what the tasks require and according to the standard rates in each requirement level. The collective agreement gives rather detailed guidelines on how the different tasks should be classified in the different requirement levels. This is done by the employer, but the shop steward also has a say in the process. The purpose of the requirement classification is to categorise tasks, not people. There is a special mention in the agreement that the person who does the tasks, for instance his or her sex or education, is of no relevance. In addition to the standard rate of pay, the employer can pay personal bonuses to the white-collar workers which are rather extensively used. An unusually explicit statement in the collective agreement says that 'the sex of the white-collar worker is not a personal factor having an effect on the wages'; in other words, sex should have nothing to do with the fact that the employee gets the bonus or how large it is. In practice it has turned out to be impossible to keep the employee's sex and tasks separate (for example, Acker, 1989a). Sex also tends to affect personal bonuses, because male white-collar workers in industry get substantially bigger bonuses than women.

In the official statistics describing socioeconomic positions wages clerks are classified as lower-level employees who do ordinary clerical work. What is essential to their job according to that definition is dealing with symbols either manually or by using machines. The classification says that lower-level white-collar workers work on the performance level of the organisation and their tasks require more limited and less theoretical knowledge than those of the higher-level white-collar workers. More than half of all female employees in Finland are lower-level white-collar workers, and almost all wages clerks are women. Quantitatively, it is women's work. But there is more to it than numbers.

As feminist scholars researching working life we make the interpretation that situationality is essential to the wages clerk's job. The changing daily situations define the contents of the work. Many aspects of their work are left outside the textuality of job descriptions, collective agreements and statistical classifications thus making it very hard to describe their work process. As researchers we think of their job as women's jobs, where women are responsible for the everyday running and continuity of the work community, taking care of several tasks simultaneously and anticipating other people's needs when dealing with them (Rantalaiho, 1990).

The workers, their superiors, the written job descriptions, collective agreements, statistical classifications and our feminist understanding of women's work all have different perceptions of the contents of work. Sex and gendering come up when the concrete daily work is being talked about, but they remain largely hidden when one has at hand a document describing the contents of work. However, these perspectives cannot be separated from one another. What is essential in all these cases is some kind of a cultural interpretation of the differences between women's and men's actions and that the actions are constructed as dichotomous. The interpretations are cross-cut by many of the cultural meanings of women's position and waged labour, relations of ruling (Smith, 1990a) and the processes whereby they become hegemonised (Laclau and Mouffe, 1985) in waged labour and in local institutionalised contexts.

We examine how the practices which differentiate between women's and men's actions naturalise the gender hierarchy in the world of waged work. Our aim is to deconstruct the ways in which sexual difference is done and the ways of thinking which produce the hierarchies between women and men. From concrete practices we read the different technologies of doing gender (de Lauretis, 1987) and their alterability from 'an iron cage' to women's chances of autonomous action. We place emphasis on the fact that femininities and masculinities are local, situational and embodied. The following chapters also bring up different visions of how the established ways of thinking and acting connected with individual women and men could be deconstructed.

NOTE

1.   The example is based on the study of transformations in white-collar workplaces (Korvajärvi, Järvinen and Kinnunen, 1987, 1990).

3 Making Gender with Classifications
Merja Kinnunen

How do the classifications describing waged labour relationships engender practices which reproduce the hierarchical differences between women and men in working life? Here I examine how employees' own definitions at the workplace level and the institutionalised classifications used by statisticians and social scientists are intertwined with each other. Simultaneously I aim to bring up the cultural perceptions, symbols and images included in the classifications describing the structure of society. My focus is on the classification of the so called lower-level white-collar workers, such as wages clerks (see in the Introduction above), and their work and positions.

As producers of knowledge about the society in question, official statistics and social scientific research have the power to produce classificatory categories which describe people's social positions and their changes. Statistics and theoretical analyses may reproduce the existing ideas or create new interpretations about gender and their relationship to waged labour. As institutionalised texts, classifications are also a means to manage and control the material world (see Smith, 1990a: 61–80). In view of people's everyday actions, or the way in which they organise themselves or make self-definitions, it may not necessarily be of immediate importance in which class, socioeconomic position or so on they are placed by statisticians or social scientists. But at the same time one can ask how people's self-definitions and the ruling textuality are interwoven. The difference in definitions between groups of people always brings about one certain kind of idea of people's positions in the society in addition to what differences are thought to be important. In this way the definitions shape the society according to their descriptive system (cf. for example, Berger and Luckmann, 1972; Foucault, 1973 and 1991; Lévi-Strauss, 1966).

As a sociologist and a researcher of working life I also interpret work content, occupations, hierarchical positions and gender. Classifications are a contested ground, and researchers participate in these struggles with their own voice whether they want to or not. In my previous research on the subject I participated in the research project 'Transformations at white-collar workplaces in the 1980s' (Korvajärvi, Järvinen and Kinnunen, 1987,

1990) where we investigated white-collar workers' work content and positions in nine Finnish workplaces. Below I will weigh the observations and interpretations we made in the previous study against other classifications describing social positions and gender. However, I start with a general overview of how people's own definitions of their work and position intertwine and overlap in concrete terms with the classifications made by official statistics and social scientists.

WHAT IS YOUR JOB?

It is most likely that as a citizen every person has to, or is able to, define her/himself in relation to waged labour and gender at some stage of her or his life. If we do not do it ourselves, someone else, authorities or a guardian, does it on our behalf. There are questions relating to an individual's occupation and sex on numerous forms, as for instance when one registers a change of address, hands in one's tax return, registers with the employment office, reports an offence or answers social scientists' questions.

Those who are outside paid employment are usually expected to define their status or stage of the lifecycle in relationship to paid work, such as people doing home-based work, entrepreneurs, students or pensioners. Employed respondents, as much as those unemployed, form their ideas of work or occupations largely on the basis of how their occupational or job titles have been defined at the workplace and also how they have been legitimised by education.

This information about work and occupations, first collected from people and then documented, is the data used when the population is classified according to social positions by official statistics and social scientific research. When the statistical offices make textual classifications of the population's social status in the 1990s, the most essential basis for distinguishing between groups of people is connected to the ways in which the labour force, occupations, occupational statuses, education, industries and ownership are being defined. When socioeconomic groupings are being classified occupations are the most important criterion. The distinction between women and men in population statistics has indeed been self-evident ever since modern official statistics were founded in the eighteenth century. When regular censuses in each decade were first established in USA in 1790, people were differentiated into women and men, black and white, free and slaves. These distinctions were important for an evaluation of military and industrial strength (Davies, 1980: 548). The first governmental statistical office, established in 1756 in Sweden, divided the population into women and men of different age, marital status and estate position (Pitkänen, 1982: 109–10). There the government's interest was mainly in the preconditions of population growth. Social scientists' emphasis and criteria for classifications vary according to their theoretical background and framework. Social scientists make use of population statistics, despite the fact that they often criticise them and make new categories. Nevertheless, social scientific research also produces classifications for statisticians' use. In practice researchers also participate in the formulation of statistical classifications as, for example, by giving expert advice or through committee membership. The most usual criteria for describing social positions that researchers use are the same as the ones used by statisticians: occupation, education, occupational status, income, relationship to production and ownership. So in many essential ways there is not much difference between the classificatory systems in the modern society and the ones researchers use. But compared to how self-evident the classification into women and men has long been in the censuses all over the world, it is really astonishing that gender became an analytical category in social science only in the 1970s.

The categories researchers use may be different from the ones used by statisticians, but empirical observations are nevertheless gathered from people themselves who in turn can be classified in either one way or another. All this sounds rather logical, although circular. People's own definitions and the institutionalised groupings are intertwined with each other as if they were a self-perpetuating continuum.

Below I will examine the hierarchisation of women and men and take a closer look at the contents of the classifications describing waged labour positions. I will start with people's own classifications at white-collar workplaces.

THE CLASSIFICATION OF WOMEN'S AND MEN'S WORK AT THE WORKPLACE LEVEL

The view that the male body is the source and sign of physical strength is very persistent in our culture. Especially in industrial work hierarchical divisions between women's and men's work have been produced by associating heavy work with men and light work with women (Game and Pringle, 1983: 28–9). We know that both the heaviness and lightness of work are relative and that they change historically and culturally. For instance, metal factory work, which requires physical strength, is thought of as strenuous and being the job of muscular men. Despite its physical

Table 3.1 Distinctions between women's and men's ways of doing things at
white-collar workplaces

Women	Men
Personal commitment	Factual orientation
Reliability	Responsibility
Compassion	Problem-solving
Details	Comprehensiveness
Coping with stress	Physical strength

stress, work in a textile factory has been regarded as suitable for young
girls.

At workplaces white-collar workers are unanimous that clerical work
is basically suitable for both women and men.[1] A female tax clerk gives
this explanation: 'There is hardly any heavy work in the office, except that
janitors have to move things about, and that would be too heavy for
women.' White-collar workers think that they are doing mental labour and
so women's and men's suitability is not directly differentiated by using the
physical dimension of lightness and heaviness of work. But yet gender is
present when the tasks are defined: the suitability of a job is reasoned with
by saying that it is equally suitable for women and men because the job
does not include such heavy tasks that women would be unable to do
them. The physical strength associated with the male body is the standard
used.

When the question is posed in another way it becomes apparent, however, that both women and men think that there are tasks to which women
and men are differently suited. The sexes are thought to be different because of their characteristics and ways of doing things. The distinctions
between women's and men's way of doing things that become apparent at
white-collar workplaces can be summarised in the opposite pairs listed in
Table 3.1.

Without changing the discourse this list could as well be extended by
quoting the observations the classic sociologist Georg Simmel (1984: 65–
101) made of life in turn-of-the-century Germany. Simmel describes how
men have the ability to separate themselves from facts and actions and
how women cannot make this distinction and personalise everything instead. Men are capable of grasping objective facts and women have the
ability to interpret other people's inner worlds and feelings. The similarities between what a German sociologist has written almost a century ago

and how Finnish white-collar workers define themselves today illustrate the fact that the overall cultural structure, within which we understand reality, is fundamentally rather permanent.

The definitions given to women's and men's actions express not only the gendered work content but also produce notions of feminine and masculine embodiment. Women are defined as committed, feeling, understanding and enduring. Men are defined as solving problems, controlling and bearing responsibility for things that are outside themselves. The different tasks and jobs are routinely coded as difference.

The categorisations of femininity and masculinity related to work tasks do not mean that 'in real life' women's and men's actions could be reduced to a mere femininity–masculinity opposition. Whether the worker is a woman or a man, as a worker s/he can simultaneously understand and solve problems or be accurate with details and deal with things comprehensively. But when there is a strict segregation between women and men, the different tasks and jobs are rather smoothly coded as difference in a way that women's spheres are associated with feminine skills and the female body, and men's tasks with masculine skills and the male body. At the same time we uphold a view that women could not possibly have skills that are thought of as masculine and that correspondingly men could not have feminine skills.

However, it is not a logical conclusion of the differences and divisions between women's and men's skills that one would be better or worse, or higher or lower esteemed, than the other. For example, the ability to feel compassion and understand other people's problems is as important as problem-solving skills. The definitions just sustain the idea of what jobs are thought of as suitable for women and men. The different definitions and splits related to women and men form the cultural grounds for segregation between women and men. These cultural categorisations of women and men are not, however, hierarchical as such.

LOWER AND HIGHER GROUPS AT THE WORKPLACE LEVEL

In the metal factory (see the Introduction above), on the ground floor in a well-lit, clean and almost noiseless space we can meet male workers wearing overalls and overseeing and controlling the material flow on their computer monitors. On the first floor of the factory, in the noise and clamour of an open-plan office, female white-collar workers oversee and control the factory's material flow with their computers. There is not necessarily an apparent and concrete difference between the nature of the work of these two groups of workers, or in its autonomy and decision-making power. The work is defined by the company's material flow and both groups share a common schedule.

Physical space and overalls separate the workers and other personnel. All other differences are harder to detect with 'bare eyes', such as the positions, esteem and work content of the different worker groups. The occupational titles used at the workplace do not always tell anything to an outsider about work content, education or the worker's hierarchical position. Occupational titles are based on a division of jobs and tasks specific to the workplace. The three hundred white-collar workers have nearly a hundred different job and occupational titles related to the design, planning, supervision and control of production. There are technical employees who are mostly male. There are people in supervisory positions and higher-level white-collar workers, most of whom are men. Then there are clerical workers, the majority of whom are women.

The production workers, clerical workers, technical employees and the management have different tasks within the division of labour. However, when asked, the clerical workers wonder about the difference between production workers and themselves, because there is no visible dissimilarity in the work content. The distinction between production workers and white-collar workers is also not so self-evident. There are examples of people on the factory floor who could have 'made it' and become white-collar workers, but they are reluctant to do this because it would mean less pay. There are no corresponding examples of people switching over from white-collar classification to production. In everyday speech white-collar workers make differences among themselves by talking about the different tasks and departments. They talk, for instance, about wages clerks and people working in the computer department. The various supervisors and managers are not talked about in connection with their different areas of responsibility or departments but as 'bosses', a hierarchical position written in their occupational titles.

The definitions within groups of production workers and white-collar workers are based on the way the work is organised by separating planning and performing, but these divisions also correspond with membership in different unions and the way wages are calculated. The classificatory systems of work are also different. The higher-level white-collar workers and managers are paid according to various criteria of responsibility, targets and output. The wages of the lower-level white-collar workers, which are the concern of collective bargaining, are determined on the basis of job descriptions. The clerical workers can themselves, or with their shop stewards, participate in job classification by compiling job descriptions of their work. Supervisors approve of the job descriptions and define the task hierarchy in relation to the other clerical workers. The divisive line between clerical workers and higher-level white-collar workers is that the first mentioned are defined according to their tasks and the higher-level employees' position with regard to their areas of responsibility. The clerical workers' tasks and the higher-level employees' areas of responsibility are not compared. Consequently the classificatory practices already include an inscribed hierarchical difference in which tasks and responsibilities are separated from each other.

The clerical workers, who are women, think that they are the weakest and lowest esteemed worker group in the factory. They compare their position with the workers by saying: 'It was a long time ago that clerical workers were thought of as being better. Now production is grand [. . .] It used to be a great thing to be working in an office. Now it's just the opposite. Workers are more highly esteemed and they get better wages.' Why do the female clerical workers think at the end of the twentieth century that they are the least valued group in the factory? A hundred years ago these jobs were done by highly respected men in suits and ties who used pen and ink to write business correspondence and keep the books. In concrete terms the low esteem is shown in the size of the pay cheque and also in the fact that from the clerical workers' own standpoint the other worker groups do not know what their jobs are actually like. 'Our work does not have that kind of a visible effect on production, although what we do is indispensable.'

Why does the clerical workers' work remain invisible? One reason could be that work which does not have visible results and produces the everyday continuity of things by taking into account other people's needs instead does not fit into the existing systems of classifying the relationships, positions and content of work. For instance, the wages clerks' work combines physical performance (entering the numbers accurately on the computer), knowledge (basic knowledge of computers and the contents of collective agreements), experience (how the wages of the different personnel groups are formed in that particular workplace) and emotional commitment (responsibility for the running of things, interpersonal skills). However, in the workplace's documented job description work requirements are reduced to two things: knowledge on the one hand (basic knowledge of computers) and physical, practical performance on the other (accuracy). Experience and emotional skills are not defined in a way that would give them the status of standard requirements in job descriptions.

The classification which determines the wages lacks the wages clerks' own view of their work as 'cooperation with many different people' and

'everyday running of things'. Nor does the classification include the requirements their supervisors listed, such as 'flexibility', 'coping with stress',
'help and consideration', 'commitment', 'taking work to their hearts'. Sub-
sequently the cultural definitions which are associated with the women's
work at the workplace disappear from the official work classification. The
qualifications of the embodied female wage worker do not become an
established and documented job classification at the workplace level.

LOWER AND HIGHER SOCIAL POSITIONS

What happens when the wages clerks are located into the socioeconomic
positions representing the whole population? Within the model that population statistics use to describe society, wages clerks become lower white-
collar employees. The classifications and criteria of socioeconomic position
vary from country to country, but internationally they are connected by the
United Nations' recommendations. Population statistics are indeed special
as a descriptive system of social positions in that their content is defined
by international comparability. In a way, population statistics integrate
concrete local realities with abstract global models of society. The universal models that make international comparisons possible may have grave
problems in describing local realities. On the other hand, the country-
specific classifications are not unambiguously local in the sense that they
are formed after the models of international classifications, particularly
those of the United Nations.

   In international comparisons the occupational classifications have proved
to be especially problematic. Occupational classifications are central when
populations are grouped into socioeconomic positions. The development
of occupations and professions, their social significance and prestige all
retain ways of conceptualising the economy as also local histories and
cultural specificities. For instance, in a comparison (Lane, 1987) of the
positions of lower white-collar employees in two countries, Britain and
Germany, which are economically rather similar, several country differences appear. In Britain there is a clear and marked tendency towards an
increasing division of labour, deskilling and deterioration of market chances,
whereas the same tendencies are not evident in Germany. There has occurred
a polarisation of the clerical labour force with the creation of a large
proletariat at one end of the pole in the British financial services sector,
but not in the German one. These differences cannot be explained by
economic factors; instead, cultural differences play a crucial role, especially
the attitude towards occupational training and skills which traditionally

have high prestige in Germany. Both countries, however, have in common that women are the majority in the lower positions of the labour market hierarchy.

The local history of the development of occupational classifications may be very different, as, for example, in the comparison of Britain and the USA (Davies, 1980). When the model of occupational classification was developed, the concern in Britain was with the changes in the traditional status order and the problem of assimilating new occupational groups in the social evaluation. In the USA by contrast, the issue was far less on this diversity of persons and more on the need to document or monitor economic growth and development. Yet both had in common the idea of a value difference between men's and women's occupations.

What, actually, are the ideas and conceptions contained in the classification of socioeconomic positions that legitimise the value difference of women and men in working life? The arguments that are used for the classification of socioeconomic positions in each country vary from case to case, but cultural conceptions can be found in all classifications.

In the socio economic classification (Sosioekonomisen aseman luokitus, 1989: 19–20), which is based on the United Nations Recommendation for the 1990 Population Censuses (1987), lower-level white-collar employees, such as for instance nurses, are said to be on a performance level in which responsibility for performance, instead of the whole undertaking, is characteristic to the job description. Their tasks are characterised by saying that 'dealing with symbols, either manually or by using machines or equipment which substitute manual work, is essential' or that it is their job to 'care for people or deal with information concerning them or other information'.

In the classification of socioeconomic groups (Ibid.) upper-level white-collar employees, such as for example engineers, are said to take part in decision-making or to be working in specialised controlling, managing, planning and service jobs, or in productive occupations. The tasks are characterised as independent, responsible, indivisible and as requiring extensive theoretical knowledge.

The boundaries between upper- and lower-level white-collar workers are defined as the places they hold in the organisational hierarchy and the theoretical knowledge their work requires. The upper-level employees are located in the higher levels of decision-making organisations, and lower-level employees work on the performance level. According to the classification upper-level employees need extensive theoretical knowledge whereas lower-level employees need limited and less theoretical knowledge and experience.

The grounds for differentiating between upper-level and lower-level

Table 3.2 Criteria for upper and lower socioeconomic positions

Lower-level	Upper-level
Responsibility for performance	Overall responsibility
Dealing with symbols	Decision-making
Routine	Specialisation
Replaceability	Irreplaceability
Limited knowledge, experience	Extensive knowledge, theory
Unautonomous	Independent
Caring	Productive

employees in the classification of socioeconomic groups can be summarised as in Table 3.2.

When the differences between upper-level and lower-level positions in the socioeconomic classification and the above mentioned divisions of women's and men's work at the workplace level are compared, it is obvious that the cultural qualifiers attached to women and men are easily associated with the definitions of upper- and lower-level positions. Responsibility for performance presupposes reliability, decision-making requires problem-solving skills, caring calls for personal commitment and so on. I would argue that the qualifications of an embodied male wage worker are transformed as upper and those of an embodied female wage worker as lower in the classifications which describe social positions.

The classification of socioeconomic groups, which is based on occupational status, describes the hierarchical power relationships in working life on a highly general level. Office workers are usually on the lowest position of workplace hierarchies. Women's caring jobs in the welfare state are as a general rule lower in hierarchies than men's technical fields. However, the titles of classificatory groups and the things classifications are based on (responsibility, performance, decision-making, caring, independent, unautonomous, specialised, routine) refer to work content and at the same time produce presuppositions of work requirements.

There has been a theoretical debate in social research on whether lower-level white-collar workers belong to the working class, lower middle-class or middle-class. In their criteria for classifications, researchers have simultaneously produced conceptions of 'typical' women and men. For example, in an international comparative study influenced by Marxist theoretical traditions and directed by E.O.Wright, the researchers suggested (Luokkaprojekti, 1984: 190) that the mental picture of 'the worker' as a brawny, strong-jawed man lugging a sledge hammer should be replaced by an office worker typing at her word processor with dainty fingers, or by a slender health worker lifting a fragile patient. Researchers in cultural studies, who are inspired by the French sociologist Bourdieu, brought up the fact (Kinnunen, 1989: 21–2) of how, for instance, female bank employees and male blue-collar workers clearly differ from each other as regards their symbolic 'cultural capital' and lifestyle. Whereas women read magazines on interior decoration and wear trendy clothes, men drive used cars and go ice fishing every weekend. These researchers representing different research traditions have, as if in passing, produced gender stereotypes in the examples with which they illustrate their classifications, namely dainty women interested in clothes and interior design, and strong-muscled men who drive cars and go fishing.

Researchers' debate on female white-collar workers' class position continues. What is essential is that in Finland married women gained independent status in stratification research in the 1980s. The self-evident starting point for the Finnish team of the International Class Project (Luokkaprojekti, 1984) was that women's social position can and should be studied independently and separately. In the mainstream research tradition this solution can be regarded as radical. The team had to justify, in particular to their British colleagues in the project, why married women also can have their own social position. But what is also essential is that after women are 'let in' to the wage worker status acknowledged by official statistics and social scientific research, the majority of them are then categorised as having lower social positions. The lower-level white-collar worker classification has become the growing and scientifically contested 'leftover class' for wage worker women.

THE DICHOTOMY OF THE HEAD AND THE HAND

In the classification of socioeconomic positions the difference between lower-level and upper-level white-collar workers is argued for by using the same criteria as when the distinction between workers and white-collar workers has been justified. The difference is made by separating mental labour from manual work. Theory is detached from practice, responsibility from performance, heading from handling. This is a dual structure in which the difference between the head and the hand is being produced and made hierarchical so that the head ranks higher than the hand.

The cultural separation of theory and practice, mental and manual, produces divisions between women and men, between workers and white-collar workers and between the different white-collar worker groups. The same structure can also be interpreted in the struggles for classification and status which women, who are categorised as lower-level white-collar employees, go through in hospitals, day-care centres, in home helping and other caring and nursing jobs. When people try to reach higher in occupational hierarchies, it is also attempted to define work content in a way that excludes concrete, everyday and bodily practices from the 'actual' professionalised work content. Hence there are conflicts at the workplaces: Who cleans up afterwards? Who takes patients to the toilet? Who feeds them and helps them get dressed? Worker groups try to climb higher in occupational hierarchies in the name of education, science and theory.

We all know that the mode of thinking which separates the world of ideas from the material world, theory from practice and the head from the hand is deeply embedded in Western culture. In ancient city states, where slaves represented corporeality and free men spirituality, the superiority of mind was reflected in the division of labour and ownership. In industrialised Western societies the separation of the mind and the body is intertwined with the separation of waged labour and its control. When we talk about mental and manual labour, the opposition can be regarded as an expression of the division of labour in society. But simultaneously this contrast is also a cultural convention which is legitimised by the fact that ideologically the difference between mental and manual seems self-evident because it looks as if it originates from 'nature', in other words it has been adapted from the Western world-view.

The analogy of the head and the hand is a common way of justifying social inequalities in modern industrialised societies (Douglas, 1986: 49). It is hard, however, to imagine even one occupation, job or task which could be done in practice without joining together head and hand, mental and manual. Such work simply does not exist, not even in Tayloristic factories. In wages clerks' work, physical performance is combined with knowledge, experience, and emotional and interpersonal skills. Wages clerks' work content does not 'fit into' the dual separation of theory and practice. Instead it has a third dimension: the 'invisible' skill of understanding and feeling, which has neither a linguistic expression in the documented job classification at the workplaces nor in the textual classification of socioeconomic positions. In the female domains of the welfare state, in personal services, nursing and caring jobs, the separation of theory and practice is especially problematic. In concrete work content 'mental caring', in other words dealing with other people's problems (responsibility, head and theory), is combined with 'the physical body' (performance, hand, practice) as for example in washing, feeding and lifting patients.

Work is no more purely physical than it is purely mental. It is impossible to grasp the content of these jobs on the basis of two-dimensionality because emotions, feelings, bodily experience, knowledge and physical touch are all combined in them.

CLASSIFICATIONS AS BLOCKS AND POSSIBILITIES

Mine is a truly love–hate relationship with the classifications which describe social positions. Love because the classifications produced by official statistics and social sciences give, for their part, a means for understanding the world. I find it important that we get information about local and global populations, changes in the industrial structure, the ways in which women and men make their living, family forms, etc. The world would seem a rather narrow and local place if people, objects and things were not somehow organised and compared. Hence I do not draw the conclusion that objectified classifications and forms of knowledge as such repress and control people's own chances for action (cf. Smith, 1990a: 61–80). I rather think that classifications enable social planning, comparison and prognosis.

Hate comes from the fact that institutionalised classifications have also been used to legitimate social inequalities. Every concept, criterion and classification includes the idea of who are lower and who are higher in the hierarchy. These are shifted, interpreted and negotiated from one generation to another. The 'natural' starting point for classifications describing social positions has been the difference between productive and unproductive work, occupational classifications based on men's work and the patriarchal family ideology. Feminist research too has presented the interpretation (Acker, 1980, 1988) that the very ways in which the economy, occupations and division of labour have been conceptualised have in themselves produced and then legitimised inequalities between women and men.

There is nothing 'natural' in the textual classification of social positions; instead they are agreements produced in social power relations. Yet the classifications include numerous analogies derived from nature. Argumentation which uses physical and biological metaphors reveals a more general way of talking in which the inequality produced in a social relationship is legitimised with analogies from the nature.

The difference between higher and lower is defined as the difference between the head and the hand, the mind and the body. The head and the mind are analogically linked with responsibility, theory, independence and higher positions. The hand and the body are combined with performance, routine, dependence and lower positions. When a concept which describes social positions is connected with a metaphor denoting physical space, such as 'lower/higher', the abstraction becomes understandable because it has to do with everyday experience (Lévi-Strauss, 1966: 135–60). We walk up and down the stairs. We have upper and lower middle classes. We have higher-level and lower-level white-collar workers. The image of social positions is a vertical ladder, not a horizontal line (see also Fiske, 1990: 93–4). When experiences of the physical world and the concepts produced in social relations are combined in linguistic metaphors, this connection is ideological. The classifications' linguistic analogies of nature and social relationships make them to be seen as if they were 'natural' and self-evident (Douglas, 1986: 48).

In the above I have shown, especially from the standpoint of women, who are classified as lower-level white-collar employees, how classifications which describe social positions include structures and ways of thinking that also maintain and reproduce the hierarchical order of women's and men's areas within waged labour relationships. When a rigid segregation prevails, the images of femininity and masculinity associated with different jobs include a view of gender as a difference between women and men in particular. Gender does not appear as a neutral matrix of a variety of differences, but as a rather solid women–men heterosexual dichotomy.

The white-collar workers' own classifications maintain a cultural differentiation of women's and men's jobs. However, these classifications are not hierarchical. The documented work requirement classifications, which determine the wages at the workplace, lack the diverse skills and abilities which are connected to the tasks done by women in lower-level positions. The distinctions between upper- and lower-level white-collar workers in official statistics show the hierarchical power relationships in working life practices, but they do not have the competence to describe work content or requirements. However, the linguistic namings and criteria in classifications, such as independent and routine work, refer to work content and requirements. When work, for example women's office work, includes different interpersonal relationships, its classification as routine performance creates a simple and uninformed image of the actual work requirements. Consequently the language of classifications ideologically justifies and sustains the hierarchical order of work and positions. The structural definitions of lower and higher positions are intertwined with the cultural production of dichotomous differences between corporeal and incorporeal, feminine and masculine. Dual classifications constructed by separating theory and practice do not incorporate the work content of female lower-level white-collar workers. The dichotomous principles in classifications also tell us about the structure of the existing culture, but simultaneously they also maintain and legitimate this structure. Dichotomising always involves an indisputable possibility for repressive hierarchisation.

NOTE

1. The white-collar workers' definitions of women's and men's different suitabilities to different tasks are based on our interview questions. The definitions were not necessarily apparent in any way in everyday work situations. Päivi Korvajärvi gives a more detailed account of this in her chapter.

4 Gender Matters in Collective Bargaining
Riitta Martikainen

Collective agreements are one way of improving women's position on the labour market, a way which the United Nations' Fourth World Conference on Women (1995) also emphasised in its platform for action. From a European perspective, the issue of collective bargaining in the context of equal opportunities has additional importance given the increasing feminisation of the European labour market and the need for employment policies and trade union strategies to respond to such change. In many countries workers and employers have agreed on wider or more specific programmes with the aim of promoting equality. Collective agreements are a valuable way of trying to explicitly address discriminatory practices (e.g. Bercusson and Dickens, 1995).

Agreement texts are usually regarded as gender neutral and at first glance that is what they actually seem to be like. But when the texts are read more carefully and in connection with the practices in which they are applied, it becomes apparent that the neutrality is largely ostensible. The aim of this chapter is to highlight the curious tension created when gender neutral thinking and writing collide with gendered practices. The focus is on agreement texts on the one hand and on the practical processes in which the texts are being produced on the other. I do not find agreement texts interesting as such but in relation to the context of their formulation and application. The principal actors in the process are the negotiators in labour market organisations and at the workplace level.

THE BARGAINING SYSTEM

Terms of employment are negotiated differently in different countries. Typical for Finland is that collective agreements are generally binding which means that, with certain conditions, unorganised employers are also obliged to apply the collective agreement in the branch to all their employees. Because the agreements are generally binding and because the rate of unionisation is high, the majority of all wage earners are covered by collective agreements. This means that collective agreements are in a key position when wages are fixed. They include provisions on base pay, working hours, annual holidays, sick pay, etc. Negotiators delegated by workers and employers draw up the contents of the agreements. The bargaining system is highly centralised in Finland, as in the other Nordic countries, Austria and Belgium (Kauppinen, 1994: 120–1). The USA is an example of a quite different bargaining system, because collective agreements there are made mostly at company level. Since 1968 the Finnish employers' and workers' central organisations[1] have mostly devised so-called incomes policy agreements. The aim is to find the general conditions by which sectoral collective agreements can be reached. Usually the agreements are valid for a two-year period. In the corporatist system prevailing, for instance, in the Nordic countries and Austria the state is the third party in incomes policy agreements. This usually involves decisions on income tax and government social policy as well. For example, the provisions for maternity and paternity leaves have been negotiated in this way in Finland. Later on they have been decreed as legal benefits which the collective agreements may exceed but not undercut.

The incomes policy agreements have also to some extent been used to regulate the wage distribution in different branches and, if desired, they can be used to reduce the wage differentials between female and male dominated branches. The 1970s agreements were designed to improve the situation in branches with low pay, and these also benefited the lowest paid women workers. In the 1988 negotiations the negotiators for the female dominated white-collar unions brought for the first time to the negotiation table a demand for a wage increase which was clearly based on gender. This was the so-called equality bonus with which a certain percentage of all pay rises was allocated to female dominated branches. The equality bonus has been included in incomes policy agreements several times.

In the incomes policy era the wages gap between women and men was at first reduced, but the late 1980s marked the end of this progress. New incomes policy agreements have not been entered into in recent years, at a time of economic recession and mass unemployment. Finland is at present undergoing a decentralisation of labour markets which means that the emphasis of agreement practice is gradually moving away from central organisations to the workplace level. As a result of the latest union-level agreements wage differentials have started to increase. The male dominated unions in export industry have been the main beneficiaries of pay rises. The female dominated service and public sectors received no wage increases, and in the public sector wages were even reduced. This means that the overall wages gap between women and men may start to grow.

The effects of decentralisation on gender equality in the labour market are not simply negative, however. There are examples of company-level agreements granting women benefits that could not have been achieved on a central bargaining level in the difficult economic situation (Brumlop, 1995).

The bargaining system is usually male dominated (see, for example, Colling and Dickens, 1989: 29–30). This is also the case in Finland, although the majority of organised labour are women. Most of the trade union negotiators are men, and there are even fewer female delegates in employer organisations. The proportion of women among union negotiators began to grow in the latter half of the 1980s when women were elected, often after serious debates, for example as leaders of female dominated unions. According to Cynthia Cockburn the number of women officials in British trade unions and their influence in collective agreement negotiations also started to grow at the end of the 1980s, but not without resistance (Cockburn, 1991: 112). Collective bargaining is nevertheless still largely a male bastion in our country, and there are hardly any women at incomes policy negotiation tables. All the top negotiators in incomes policy negotiations are men. In May 1992 the female dominated central union for white-collar employees elected its first ever female chair. In the same year, before even the first negotiations took place, the central union was declared bankrupt and she became unemployed.[2]

Unlike employer organisations, trade unions are ideologically committed to equality. However, the trade union movement has traditionally given first priority to economic equality. Gender divisions have not been emphasised; instead there has rather been a tendency in trade unions to ignore them. In many countries employers use equality plans or programmes, but in Finland such instruments are still new. Employers are not committed to equality. In principle the fullest possible use of human resources, including women's labour, is advantageous to employers. On the other hand, reducing the wages gap between women and men means in practice that, if women get pay rises, employers' labour costs also increase.

FROM A NEUTRAL TEXT TO UNEQUAL OUTCOMES

The following two examples are taken up in order to illustrate how collective agreements and their application make for women's and men's unequal positions in working life. The first example shows how a seemingly gender neutral text does not result in equality of outcomes. The second example is from the grassroots level and elucidates how a productivity bonus system used in a paper mill functions from the standpoint of gender equality. Gendered reality and gender neutral thinking are maintained through textually mediated processes (see Acker, 1992). The salespeople's collective agreement is to my mind a good example of how, under closer scrutiny, a seemingly gender neutral text turns out to produce inequality. It is interesting to see how occupational skills are gendered in this agreement. How does this work?

Salespeople are one of the biggest occupational groups in Finland. Three-fourths of salespeople are women and the majority work full-time. In 1990 about one-third of the salespeople in retail trade worked part-time, and during the present recession the figures have risen to slightly over 50 per cent. The number of part-time workers in retail trade is exceptionally high because part-time work (less than 30 weekly working hours) is rare in Finland, even among women (see Chapter 2). Part-time salespeople are covered by the same collective agreement as full-timers and they have basically the same terms of employment and wage as full-timers. In this respect Finland is different from, for example, Britain where part-timers can be paid lower hourly rates and they have poorer social security, e.g. maternity leaves, than full-timers have (Cockburn, 1991: 43).

In the collective agreement salespeople are divided into two categories according to how demanding their tasks are. About 90 per cent of all salespeople belong to the first category whose tasks are not considered to be very demanding. Only one-tenth of all salespeople belong to the better paid second category. The collective agreement gives the following definitions:

- Salespeople, who by virtue of their tasks are not placed in category II, are placed in category I.
- If the work of a salesperson is particularly demanding, and the performance of the tasks requires special training or professional skills acquired through extensive work experience, the salesperson is placed in category II.

The tasks of a worker placed in category II include, for example, those of a senior salesperson in the meat and poultry department of a supermarket which has a wide assortment of products and a high sales volume, or sales tasks of similar standard in other departments.

The sale of building materials and heating and ventilation equipment is an example of such demanding sales tasks in cases where the salesperson makes quotations based on cost estimates made according to the blueprints or other instructions given by the customer.

If the sales tasks require of the worker the ability to offer deliveries based on the complete working plans provided by the customer, the worker can be considered as belonging to category II.

In order for the tasks to qualify for category II wages, the worker is required to have a special expertise related to the articles on sale and to be able to provide guidance to customers on the principles of operation of the products concerned (salespeople's and warehouse workers' collective agreement, para. 5.)

The more demanding jobs mentioned in the guidelines are all in branches in which the proportion of male workers is relatively high, for instance in meat and poultry and hardware departments. Why, for example, does the selling of cosmetics not rank as especially demanding work? Cosmeticians often have extensive expertise on the various beauty products and some of them have special training. Salespeople selling fabrics and clothing are not mentioned as having demanding tasks either, even if their job can involve choosing fabrics on the basis of the customer's work design. No job evaluation system was applied when salespeople were divided into the wage categories.

According to the guidelines, entry into the better paid category requires special knowledge of the products on sale and the ability to guide and instruct the customer on their *principles of operation* (emphasis mine). This formulation connotes machines and equipment. The articles typically sold by women such as groceries, books, fabrics, clothes, shoes and so on do not 'operate'. Instead they have qualities which the salesperson must be familiar with and know how to explain to the customer. On the other hand a moisturiser could be said to operate when it is absorbed by the skin, or a garlic presser operates when it crushes the clove. Some of the products men sell can undoubtedly be said to operate, such as car parts, different kinds of machines and many hardware and building supplies. But how does a nail or concrete operate? 'Principles of operation' brings to mind highly developed automatic operations. But not even the sale of all domestic appliances is considered as belonging to the more demanding task category. Women sell smaller domestic appliances for smaller wages than men do the bigger ones.

The definition of category II salespeople has been written up to suit selling jobs in which the proportion of men is high. Yvonne Hirdman (1988) uses the concepts difference and hierarchy to describe the two logics of the gender system. By hierarchy she means that men are the norm. What men do is worthier and preferable. Could it be that the high cultural esteem of men's work underlies the division of groups of salespeople, or why is it that the typically male occupational skills are better paid than feminine skills? What do the negotiators have to do with all this?

GENDERED ACTORS IN THE BARGAINING PROCESS

In the retail branch both the employers' and workers' top negotiators are men. Also the female chair of the trade union participates in the negotiations, but the majority of union officials at the agreement level are men and they have an important role in both the negotiations and the draft stage. So the negotiations in this branch are generally dominated by men (cf. Colling and Dickens, 1989; Kumar, 1993: 209). Before the final signature the outcome of the negotiations is presented to the decision-making organs in the union which have a female majority.

How have the definitions of salespeople categories been negotiated? The union's male top negotiator told me that when these two categories were adopted, salespeople were divided into groups roughly on the basis of what employers were paying to workers at that time. In other words the trade union gave their blessing to the employers' opinion of work requirements.

Unlike all the others, one of the female negotiators saw the gender bias in this part of the agreement: 'Yes, that's it exactly, although it's not written down, it's men and women. But when you read the definitions you can't fail to notice it.'

Why is the definition still there in the agreement although the trade union knows that it results in better wages for male than female salespeople? The male top negotiator, who used to work in a hardware store, regarded the discussion on the fairness of wage categories as a battle between different groups, which the union did not wish to encourage. He did not say that it is actually a question of conflict of interests between groups of men and women. Trade unions often tend to avoid making the hidden gender conflict an open issue (cf. Lukes, 1986). The unions would rather see their members as a homogeneous group, and bringing up gender divisions would spoil this image. Talking about the conflict between women's and men's interests still arouses strong opposition among many male trade union activists in Finland (cf. Cockburn, 1991: 112).

Wage workers have to define their common interests in a continuous debate and solve conflicts in order to be able to act collectively. Just like the male negotiator I interviewed, male social scientists Offe and Wiesenthal (1980) omit all mention of gender as a basis of interest formulation when they write about the difficulties in making workers' interests compatible. However, the interests of trade union members can be partly based on gender and thus divide the membership in two. The employer organisations also may have varying conflicts of interest between them depending on whether the branch is female or male dominated. Gender is a dimension which may divide not only trade unions but also employer organisations in a new way.

A British study noticed some gender differences in the negotiating styles and issue priorities of the local negotiators of a public sector union. Women shop stewards gave a higher priority to low pay and equality issues than men; on the other hand the researcher comments that the similarities between female and male negotiators were on the whole greater than the differences (Lawrence, 1994: 130–6).

In order to achieve equality bargaining pressure is needed which is aimed at the union either from workplaces or from society, the media, etc. What is also needed is receptiveness to pressure and the ability and preparedness to act (Colling and Dickens, 1989: 48). What the female negotiator wished for was pressure from below to change the salespeople categories.

Why then have the female salespeople not started to demand more tasks to be included in the definition of the better paid category? I assume that people at workplaces think that the categories are unchangeable, in some ways self-evident. The agreements have the status of a law in workplaces, and who would think that they can change laws? It would be a very time-consuming and bureaucratic process to start making demands for changing the application practice and therefore it is no wonder that not many people take it up. Employers do not wish to expand the better paid category because they want to cut labour costs. The employers' top negotiator said that salespeople placed in the lower paid category were 'an underclass' which describes his understanding of work requirements. From the point of view of the trade union, changing the categories would involve problems of organisational policy: they would like to recruit all workers in the branch into their membership because a high rate of unionisation means more power in negotiations. 'Ordinary salespeople' are rather highly unionised but there are many special groups that are not members of the union, and these are the people the union wants to win over.

As a part of the corporate system trade unions have to take into account the actions of the other parties in negotiations and cope in a conflict situation (Regalia, 1988). The union negotiators have to choose whose interests they prioritise and also take into account the employers' point of view. The conflict can materialise in the negotiator's everyday practices in the following way:

I've found it extremely frustrating that although it's completely clear that we should decide that salespeople get 10 per cent more than the others, employers oppose to it strongly. It's easy to get higher wages for all the other groups, but not the salespeople group. It's always hard to get.

(Female negotiator)

When studying the equality initiatives in a British retail company, Cynthia Cockburn (1991: 42–4) has also observed that it is hardest to improve the situation of the lowest paid women. It was easier for the better paid women, of whom there were fewer, to gain improvements. Cunnison and Stageman (1993: 48–54) report a case where the male workers, the union and the management bonded together against women when these wanted a flat-rate raise to the low paid women's wages instead of the usual percentage raise. Examples from both Finland and Britain would seem to point to the fact that advocating the interests of large and relatively low ranking groups of women is met with most resistance by employers.

Does the female dominated trade union for commercial employees prioritise the interests of small groups of men at the expense of great numbers of women? This would not be totally unheard of. In trade unions the conflicts between female and male workers have often been settled in the men's favour. Men's interests have been the first priority (Alasoini, 1990; Bergholm, 1991; Cockburn, 1991).

I don't know where it comes from that we think that the male special groups are so important. That's why we make these kind of decisions, in order to make them happy, and the salespeople are always unhappy.

(Female negotiator)

THE BASIS FOR BARGAINING POWER IN A PAPER MILL

The next section deals with the grassroots level and looks at how terms of employment, or rather one aspect of terms of employment, are decided upon at one workplace. Production bonus is an essential part of the wages at this particular workplace and it is interesting to find out how it is being distributed to female and male workers.

The following example is from a big paper mill in southern Finland which produces magazine paper. The mill has several production bonus systems which means that a part of the wages is paid according to the quantity and quality of production. The decision on the introduction of production bonus is made at the workplace between the employer's and workers' delegates. There are a number of different bonus systems and criteria for productivity. The productivity bonus may be as high as 20 per cent of the wages. The paper mill has three personnel groups, and each group has its own trade union. By far the biggest group is that of the paper workers, who are mostly men. The male dominated technical employees are the second biggest group, and the female dominated office workers are the smallest group. More than 25 per cent of all workers in paper mills are women.

Each group has its own collective agreement. On the Finnish scale an exceptional amount of things connected to the blue-collar paper workers' terms of employment are decided upon in the workplace. Their chief shop steward negotiates all wage issues with the employer's representative. In other words individual workers never negotiate their own wages. Office workers and technical employees have so-called personal salaries, which means that each worker negotiates her/his salary with the employer's representative. However, the collective agreement specifies minimum wages for each job. Shop stewards from each worker group negotiate the productivity bonus with the employer.

Most of the workers at the paper mill get the productivity bonus; only cleaners and the security personnel are left outside the scheme. Colling and Dickens (1991) have also discovered that cleaners are the group which is most often left outside bonus schemes. Most of the technical employees, but none of the office workers, get the bonus. In other words a large number of women workers in the mill are outside the bonus scheme.

According to the employer's negotiator the productivity bonus is paid in all the jobs in which it has been possible to build adequate indicators for evaluating the relationship between production and work. The office workers' female shop steward has repeatedly, but in vain, demanded from the employer a bonus scheme for those employed in office work, but the employer's negotiator has said that it is impossible to find relevant criteria for evaluation in office work. In the shop steward's opinion these indicators could be created, but the employer is unwilling to even try.

Membership in a blue-collar union seems to make it easier for some groups in the mill to get the bonus. One example of this are the cleaners (women) and security personnel (men), who belong to the same union. As they were unable to be included in the bonus system, a fixed extra sum was added to their hourly wages as a compensation. Why is it that some groups in the mill succeed in bargaining for productivity bonus and some do not? In labour market jargon the term negotiation power is used to denote a group's chances of improving its status in negotiations. There are stronger, more prestigious unions, and weaker unions with less influence.

When I interviewed the mill's negotiators I asked them what they thought their negotiation power was based on. The size of the group was the most frequently mentioned explanation, but there are other issues involved as

Table 4.1   Occupational groups according to size and gender structure

	Gender structure	
The size of the group	*Female dominated*	*Male dominated*
Large	Cleaners	Paper workers
Small	Office workers	Machine operators

Table 4.2   Negotiation power by different occupational groups

	Gender structure	
The size of the group	*Female dominated*	*Male dominated*
Large	Cleaners Little negotiation power	Paper workers Considerable negotiation power
Small	Office workers Little negotiation power	Machine operators Considerable negotiation power

well. Tables 4.1 and 4.2 illustrate the basis for the negotiation power different groups have.

It seems that negotiation power is not determined by the size of the group but by the sex of the majority in the group.

- Paper workers are the largest personnel group in the mill. They have a lot of advantages defined in both the collective agreement and local negotiations. They are the least educated personnel group in the mill. According to all interviewees paper workers are definitely the strongest group in terms of negotiation power.
- There are only a few machine operators and they are some kind of 'kings' at the mill. A machine operator's job is at the top of a paper worker's career ladder. Machine operators have always had a special position in paper mills and by far the highest wages of all blue-collar

groups in such mills. Their wages are often better than those of many of the technical employees or even of their immediate superiors, and they seldom change jobs. All machine operators are men and will be for many years to come because the prohibition of women's night work in 1955–88 was effectively used to bar women from working with paper machines. Nevertheless during that same period women were still allowed to work at the mill at night in other jobs (cf. Cockburn, 1983).

• Cleaners are the biggest occupational group in Finnish paper mills, and they are all women. Cleaners have the smallest wages of all the blue-collar workers, but their wages can be on a level with office workers who have a much better education.

• Office workers are the smallest occupational group, and they are mostly women. The average wages for office workers are clearly smaller than the wages for paper workers or for technical employees, even though they have a better education than the blue-collar workers and about as much education as the technical employees. None of them gets the productivity bonus or any compensation for its lack.

Estimating negotiation power with the help of only two characteristics, the size of the group and sex, is of course simplistic. Many interviewees thought that the closer people work to production the more negotiation power they tend to have. This criterion is even used as the basis for grading the technical employees' productivity bonus.

Women are generally defined as working far away from production. Although a cleaner wipes the machines with her own hands or crawls underneath them in order to clean, she is 'far away from production', obviously further away than the machine operator who, for the most part of his working day, checks figures indicating the paper-making process on the control room monitors. So being 'near the production' does not mean being physically close to the machines. Maybe 'nearest to production' is the person who is capable of stopping the machines and in so doing is able to cause the most financial damage to the company. Men's negotiation power systematically produces masculine interpretations of the criteria. We could say that this reflects hegemonic masculinity at the paper mill (Connell, 1987: 183–8).

Sheila Cunnison and Jane Stageman (1993) have conducted a feminist study on the local trade union of a large hospital in Britain. Nurses, porters, cleaners, barbers, etc. belong to the union. Both the local trade union and the employer are of the opinion that bonus schemes are better suited to men's jobs (like portering) than to women's jobs (like cleaning). As at the paper mill, they argue that bonus schemes are easier to apply in jobs in which it is easy to measure productivity. However, it is hard to see what the difference between porters and cleaners might be in this respect. According to the researchers the situation is an example of how men use power in the local trade union in order to promote their own interests (Cunnison and Stageman, 1993: 43–4).

In the paper workers' local trade union cleaners' wages had not been completely forgotten; instead they had been negotiated 'a compensation' for not getting the productivity bonus. In other words the female cleaners benefit from belonging to a large and strong male dominated blue-collar union.

CONCLUSIONS

In recent years women have openly brought up the issue of gender in Finland. In the 1980s women were mobilised to promote their interests at workplaces and trade unions, and the public discussion on discrimination became more heated. This resembles what Connell calls 'working class feminism' (Connell, 1987: 265–70), but unlike Australia both white-collar and blue-collar women are involved. Comparable worth movement is an important element in trade union women's activism (see Chapter 11).

Collective agreements contain a number of individual conditions and structures which, despite their seeming gender neutrality, place women and men in different positions. It is this indirect discrimination that has become a universal topic especially among women active in trade unions. Therefore women have started to demand gender proofing of texts and agreements, which means that the issues should be considered explicitly from a gender perspective. Collective agreement texts are largely compiled by men. Although some women are involved in the negotiation process, men still mostly define the agreement content and their application.

In principle a centralised agreement system presents many opportunities for enhancing equality between the sexes. However, these possibilities can only come about as beneficial to women if they are strongly enough supported by the labour market organisations. Equality bargaining needs concrete agents in places where the important decisions are being made: someone has to take up initiatives and defend them at the negotiation table. Female negotiators are on average more sensitive to equality issues than male negotiators (Colling and Dickens, 1989; Kumar, 1993; Martikainen and Yli-Pietilä, 1992). In order to increase equality bargaining it is important to have more women in the strategic positions of the negotiation process.

Most of the negotiators I interviewed are gender blind; in other words they act as if workers are sexless creatures. As a result the decisions on terms of employment are made in a process in which nobody stops to think about what effects the decisions have for women and for men. As Colling and Dickens (1989: 46) say, negotiators can hardly understand what indirect discrimination in collective agreements means. This kind of action maintains the dominant hierarchic gender divisions with the help of seemingly gender neutral agreement texts. All negotiated issues should be regarded from a gender point of view and this kind of gender proofing requires of the negotiators that they be familiar with equality issues.

Although a single negotiator can be aware of the meaning of the worker's sex when negotiating the terms of employment, the chances for change are slim because the suggestions are met with opposition. Women in particular have a potential power of change in both workplaces and trade unions. Women's cooperation in trade unions is endangered not only because of opposition from men and their own prejudices against feminist action, but also because of the party political divisions among women and membership in competing unions. Women's interests also conflict with one another in many cases which makes it difficult to formulate common political goals. However, cooperation among Finnish women trade union activists has clearly become more intensive since the end of the 1980s, and a permanent unofficial organisation has been created.

On the basis of the Finnish experience it can be said that the high rate of unionisation together with a centralised bargaining system does not guarantee women equal terms of employment. From women's point of view there are naturally things that are relatively well taken care of, such as the provisions for maternity and childcare. Yet despite full-time employment and good education women's wages are nevertheless clearly lower than those of men and collective agreements include a lot of indirect discrimination. The application of gender proofing and more negotiators committed to women's interests are needed at all levels of collective bargaining.

NOTES

1.   At present, wage earners have three central organisations in Finland: Central Organisation of Finnish Trade Unions (SAK) with member unions in industry and the private services; Confederation of Technical Employee Organisations

(STTK) with member unions in white-collar and health work; and the Confederation of Unions for Academic Professionals (AKAVA). Employers have five central organisations who represent industry (TT), the private services (LTK), the state (VTML), the municipalities (KTML) and the church (KSV).

2. Most of the trade unions that were formerly members of this central union later joined the central union for technical employees which as a result got a female majority.

5 Working Within and Between Hierarchies
Päivi Korvajärvi

Is the relationship between women and men defined as hierarchical differences and dichotomous divisions also in the everyday work situations in the workplaces? How is it possible for female white-collar workers to change their places in the hierarchy and do their jobs discarding the hierarchies and yet making space within these hierarchies?

DOING GENDER

I understand 'gender' as a verb. This means that 'gender' is the continuous process of 'doing gender', concrete activities people do in different subject positions. Furthermore, 'gender' is not only the creation of the meaning of gender, but also the ongoing constitution of divisions between women and men, feminine and masculine, in all social interaction (Acker, 1990, 1992; Gherardi, 1994). Apart from making differences gender means managing situations in a way in which gender differences are rendered a self-evident fact. Human interaction, culture and institutions are all interwoven in doing gender (West and Zimmerman, 1987).

Gender and the relationships between women and men change in character, and the contents of the feminine and the masculine are continuously reconstructed in workplaces. The work organisation is a melting pot which takes advantage of the existing images of femininity and masculinity and in which these images are also produced (Alvesson and Due Billing, 1992; Kvande and Rasmussen, 1993). My emphasis is on the situational construction of gender in white-collar workplaces.

The concept of 'doing gender' means elastic, amoeba-like and nuanced processes in organisations. Some writers emphasise the continuous creation of distinctions as a way of maintaining women's subordination, in other words as a way of reproducing the hierarchical relationship between the sexes (e.g. Acker, 1990, 1992). Other writers maintain that organisations in general are masculine arenas. However, the content of masculinity varies and it is possible, in fact, to find a number of dominant masculinities in different organisations (e.g. Kvande and Rasmussen, 1993; Collinson and

Hearn, 1994). The changeability of both femininities and masculinities has also been discussed, and the view that organisations are merely places enabling masculine action has been criticised. Instead, there may also be compatibilities between women and the function of organisations (e.g. Alvesson and Due Billing, 1992). In the context of this book, it is worth emphasising that theories developed in Britain (Collinson and Hearn) and in North America (Acker) focus on practices which exclude or subordinate women in organisations, whereas some theoretical suggestions made by Nordic researchers (Kvande and Rasmussen, Alvesson and Due Billing) also tell about a possible 'room of women's own' inside organisational structures. This distinction in the conceptual ideas argue for the existence of culture- and country-specific variations on how gendering practices operate at concrete workplaces.

However, in concrete waged labour[1] gender becomes apparent, but in an obscure way. Interviews with the white-collar women gave rise to questions of, firstly, which ways gender and the gender conflict are hidden in organisations, and secondly, how gender appears as a subtext in speech and actions (cf. Martin, 1990; Calas, 1992). Two workplaces were chosen as the focus of the study, an employment office from the public sector and the head offices of an insurance company from the private sector. Both of these offices are vertically gender segregated so that the male employees hold the superior positions.

I have written this chapter from the standpoint of the voices and practices of women white-collar workers and given consideration to the kind of cultural categorisations they have made and used when we researchers have been present. As a writer I am nevertheless an interpreter, not just an annotator. I cannot show gendered relationships in the white-collar workers' worlds 'as such'. Instead I make my interpretations through the relationship I have as a woman and a researcher to the gendered subordinating practices in working life. In other words my writing is situated knowledge (Haraway, 1988; Bhavnani, 1993) which has been built into the research relationship at the workplaces.

A BALANCE WITHIN THE HIERARCHY

The first workplace in the case study is a small employment office which has a male director and twelve female counsellors or secretaries. The office operates on the local level as a part of the state labour administration. The women workers have at least a two-year commercial college education or a lower-level academic degree. The workplace is one case by which I describe the ways in which women can develop their own goals within the hierarchy with the male management's support. However, being a woman in the workplace entails contradictory dimensions. The women partly conformed to a femininity which emphasises responsibility for other people including customers and clients, colleagues and superiors in the organisation (Rantalaiho, 1990). At the same time the same women kept their waged work strictly separate from their lives outside it. They did not describe their working relations with family images (see, for example, Pringle, 1989) which seems to be quite usual in the Anglo-Saxon context.

Own professional space

When we talked about the actual work content, the introduction of computer technology or the job's esteem at the workplace, the workers never brought up gender as a significant issue. Clear-cut places for women's and men's tasks in the hierarchy did not lead to a conflict or a discussion of the gendered divisions and differences in this workplace.

The women workers had chosen 'good service' as their goal within the limits set by laws and guidelines. They were partly able to adjust these limits with their practices. When asked to define their work requirements they said that the most important of these were empathy, knowledge, courage and personal service. They were also able to put these ideals into practice, although not as much as they would have wished, but the values they held were in general appreciated in the workplace. The manager also supported the goal of improving the services and the education it entailed. His by-word was 'We are, and know how to be, experts in this field.' None of the women said that they would be interested in career advancement or holding a supervisory position. On the contrary, the women wanted to develop their current jobs and were not interested in promotions in the organisation. For example, Paula, who was the acting director in the manager's absence, emphasised the same work requirements as the other women. She wanted to take responsibility for her clients, to take proper care of the clients' problems and create intensive cooperation and a common goal with the client.

Paula considered that during the research process her situation had improved in the sense that she no longer had administrative tasks. But from the standpoint of her goals the situation had, however, also taken an opposite turn. There was less and less time for clients and preparation before appointments. With rising unemployment and ever more complicated benefit systems the problems clients faced had also gradually become more severe. The goal of in-depth client contacts had, in practice, been replaced by ever greater numbers of clients.

Both the removal of administrative tasks and the number of client contacts had a gender dimension. A new post was created in the office and its job description included the acting supervisory tasks that Paula had been doing. The post was given to a man. Paula did not want to apply for the job. She had earlier been the person organising schedules with clients and she also sorted out problems in personal relationships at the workplace. Paula said that she was a go-between in the arguments that came up among colleagues. I asked whether it mattered if such a position was held by a woman or a man. 'Yes. It might be easier to come to talk about these things with a woman.' Paula said that the male consultant '[. . .] was not drawn into the things that I was. Keeping to the weekly schedule used to be pretty hard, and now it seems it's become easier when the new consultant has not taken that much responsibility or worried too much about it. He has quite rightly given the responsibility to other consultants, so that they must look after the schedule.'

Paula was not satisfied with decision-making power because she wanted to devote herself to the job and clients. In this case a man had been 'better' at exercising power because compared to him Paula had, in her own opinion, cared too much. At no point in Paula's story did gender come up as a subordinated relationship. The man had just done the same job differently. Instead, gender comes up as a cultural Woman whom people can easily approach to tell their personal problems, and as a cultural Man who knows how not to care too much.

The female white-collar workers wanted, and created, their own space in the client work. In this they were also supported by the male director. There were possibilities and room at the workplace for activities which both the women and the men desired within the hierarchic and gender divided work organisation. Occupational hierarchies were not absolute; instead women were able to create autonomous room for themselves between them. Hierarchy in terms of organisational positions or decision-making power never came up, although these were the watershed between the women's and men's goals.

Job model and gender model somersault?

It has been argued that the malestream sociology of work regards people only as wage labourers whose whole lives are located in waged work. This means that a gendered substructure operates in organisations which assumes that work is a sphere of life separate from all other spheres. At the same time it assumes that the abstract bodiless worker engaged in waged labour is a man. Reproduction, sexuality and caring for and about other people are transferred outside the work tasks and the organisation. It has been argued that a working woman does not conform to these presuppositions (Acker, 1990, 1992).

When men's relationship to waged labour has been considered the commonly proposed framework has been that of the job model. In this case people's relationship to their employment is assessed from the perspective of waged labour only. Women's relationship to employment has been estimated on the basis of personal characteristics and family situations. This framework has been called the gender model (Feldberg and Glenn, 1979).

At the employment office Paula and the other female white-collar workers wanted to develop their work, to take into account their interest in immediate contacts with clients. Family duties were excluded when they reflected on their relationship to work. The women did not use a definition of femininity which was directly connected with the family. For them femininity meant that it was easier to make social contacts with women. They too left the world outside work, family relations or its symbolism outside the reasoning.

The women white-collar workers gave direct hints of what, in relation to one of the men in the organisation, could be called the gender model. This male consultant was respected by many women because he took a four-month paternity leave;[2] in other words the man combined waged labour with parenthood in his lifestyle. The women said that this kind of masculinity is very positive, even admirable.

The independent professional spaces enabled the testing of cultural gender divisions. A woman tried to break the boundary between the masculine and the feminine in her work by using her decision-making power but soon came to realise that this was not a very good option. A man tried to break this boundary outside waged work and by doing this earned his female colleagues' respect. The women allowed the man to combine family and work duties, but it seemed that they were not so generous with their esteem when it came to themselves.

IS OPPRESSION DISTANT BUT EQUALITY CLOSE AT HAND?

When we started to discuss issues other than the immediate tasks, the conflict between women and men nevertheless surfaced. When I asked what it means when the field is generally female dominated, the women's typical first reaction was that it means low wages. Another remark was that in this field, too, men tended to have better advancement prospects and that men were usually favoured in recruitment processes. The women never problematised the reasons for this and could find no examples in their own workplace.

Regular meetings dealing with current issues were held at the workplace. Most of the women felt that they had some influence: 'They always take your suggestions seriously.' I attended a meeting in which available posts were dealt with. In practice the male director had already made arrangements and proposals concerning suitable people. The male director presented the topics very thoroughly and formally. He emphasised the functionality of the work organisation as a basis for his decisions. In his speech this meant that the people proposed for the jobs were already well known in the organisation. Following the male director's proposal two men were hired in the office without having to apply for the posts.

This did not cause any protests whatsoever. On the contrary, in the interviews the women had expressed the wish that there were more men in the workplace because it would have a stimulating effect: 'It would create positive tension and make people more energetic.' In addition they thought that wages would also increase if the field attracted more male workers.

When I asked what could be done about women's position in general, the suggestions largely pertained to matters outside the workplace. The female workers demanded that women should be taken into account because they had the same abilities as men. But how could this be done? The Equality Act and better education were both given as solutions to this problem, although the women usually quickly added that they do not seem to be of much help. 'Women should have more cooperation,' was another comment. She added that the men in the field were not an obstacle to women's cooperation but that the other women were, those who were earning pin money for the family's consumption and were not interested in improving women's position. This sounds rather surprising in a society where women's incomes are absolutely necessary to support the family and are thus as important as men's. But on the other hand, women's incomes are still in general smaller than men's and so they may also seem additional just as they do in the family wage ideology (Hartmann, 1976).

The women also said that they themselves should be partly blamed for women's lack of power. A trade union activist said that 'we women' do not exercise power although this would be possible in the spirit of workplace democracy. People do not have enough faith in workplace democracy and in her view one answer would be manipulation and campaigning. 'We remain rather silent and just wait, and grumble only when the decisions are made.'

The flexible functioning of the work organisation was the most important thing from the male director's point of view and this gave room for recruiting more men without any need for explanation. Yet, simultaneously, the male director supported the women's attempt to develop client work and women the director's decision-making power. Women were aware of the gender conflict; it affected their wages which they were unable to settle at the workplace. But they still thought that the conflict existed somewhere else, in the society at large, and did not affect them personally or take place in the workplace. The women were not threatened by the fact that men took up some of their jobs in the workplace. On the contrary, the women's space was open for men, because having more men would resolve at least part of the social equality issues by improving the wages in the field, and it would also give more diversity to the workplace atmosphere.

In short, the way in which gendered divisions were constituted in the workplace suggests that participation, influence and culturally recognised spaces for women's and men's expertise do reduce consciousness of the hierarchic relationships. Gender disappears from the immediate work process when the male-oppressor and female-oppressed pattern does not exist in this sense. When the concrete things present in the work organisation were discussed, the women's context of relating to their job was that of their waged work as a gender neutral issue. But at the same time gender as a factor affecting wage determination was very important in the interviews. At the workplace level the women considered themselves as individuals, but at the society level as a group which had common interests (cf. Buswell and Jenkins, 1994). They both upheld and broke the gender boundaries, but then their evaluation was based on a very exceptional cultural conception of gender compared to research done in other countries (cf. Feldberg and Glenn, 1979; Pringle, 1989).

FENCED IN WOMEN AND MEN

The other example that I have chosen is one department in the head office of an insurance company which is divided into several smaller units. The department employs about 100 people. The majority of them, in other words the insurance clerks and their immediate superiors, are women, but the higher rungs in the hierarchy are taken up by men. I use this case to illustrate the ways in which a strict hierarchical order between women and men includes living and dynamic processes, and how even the strictest hierarchy between the sexes is not permanent. In contrast to the employment office the female insurance clerks brought up the bodily aspects of their work.

The abstract worker and the embodied woman

The department manager wanted to control what we researchers did at this workplace. The employees we were allowed to interview and observe had already been chosen for us when we came to do the research. The male department manager had enclosed with our questionnaire his own letter which was an order to fill in the questionnaire. Gender came up spontaneously in the interviews in this workplace, although basically this required some prompting from the researchers in this case as well. Contrary to the employment office the female insurance clerks connected gender with the situations and events in their workplace and in their opinion gender conflict was present in the company. However, gender conflict did not exist in the speech of the men on the supervisory level. To them, the clerks were abstract workers whose most important characteristic was speed.

The insurance clerks criticised two things in particular: the managers' control of work and their ignorance of the insurance clerks' work content. The clerks had to keep a quantitative watch on their work. Everyone took down the numbers of client contacts and the cases they had dealt with, and these were given to the supervisors. The women got detailed instructions on how and where to have coffee at the workplace and some of them compared the workplace to a prison. Compared to the employment office the managers' offices were far away from those of the employees, and the women thirsted for encouragement and feedback which they hardly ever got.

There was a strong conflict between the managers and employees in the women's speech: 'I feel that the managers do nothing. Many have very important jobs, but somehow I feel that the real work is done somewhere else.' The women said that there was one exception among the managers. They respected their male department manager who asked for their opinion and gave them feedback. 'The new manager has told us how important our work is. If you think of the whole company, our work includes a lot of responsibility.' The women pointed out, for example, that sorting the mail and keeping up the files on clients was also important because then the information was conveyed further in the organisation. We asked the department manager what he thought of the fact that the employees were women. He said that in problematic situations women tend to pay too much attention to details. In addition he thought that female and male employees have different problems because in his experience women's problems have more to do with children and illness than men's.

The women's accounts of work content varied from boring routine to lively exchange of ideas with other women. The women all agreed that they were doing a woman's job. When the researcher asked them whether they could think of a man doing the same job, the answer was that this is a feminine job. 'A man could sign papers but not work with such small details. This job requires accuracy and a good memory. Men are much more careless.' To women 'feminine' equalled paying attention to details, boring work content and low pay. In short, although the women had their own space also in this workplace, contrary to the employment office the women were forced into it. There seemed to be no avenues into the men's space and the men and women working within the men's space controlled the insurance clerks' work. The grounds for the division between women and men could be found in wages, the contents of work and the glass ceiling. Yet in this workplace, too, the interviewed women avoided making any connection between their jobs and their lives outside work. These things interacted but were not an obstacle to work as such or to career advancement. Male managers brought up the difference of women's problems because these had to do with issues that were outside work.

In the workplace the female insurance clerks and both male and female managers occupied different material and cultural spaces. Contrary to the employment office the conversations that took place in these spaces did not have any common ground. The managers talked about 'employees' and at first the word seemed neutral. But simultaneously they confused 'women' with 'girls' in their categorisations. In their opinion 'girls' had nothing to do with the Important Issues, like productivity and efficiency. They thought that the women were some kind of a herd and they only expected them to be quick. The women were different because they had problems outside waged work. Their lower status was self-evident and it did not need to be mentioned. The women themselves made a clear distinction between women's and men's jobs: women's jobs were badly paid dead-end jobs. Men's jobs had grander titles and better wages, independent of what the actual job entailed. This opposition, which was justified by life both inside and outside the organisation, was extremely strong. But in spite of that women too had some chances of overcoming these boundaries.

Across space – managing and selling

The only way the fence could be surmounted in the insurance company was that the women had to enter the men's field. This could be done either by entering management positions or by including more marketing, which was encouraged by the management, in client work.

At the beginning of the research period Leila worked as an insurance clerk. Later the department manager had asked Leila whether she wanted to start working as the insurance clerks' immediate superior. Leila felt very unsure about this. She was apprehensive of the responsibility because of the personnel management duties she would have to take on. She accepted the offer but asked for a trial period, because 'I can't be bothered to take on a job which I wouldn't be good at.'

After the initial trial period Leila decided to cross over the fence. She felt that 'if I don't take this opportunity I will never be offered anything else'. Just as the male managers she referred to the 'girls' when she talked about the clerks, but unlike the male managers she also relied on them. She thought that 'the girls' were a resource at the workplace. Leila valued what the workplace discussion groups did in planning detailed work contents, like designing the forms the company used for the computer system. Her goal was to make the company's leadership a bit more 'humane'. According to her the managers should know what happens on the levels below them in order to base their objectives on something else besides workplace statistics.

In addition Leila developed the same incentive in her work as the male managers: 'We will have to be able to compete.' Compared to her job as an insurance clerk the most essential change in her work content was that it now involved more social contacts. Previously she had been able to see the results of her work immediately in that the papers disappeared from her in-tray. Now at the end of the day she might wonder what, in fact, she had actually been doing all day. 'My mouth is dry, my throat is dry and I have no strength left. The whole day goes in just organising and talking.' Management and its social content was also physical work.

Gender did not come up in the interviews with Leila. Her position was close to that of the insurance clerks, but at the same time she had a superior position in which 'I have to make decisions myself and stand by them and take responsibility.' From this contradictory position her arguments were both similar to and different from those of the female insurance clerks and the male managers. She considered things in relation to waged work just as the insurance clerks and managers did. She never said that women's problems were any different from men's, nor did she talk about men's or managers' problems or her relationship to them. Her views on keeping up with the competition were rather close to the managers' views. Her relationship to the insurance clerks was built on acknowledging both the women's and male managers' views, but she kept these two separate in her position as the immediate superior. In practice she worked between two personnel groups, between the employees and managers, and at the same time, between women and men.

During the research period, marketing and selling became more substantial issues in the interviews and observations when we talked about transformation processes. The male manager who was esteemed by the female employees changed his manner of speaking about the contents of the work during the research process. He spoke of selling in terms of good service.

The many enquiries and questions from clients were all received by the telephone service. Ida had worked in the telephone service for a considerable time. She compared her tasks with tasks that were even 'worse' with the following comment: 'At least I am not a messenger girl.' In the same breath she too said that it would be 'wonderful if there were career prospects', but the chances for this were rather slim in an insurance company. Client contacts made the work dynamic, and she also said that she was able to influence clients with her own conduct. She defined her work by saying that you always have to cope and somehow get the information the client is looking for. However, this work was done not only by using one's brains, but the whole body: 'I have to strain my hearing very much . . . in a way I have to strain my whole body when I try to listen to what the client is saying.'

At the beginning of the research process client work and insurance selling were incompatible in Ida's opinion, but later she came to the conclusion that 'you have to fit selling somewhere into your work.' Her criteria for good client service changed in a way that was in accordance with the management's objectives. She said, 'there is no client to whom you could not sell something more.'

Ida had gradually taken on the two sides to this issue during the research process, that is both the client's and management's. She tried to separate these two in her thinking, and she did not associate them with gender in any way. This type of action has been analysed in terms of emotional labour (Hochschild, 1983), bounded emotionality (Mumby and Putnam, 1992), reproductive work orientation (Rantalaiho, 1990) and responsible rationality (Korvajärvi, 1990). Ida assimilated both the management's and clients' rationality, in practice, in interaction with clients, although the interaction took place on the clients' terms. She was the one to define how she would combine the different standpoints in each situation, because the male managers, who set the marketing goals, worked practically and culturally very far away from the everyday sales work. This gave her pleasure and independence to a certain extent, but at the same time it kept her within the masculine values and power. From her own point of view she pushed the masculine hierarchy a bit further away.

WOMEN AND MEN IN ORGANISATIONAL CULTURE

The analysis of these two cases shows that in their daily activities women white-collar workers had contradictory ways of maintaining, reproducing and trying to break the hierarchic divisions between women and men. In other words they gendered ambiguously. Women had some chances of moving away from their places on the lower levels of the hierarchy, but in both workplaces it happened with the help of the male managers or within the conditions set by their goals. Support could be encouraging as in the case of the employment office, taking advantage of the opportunities offered to a woman, or adapting one's own initiatives in accordance with the organisation's goals as in the insurance company.

Analysing just two cases is enough to illustrate the fact that organisational hierarchies offer not only limitations but also many possibilities to women. It is essential to come to terms with how gender is culturally understood in organisations. The crux of the matter is thus not only the ways in which women and men define their work but how their work is defined in the organisational culture at large. One of the fundamental questions is in which and on whose terms women's goals are expressed.

In the first case, in the employment office, the differences between women and men did not come up as dichotomous divisions in everyday situations. The women, just as the men, were subjects. The women were able to attempt to achieve practices that they enjoyed, in other words to make client work more varied. Client work was also an essential part of the goals of the office which means the goals of the two were easily compatible. At the same time men's and women's areas were clear-cut within the vertical hierarchy. The women had their own professional space and could take advantage of this space. They were able to develop their work content on their own terms and were even supported in this by the men. Simultaneously, the goal upheld by the women remained a separate discourse in relation to the decision-making systems of the workplace or the whole administrative area. Both cultures supported one another and so the women's powerful personal space did not, nor was it meant to, work as a counter discourse for the decision-making system dominated by men.

In this sense the hierarchy between women and men disappears in the turmoil of everyday practices. But if the hierarchy is examined from a distance, for example measured by wages, it still exists. From an outsider's point of view the hierarchy is bound up with individual women and men, but for the insider the hierarchy largely disappears. Women and what is defined as feminine have a space within the structure and so have men and their occasional expressions of cultural femininity. Women and men are mutually supportive. However, masculinity is more or less invisible. For example, chances for career advancement – one of the main strategies of liberal feminism for improving women's position – did not appeal to women in this case. Thus femininity can be detached from individual women and men, but masculinity as an established discourse is not bound up with individuals in the workplace. The lack of concrete masculine culture obscures masculine structures at the workplace level. Activities that are defined as masculine rather seem to remain a faceless machinery inside the organisation.

In the second case, in the insurance company, women and men produced dichotomous gender distinctions. Both women and men had different understandings of women's work activities compared to the employment office. The work that women did meant to the insurance company's men something small and detailed for which they also were accountable to the men. Men did not regard it highly, although some of them used to tell the women that boring work is also important to the organisation. On their side, the women had no room of action to enjoy their jobs without special effort. They constructed a dichotomy against the men because of the remoteness and strangeness of each other's work.

It is also interesting to note that in the strictly hierarchical organisation men constructed a different image of women because of the women's domestic responsibilities, creating a dichotomy between public and private. This same type of domestication of women (Cockburn, 1991: 82) may be worldwide. However, locally on a workplace level its realisation seems to call for strict distinctions between women and men.

The women under observation lacked recognition and appreciation and sought this from the researchers. The detailed work defined as feminine by the women was also worthless in view of the lack of recognition from the female superiors. On the one hand the female white-collar workers want to be recognised and appreciated for what they do, but on the other, they do not always regard their jobs very highly themselves. The women who overcome the barriers take over tasks that have previously been done by men: managing, marketing, selling. What is essential here is that these jobs do not include many of the 'small, detailed things' defined as feminine in the workplace. The women's work is now controlled by the social requirements of organising and selling instead of details.

In both workplaces women white-collar workers worked within a fixed value order. Their own professional space, which was separate from the space defined as masculine, enabled them to cultivate areas of expertise which their superiors did not have. Their attempt to gain visibility and recognition for their work would, if successful, also offer an opportunity to the public and in this sense established their expertise. The legitimation of the hierarchy is questioned in both instances. The development of their expertise keeps the female white-collar workers full members of the organisation. The need to integrate the feminine and the masculine makes it possible for the women to move within the hierarchic structure, but only to an extent that does not guarantee access to the structure's male dominated core. Integration also keeps the women workers simultaneously inside and outside the organisation. Neither the development of one's own expertise nor integrating the masculine within the feminine are simply opposites to the functional rationale of the organisation. On the contrary, both, as well as women's separate sphere, are indispensable to the organisation.

In both the white-collar workplaces everyday work situations include hierarchical differences between women and men as well as possibilities to make space for women within hierarchies. Worldwide stereotypical assumptions which are included in the domestication of women and the low worth of women's work had a firmer standing in an organisation which had a strict and stable hierarchy between women and men. In a very hierarchical organisation it was not possible for women to integrate their own goals with the goal of the organisation.

Organisational practices, and their fixity or separateness from the women white-collar workers' goals, seem to define the means with which the women are able to break the boundaries between the issues defined as feminine and masculine at the workplace. In the first case, where the gender hierarchy disappears on the organisational level, the hierarchy is identified on the level of society. In the second case, where the gender conflict is strongly present and maintained at the workplace level, 'the rest' of society is not articulated as an arena of gender conflict or equality. In both cases the division between public and private lives is strong. However, it is clear that the public is also for women the more important. Both women and men reproduce this hierarchic dichotomy between public and private.

In the female white-collar workers' accounts their workplace, organisation and the society around them seem to be in a conflicting relationship. Awareness of the masculine hegemony (Connell, 1987: 183) in society does not reach its tentacles correspondingly to the workplace in the women's experience nor does the awareness of the power relationships between women and men at the workplace give rise to general demands for equality either.

80 *Päivi Korvajärvi*

The ways of defining 'women's work' are different from the Anglo-Saxon representations of femininity (Connell, 1987: 183; Smith, 1990b: 163) which emphasise sexuality, fashion and the fulfilment of male desire. In the cases examined here the women created a cultural construction of their actions located within the sphere of waged work. In that world the private, especially the family or sexuality, is hardly articulated.

Gender and organisations consist of concrete and dynamic activities which are continuously created and integrated by both women and men. In both cases, women's jobs in the organisation give the frame for their practices, and they take these frames for granted. They never question the organisation's line of action. Although aware of their existence, the women reproduce the unequal boundaries between the sexes. Thus the gendered relations, or women's and men's activities as such, cannot be separated from the function of the work organisation. Instead, they are deeply intertwined with each other so that there is no sense in a separate analysis of gendered relations within the organisation, and full understanding of organisations – regardless of the location or goals of the organisation – is impossible without taking into account gendered processes.

NOTES

1. Together with Riitta Järvinen and Merja Kinnunen I conducted several interviews with both white-collar workers and their immediate superiors regarding the transformation of work in nine workplaces at the end of the 1980s. In addition we observed white-collar workers' work on two occasions.
2. In Finland women have a statutory right to a 263-day maternity leave. The couple can decide which of the parents takes the leave after 105 days. So in practice fathers can take paternity leave for up to seven months when the baby is 3–10 months old.

Part Three
Everyday Life as
Life-Totality

Introduction
Minna Salmi and Riikka Kivimäki

The preceding part dealt with working life practices. However, people do not live their everyday lives only at the workplace. In our everyday lives we do not live in separate sectors of working life, leisure and family life. As individuals we have to fuse in ourselves our work and leisure, working life and family life, the public and the private as one life-totality. The result of this coalescence is the totality of our everyday lives.

The concept of life-totality was introduced into feminist theory by German sociologist Ulrike Prokop (1978). She defined life-totality as primarily women's activities in the area of reproduction and her aim was to bring into focus all the things produced in women's lives, in other words not just material objects but also social relationships and their continuity. Prokop was criticised by Nordic feminist researchers for the fact that placing emphasis on reproduction as the significant content of life-totality overlooks women's waged labour and the very conflicts created by the relationship of waged work and reproduction, and the way in which this relationship shapes women's lives and experience (Strandell, 1984: 204–5). If the concept of life-totality attempts to express a totality formed of different parts, the interaction between them and the simultaneous effect of the parts on the outlook of life-totality, what is essential in the life-totalities of Nordic women is the tensions brought about by combining family and employment.

Dividing life into different sectors, which is usual in mainstream sociology, does not only appear as separate fields of research such as sociology of work or family sociology. Sectors, and the way in which they are gendered, are also apparent in how the sociology of work refers to women and men by applying different frames of reference. When men are the object of research the starting point is the job model in which men only appear as workers, independent and separate from their lives outside work. On the other hand, women are researched in the framework of the gender model in which the family is regarded as an important determinant in women's lives. Women's working conditions, for example, are not studied as such; instead the point of departure is how family duties affect women's performance at work (for example, Feldberg and Glenn, 1979).

Our attempt in the following chapters is to break loose from these traditions and examine both women and men in their life-totalities in relation to the whole of their everyday lives formed by both family and work. Do the practices in time-use and everyday routines produce different daily lives for women and men? How are taking responsibility for the family on the one hand and the possibility for one's own autonomous life on the other divided between women and men? In what ways are our everyday lives gendered?

One of the crucial conflicts in everyday life is the problem of reconciling work with the family. This problem has been created by the fact that in industrial society part of work has been transferred to be done outside the home in exchange for a wage. What kind of a life-totality is constituted for women and men, and what is the relationship between work and the family like in a society in which women and men use the same amount of time in paid work? Does the fact that both women and men are in full-time employment also mean that the practices of living and integrating work and the family become more similar? Is the gendering of practices reduced, or does the gendering just manifest itself differently? Riikka Kivimäki examines these questions through the experiences of women and men in different workplaces and Minna Salmi through the experiences of people whose paid work takes place in their homes.

What is everyday life? This question seems naïve at first. We all know what everyday life is because that is what we all live. The peculiar thing about everyday life is that although we all know intuitively what it is, difficulties arise when we try to put it into words. This complexity is apparent, for instance, in the fact that there are numerous ways of conceptualising everyday life.

'Day to day', which emphasises repetition, is in many languages the basis for the word describing the everyday. Repetition and routine may be the first things that come to mind when everyday life is talked about without defining it more clearly than that. This has also been expressed in scientific discourse. Everyday life is regarded as the grey routine which is repeated unchanged from one day to the next.

Seeing the everyday as negative routine has sound philosophical roots (see, for instance, Heidegger, 1981; Kosik, 1978; partly also Heller, 1984). These can be criticised from at least two perspectives. First, in this way of thinking people are regarded as consciously reflecting and acting creatures only outside or beyond the everyday. Life and human action are thus divided into two unequal parts.

The second critical argument is interwoven with the first one. In this line of thought knowledge is hierarchised, and the knowledge gained in everyday life is regarded as second rate. Basing our argument on the views of French sociologist and philosopher Henri Lefebvre, we say that those who have developed a philosophical basis for understanding everyday life as mere monotony and grey routine have been unfamiliar with the reality of everyday life (Lefebvre, 1971: 12–18).

One of the problems with this kind of thinking is that routines are only understood in a negative way. Routines are thought of as straitjackets which terrorise people and restrict their lives. Routines have, however, other dimensions also. Routines are also practices of action with the help of which we can save time for other purposes and free our thinking for other issues. For instance, having the same routine places for things in our kitchens saves time from long searches for them each time we need them: just think of how long it takes to find the things to prepare breakfast in someone else's kitchen! Routines also create a sense of safety and familiarity (Davies, 1989). Other positive things are also connected with routines. A painter who works at home emphasised the importance of routine as discipline in her time-use. Disciplined routine is a prerequisite of her work 'because there is so much you just have to do, even if you don't feel like it at all, even if you have no inspiration, you just have to get on with these things'. Making yourself work succeeds with the help of certain routines. In this case routine means control over one's time-use.

Mihaly Csikszentmihalyi (1975: 141, according to Bloch, 1991: 35–6) offers a still wider perspective for thinking of routines as a means of control. According to him, everyday life not only contains different negatively understood routines, but also routinised actions which are done only for their own sake or for the sake of the pleasure they give. Such routines include different actions we hardly ever stop to think about, for instance chatting with a neighbour, smoking a cigarette, switching on the radio or going for a walk. They give meaning, structure and a sense of subjectivity in everyday life and create the foundations for a subconscious feeling of autonomy and control. Their meaning becomes apparent only when they cannot be done when desired. The possibility of doing such seemingly trivial and commonplace things when one wants to is essential in order for a sense of control over one's own life to develop.

Another usual way of conceptualising everyday life is to think about it as the opposite to festivities or special occasions. It has often been attempted to define everyday life as the opposite to that which it is not. In his essay on the concept of everyday life German sociologist Norbert Elias (1978) expressly analyses the everyday with the help of counterconcepts. According to Elias, it is only the counterconcepts which can help illuminate the basis of each conception of everyday life.

Elias's collection of counterconcepts for everyday life includes festivities and the unusual, as well as a view of everyday life as the life and work of masses of people as opposed to the life of those in power or in a bourgeois setting. Elias also brings up everyday life as a perspective of writing, understanding and looking at history. Everyday life is the domain of daily activities, and its opposite is the great political events which have been regarded by traditional historiography as the only significant determinants in history. Everyday life can also be viewed from the perspective of differentiating between the private and the public. Finally Elias connects the concept of everyday life with separating different levels of consciousness and thinking. Everyday life represents immediate, non-reflective thinking, whereas its opposite is analytic, especially scientific, thinking. The list Elias presents shows the numerous approaches there have been to everyday life.

Approaching everyday life by means of some counterconcept is problematic. First, the different ways of defining 'non-everyday' life are rather multilayered. Secondly, this way of thinking implies that everyday life is a special sphere of life instead of attempting to grasp a totality. What becomes evident from the list of counterconcepts Elias presents is that in conceptualising everyday life several of these counterconcepts should be included simultaneously.

In our opinion one of the central issues in the everyday life perspective is that everyday life, in particular, involves the whole of people's lives and covers the totality of their activities. That is, everyday life includes the practices of both work and leisure, both working life and family life, and everyday life is lived in the public as well as in the private sphere. The very point of the concept of everyday life is to overcome the separate sectors and dichotomies we so often use in sociology and, instead, to sketch people's lives as the actual entirety consisting of their everyday practices. Everyday life is always the life of individuals, and individuals are usually actors within a number of spheres. Everyday life unites the world of an individual into a whole of experiences (cf. Dahlström, 1987).

The study of everyday life is about the relationship between people's day-to-day lives and society's structures and institutions. The concept of everyday life focuses on daily practices, but it also strives to capture the formative role of social structures. The very point of studying everyday life is to reveal how the organisation of social relations and structures forms and defines our everyday practices. The researcher's task is to start from the subject's everyday practices and experiences and to show how they are organised by social relations, and also to show how people's actions in their everyday lives form and reproduce social structures (Smith, 1987).

One way of seeing the relationship between family and work is the concept of colouring, as introduced by Lundén Jacoby and Näsman (1989). By colouring they mean the physical, psychological and social interaction between family and work. Colouring is especially cultural, as for instance the changeover in ways of thinking and the learning of behavioural patterns from work to family or vice versa.

In conceptualising everyday life we are striving to define a concept which places emphasis on the interaction between everyday life and social structures. The concept should express the ongoing movement between actors and structures, as well as movements between different kinds of actions and different levels of consciousness.

In fact, what everyday life is all about is precisely these flowing movements; in other words the concept of everyday life is processual rather than being a fixed substance. When we study everyday life we are not searching for a certain object or substance but examining a process that produces different practices. The everyday life approach in research is, then, more a question of methodology than a conceptual problem; it is how we study rather than what we study. We are attempting to understand people's everyday activities through which they transform the social conditions of everyday life into lived everyday life (cf. Bech Jørgensen, 1988). The processes of everyday life are formed in practices which we continuously produce ourselves. Everyday life is not only a straitjacket of unchangeable routines but a cape which provides us with the basic shelter yet gives us room to move.

6 Work and Parenthood
Riikka Kivimäki

Mothers' and fathers' participation in full-time employment gives rise to questions of change and permanence. If the family is no longer supported by the man alone, are gender roles and tasks also altered at both home and work? How are the roles formed in the work–family interface? Can the worker at the workplace also be a mother or a father? Are there any differences between female or male dominated workplaces and fields?

The relationship between work and parenthood is characterised by each society's historically formed gender system (Connell, 1987; Hirdman, 1990b). The gender system is an unwritten guideline of the division of labour between women and men in society. Accordingly, customs or public opinion differ, for example, in view of whether mothers with young children usually work outside the home and how childcare is organised. Does the mother arrange for childcare privately or is she helped in this by the state or the municipality? A wide spectrum of alternatives exists in different countries. The care of children under school age can be organised mainly through private services, as in the USA or Britain, by the church as in Germany, or by the public sector as in Scandinavia. There is also great variation in how long the parents are allowed to take care of their newborn baby without losing their jobs. In the USA it took until 1993 to get a law that entitles the workers of an organisation of more than 50 employees to 12 weeks of non-paid parenthood leave with guaranteed job security. The same minimum length of parenthood leave has been proposed in the European Union but no agreement of a binding directive has been achieved. Sweden, however, has had a law on parenthood leave for 20 years, and nowadays a Swedish worker can get 90 per cent of her wage for 270 days after the baby's birth, thereafter yet twelve weeks more with a lower wage, and even after that eighteen months unpaid leave with full job security.

The changing relationship between work and family has also changed the focus of research. Rosabeth Moss Kanter commented in 1977 that sociologists have maintained the myth of the separate spheres of work and family (Kanter, 1977: 7–8). Pleck, who studied the relationship between work and family, noticed that men's and women's relationship towards reconciling work and family was asymmetrical: a woman's job has to yield in favour of her family, whereas a man's family has to yield in

New fatherhood → fathers more parents

favour of his job (Pleck, 1977: 423). In social research family has been connected to women more than men. During the last decade, instead, research on family has started to focus on fathers in a new way. There is a cultural discourse on the rise of 'new fatherhood'. Research shows that the meaning of fatherhood is widening from the traditional work-centred fatherhood, and fathers find being a parent more meaningful than the mere breadwinner role (Cohen, 1993: 1–22).

FATHERS More full-time worker than full-time father

The changes in the gender system have mainly affected women and children. Men's role has been seen as that of a full-time worker, never as a full-time father. Gender systems have corresponded to the changed circumstances in the labour market or in the state's population policy. Sometimes women have been needed in the labour market and sometimes at home caring for their children.

This study will look closer at some practices to see how the gender system works at the work–family interface. When the demands of work and family of workers in different types of jobs and different positions meet, what happens at workplaces? What happens in the interaction between work and family?

Socioeconomic position

SHAPING EVERYDAY LIFE AT HOME ...

Conditions + nature of work

The conditions and nature of work define how work and the family are combined. Working hours, workplace practices, work culture and the space allowed for action influence the freedom people have in the work–family interface. Because of the nature of work and the stage in which the family lives, the individuals' everyday lives are patterned in different ways (see Salmi in the next chapter). Socioeconomic position also influences the different variations of combining family and work (Haavio-Mannila, 1984: 187). Factory workers' lifestyles are different from those of white-collar workers or professional people, and that is reflected in their daily routines. Haastrup's study of Danish families is very illuminating in this respect. In the life of factory workers, for example, cooking can be a part of the family's daily coexistence, a sign of 'a real family' – in other words an unavoidable routine. For professional people cooking is more like a hobby in which men participate more than in blue-collar and white-collar families (Haastrup, 1993: 62–76).

I shall take a couple of illustrations from Finnish survey data[1] using health care occupations as examples that reflect the general situation of the other occupational groups in the study. The examples show a comparison between three occupational groups from three different hierarchic levels in

Table 6.1   Share of housework: cooking as an example (percentage distributions in health care occupations)

	I don't do much %	I do 25%–75% %	I do almost everything %
Doctors			
Male (n = 72)	44	55	1
Female (n = 92)	1	57	42
Nurses			
Male (n = 104)	13	87	–
Female (n = 86)	1	57	42
Assistant staff			
Male (n = 74)	16	78	6
Female (n = 51)	2	51	47

the same occupational field. Let us take the example of cooking to illustrate the everyday routines at home, as a necessary everyday task in the family. As we can see in Table 6.1, women's everyday routines are more alike, independent of the positions they hold, whereas among men there are differences according to occupational positions.

There are conflicting situations where people have to choose in favour of either work or the family. For instance, if a child suddenly falls ill someone has to stay at home in order to look after her/him at least until it is possible to make other arrangements for her/his care. In such a conflicting situation the parents have to weigh the consequences of their decision and arrangements in view of their work. Table 6.2 shows how the people in this study took care of this kind of unexpected situation which has to be negotiated. According to the study it is mainly the women's duty to be flexible in favour of the family in unexpected situations.

However, the partners of women in the highest socioeconomic groups stay at home in order to take care of sick children more often than the partners of women in lower positions. The differences among women are more pronounced in the case of unexpected situations than in the case of everyday routines. The husbands of women doctors stayed more often at home with a sick child than the husbands of nurses, nursing assistants or orderlies. Almost as a rule female nurses stayed at home in order to look after their sick children. On the other hand, the professional competence

Table 6.2   Who stays at home with sick child (percentage distributions in health care occupations)

	I do most often %	I do as often as my partner %	My partner does more often %
Doctors			
Male (n = 50)	2	16	82
Female (n = 73)	40	30	30
Nurses			
Male (n = 82)	18	55	27
Female (n = 64)	75	16	9
Assistant staff			
Male (n = 64)	12	38	50
Female (n = 33)	64	30	6

in health care occupations might have a greater influence on who stays at home with ill children than in other occupations.

These research results are concurrent with those of many other studies. Despite full-time employment women do most of the domestic work regardless of occupation, education or position (e.g. Haavio-Mannila, 1989: 135). The pattern of gender roles in domestic work shows a relative immunity to structural conditions. Bryson, who has compared Australian and Finnish families, found that the roles women and men have in the responsibility for domestic work remain the same independent of whether one of the partners works full-time or part-time. When the number of women in paid employment increases the time they spend doing domestic work somewhat diminishes, but women's employment does not increase men's participation in domestic work (Bryson, 1993: 33). When a baby is born in a Finnish family the amount of work done by women increases. Apart from childcare, women spend more time taking care of clothing, cooking, cleaning and shopping. It is still the mothers who take care of and organise the everyday lives of their children, the events at daycare or school or the purchase and care of clothes. Men's contribution to childcare is more likely to be such things as taking the children to the daycare centre and picking them up at the end of the day, playing with them or driving them to their hobbies. The other increased domestic tasks remain the mother's responsibility (Niemi, 1994: 168).

The division of housework in the family is sometimes openly negotiated, but housework is still mostly done by following the same old routine: the tasks have 'somehow gradually turned out' to be done by one partner rather than the other. Women's everyday lives are characterised by being for others and postponing the satisfaction of their own needs. The responsibility for the everyday running of family life restricts women's plans and actions. Their time includes the timetables of the other family members and the planning these entail. Women also bear most of the responsibility for the family's unexpected, out of the routine events, such as the above mentioned children's illnesses, and arrange their everyday lives to conform to the actions needed in these situations (see also Lehto, 1988; Lillrank, 1991: 7–13). The time needed for certain tasks that are one person's responsibility could be called 'socially responsible time'. Although the tasks require different kinds and levels of commitment on different days, the person nevertheless has to make sure that a particular area of everyday life has been taken care of.

. . . AND AT WORK

The situations where people try to solve the problems of integrating work and family deserve a closer examination. Workplaces have their own gender systems that segregate women's and men's jobs and hierarchies. The gender system is evident in the kinds of gendered practices there are in workplaces.

According to Joan Acker (1992: 252–4) there are different processes whereby workplace gender systems are maintained and reproduced. The most easily discernible level of the above mentioned processes is that of the gendered division of labour, hierarchy and oppression (cf. Korvajärvi in Chapter 5). The division of labour and hierarchy are visible in the workplaces as different jobs for women and men, as male management and as women having lower hierarchical positions than men. Another level is that of symbols and images which manifest themselves in the organisation as ideology, language, dress code, etc. The third level can be observed in the interaction between and among women and men at the workplace. The important decisions at the workplaces are usually prepared in smaller groups which are based on personal relationships. Hierarchical positions and 'the wrong sex' often pose an obstacle to access to these groups and participation in the background work needed in decision-making. The fourth level in Acker's analysis is the ways in which the workers' behaviour conforms to the accepted behaviour in the workplaces. In my view the attitudes to parenthood in the workplace and the gendered practices related to it are a good example of the last mentioned level. What is, then, accepted behaviour for mothers and fathers in the workplace? This has been investigated in a Nordic research project on work and parenthood. My questions in the project have been: What kind of gendering processes can be seen in different types of workplaces, and how does work and parenthood become concrete in the lives and time-use of women and men? Are women and men allowed to be in contact with children during working hours? Does the family exist in the discussions with colleagues? How are women and men treated as women or men, and as mothers or fathers? Is there a broader meaning linking a mother or a father in the workplace than the responsibilities which parenthood brings to an individual's totality of life?

There are differences between the Nordic countries in women's labour market participation. About 40 per cent of women work part-time in Norway, Sweden and Denmark. Part-time employment is often the women's own choice in order for them to help reconcile work with family duties. The situation is almost totally different in Finland where only about 10 per cent of employed women do part-time work. In Norway the father's provider role is most pronounced compared to its neighbouring countries (Leira, 1992: 51). This was also the result of the research on which this chapter is based. Different workplaces were studied by using interviews and a questionnaire. In Finland the workplaces included a health care centre, a metal industry company, a newspaper and a police station. The workplaces had been chosen as representatives of female and male dominated fields and a field in which there are equal numbers of women and men. The interviews were made with all employee groups, the employer, a trade union representative and the supervisor of one department at each workplace. The respondents had the following occupations and professions: nurses, doctors, health care workers, skilled and unskilled metal workers, journalists, police officers, textile workers and clerical workers. The following case studies are based on interviews in four workplaces.[2]

GENDERING PROCESSES IN WORKPLACES

Patriarchal hierarchy – a ward in a health care centre

The health care centre was a female dominated workplace in which the nursing assistants, auxiliary nurses and nurses were women, as well as the people in assisting positions in the office and in the wards. Some of the doctors and all of the orderlies were men. In view of Acker's analysis, the health care centre had a clear-cut division of labour between the sexes.

Especially in public health care centres the majority of doctors are women, whereas doctors who are in private practice are more often men. Nevertheless, men manage the health care centres. On the symbolic level, according to Acker's analysis, there were varied practices which, however, were more obvious with regard to profession than sex, especially concerning clothing. For example, people wore uniforms which indicated the person's hierarchic position. The doctors had the habit of wearing their white coats unbuttoned. The nurses' long white coats were buttoned all the way up and on the lapel they wore their unions' badge and the auxiliary nurses wore their respective badges. The nursing assistants had pale blue knee-length coats. Typists had medium-length white coats and the other clerical workers wore their own clothes at the workplace.

Both the nurses and auxiliary nurses wished that there were more men in the field. Underlying this wish there is perhaps the idea of seeing how a man would cope in the job, or that there might be improvements in the jobs' esteem or wages if there were more men in the field (cf. Gutek and Cohen, 1992).

As regards gendered practices, the interaction between women and men in the health care centre was defined by differences of profession rather than gender. The doctors, nurses and auxiliary nurses interacted with each other during the day, and they shared the same coffee room. The nursing assistants and the office workers spent their breaks in a different room than the people involved in nursing and care. The doctors' other contacts with their colleagues were mostly consultations and seeking advice. The nurses and auxiliary nurses had no time for breaks or interaction because the number of workers had been cut down in order to save labour costs. The nursing assistants were able to talk with each other during their breaks. The nursing assistants and office workers talked about their families and knew more about their colleagues' children than the nursing staff.

Contact with children at home was possible by using the telephone at the ward. Children were also allowed to call their parents at work although there were not many of these contacts. Children were allowed to come to the ward, for example after school, to wait for the end of the shift in the community room, but this was not very common either.

The women workers experienced fatigue at the workplace because of the lack of staff and also because they had another caring job waiting for them at home (see also Lillrank, 1991: 7–13). Work organisation and the conditions of work did not enable flexibility and this is the reason why reconciling work with the family was not any easier at this workplace than it was at the others. The fact that the workplace was female dominated was not enough to guarantee adequate solutions in this respect.

Women's and men's differentiated work cultures – a metal factory

There were extensive differences of gendered processes and practices between women and men in the metal industry company. The company had a strict gender segregation of tasks, wages and practices in its work culture and daily activities (see also Kevätsalo, 1992).

In the male dominated metal industry company men worked in a department in which vocational training was required. Women workers worked in assembly jobs which were not thought of as requiring vocational training. There was a substantial difference in women's and men's wages. The supervisors in both departments were men and the company's top management was also male.

The male workers wore blue overalls which had the company logo on the back. The female workers in the assembly department wore their own clothes. The women wished that their work was more highly esteemed, especially with respect to wages. They did not think that there was such a huge gap in women's and men's work requirements as the wage differentials seemed to indicate. The men believed that the women would be able to cope in 'men's jobs' but that there just did not happen to be any women in these jobs.

The division into female and male departments created two different cultures at the workplace and in people's behaviour. The women talked a lot about their families and knew about each other's family situations. They came to the workplace to show off their new-born babies and provide their colleagues with coffee and cake. Personal joys and sorrows were mostly shared. Things that had to do with the home were also on their minds in other ways during the day. For instance, they thought about what they were going to buy in the shops or what kind of a meal they were going to prepare in the evening. The male workers did not talk much about their homes at work, and neither did they think about their work at home. They mostly talked about sports, politics or hobbies with their workmates. They also shared quite a few hobbies with each other since these took place in company sponsored facilities.

It was possible for the workers to keep in touch with children by the department telephone during the day. The children were also able to call the workplace, but these contacts were not very common and happened only on special occasions. Bringing children to the workplace because of problems with their care was possible for short periods of time, but this very rarely took place.

Women's and men's cooperation – a newsroom

The newsroom represented a workplace in which there were equal numbers of women and men. The newsroom was big and belonged to a leading local newspaper. Half of the journalists were female and half of them were male. Gendered practices in the division of labour were not evident at first glance in the workplace. Women and men working in the newsrooms had similar tasks and were seemingly equal. However, there were differences with respect to which special department they worked for. Men worked in the financial, political and sports sections and women in the family section. There were as many women as men in the news section.

Also on the symbolic level the first impression of the differences between the sexes was that they were non-existent. The journalists did not have any actual external signs which would have distinguished them from the other staff members. Instead, they had a kind of an informal dress code, 'a journalist look'. The journalists had the habit of sitting at certain tables among themselves and discussing and laughing more loudly than the other staff members. However, the workplace culture was traditionally masculine, and the image of a 'top journalist' was somebody who was not tied down by family schedules. The 'top journalists' were free of constraining working hours and able to devote themselves to the job completely. The editor-in-chief said nevertheless that it was good that both women and men with and without families worked as journalists. He had noticed that when journalists had a family they then became more mellow and had less need to project 'a tough' image.

The journalists' working hours were ambiguous. According to the art critic it was difficult to draw the line between working hours and time off, It was vital to keep track of what was going on in the cultural scene on time off: one had to go to concerts, exhibitions and performances and read papers and magazines. The actual writing tasks were not tied up with official working hours either: drawing outlines and coming up with ideas is a constant ongoing process which is independent of working hours.

It was not until the 1940s and 1950s that the first women in Finland started to enter the journalistic profession in any greater numbers. Until then a journalist's job had been a newspaperman's job with emphasis on the word 'man'. It was work without official working hours. This meant that it was not unusual that journalists worked from morning to late in the evening. Official working hours were introduced only when women entered the field. Were women the reason for this? Perhaps it was not only that, but women did bring into the profession their own life perspective. The journalists worked in shifts which started at different times of the day, and there was always a certain number of staff present. The last journalist left at 11 p.m. The journalists were freely able to swap shifts with their colleagues as long as there was enough of them present at all times.

The journalists had pictures of their families and children on their desks, and they knew each other's families rather well. Children were also talked about during breaks which the journalists were able to have when they wanted within the limits set by work. Children were able to come to the workplace, and even spend a couple of hours there if there were difficulties in their care. It was possible and permitted to have contacts with the home during the workday. The workplace owned holiday cottages which the workers were able to rent and use with their families.

So, on the one hand, the journalists' job was flexible as regards combining work and family duties: changing shifts was relatively easy, and work was adjustable as regards time. It was also possible to choose when to have breaks or contact the family. On the other hand, the journalists had to take into account work demands on their time off to see what was going on, and the topics and contents of articles were not created during working hours only.

Women entering the tough-guy male arena – a police station

Gendered practices were strongly evident at all levels of the police station. A police officer's job is a traditional male occupation within the division of labour, and it is still highly male dominated. The office workers on the staff of the police station were women who had regular daywork. There were only two female police officers: one patrolwoman and one senior police constable in charge of the scene of the crime technical investigations, photography and collecting trace evidence. The patrol police officers worked in three shifts, during the day, evening and night, and at the crime department there were day, evening and on-call shifts.

A police officer's job can be defined on the symbolic level in one policeman's words as 'energetic activities for plucky boys'. In his opinion it was not a good idea to have women in the job because they would be carrying guns. Women told me about the prejudices they encountered when they first entered the job. The outward signs were obligatory for the patrol police officers; one had to wear the uniform on duty. Policewomen and policemen wore similar uniforms.

When policewomen entered the jobs in the police station it created a conflicting relationship between gender and the occupational image. It took time to solve the conflict and prove that women really were able to do the same tasks as men and also be competent in them.

The senior policemen said that they had noticed as they grew older that the young men, who had recently graduated from the police academy, were often far too eager and wanted to project a tough-guy image. When the young men gain more experience, and especially after they have a family, they change and start noticing different things than before, or they look at things from a new perspective. They act in a different way and become gentler and more conciliatory. Having a family was then in a way an advantage as regards doing the job. It widened the police officers' perspective on different aspects of life and increased their understanding of their clients' lives.

The office workers at the police station said that their work was sometimes too much routine. However, they had secure civil service jobs. On the other hand they dealt with different cases and human destinies every day. One female office worker said that she often thought about her son who had not succeeded in his studies as well as she and her husband had expected. In her daily job she dealt with documents recording the trouble young men of her son's age had with the law. Whenever this happened the woman said that she was happy for her son, who at least was an honest and law-abiding person. The office workers did not have very close contacts with the police officers.

EVERYDAY LIFE AND COLOURING – A TOTALITY

The connection between work and the family is more than understanding the interaction between two separate spheres. In the actions of concrete people, both work and the family are present as different kinds of perspectives and values, and, because of these, as action and practices. Work 'colours' (Lundén Jacoby and Näsman, 1989) the worker's whole cultural being in the family as well as at home. Correspondingly, parenthood is an element which affects the formation of the worker's personality and may have an effect on the person's performance at work and the things s/he notices, understands and prioritises. Life is lived as an entity, not as separate spheres. Work and parenthood can be combined in a number of different ways. Workplace culture, the conditions set by work and the worker's hierarchic or occupational position largely define the freedom for manoeuvre in relation to parenthood in the workplace. Even at one workplace many possible ways of integrating work and the family can be found. The discursive and symbolic presence of the family seems to be connected to the person's position at the workplace. Talking about the family was more usual among blue-collar and white-collar women than among their male colleagues in similar positions. A female dominated workplace does not automatically guarantee the fact that the work/family interface would be easier than in male dominated fields. The possibility of combining work and family is influenced more by work conditions and work organisation than by female dominance as such. What is important in this respect is decision-making power and flexibility. As we could see, the work organisation and work conditions in the female dominated health care centre did not allow for a flexible social space in which to combine work and the family. A modern and more flexible work organisation offers better chances for combining work and family; in the present study it was best accomplished in the journalists' job. Whatever ways people use to manage their multiple responsibilities, gender is always present in workplace practices as well as in the everyday parenting tasks that take place in the family.

NOTES

1. See note 2 for survey details.
2. The survey was done in the Nordic countries (Finland, Sweden, Norway and Denmark). Respondents were representatives of nine occupations, as many women as men from each. In Finland the questionnaire was sent to 2722 persons, 69 per cent of whom responded.

7 Autonomy and Time in Home-Based Work
Minna Salmi

THE 'TIMES' OF EVERYDAY LIFE

Everyday life is rich and complex both in its practices and as a concept. It seems therefore obvious that one always has to choose a specific perspective in order to investigate it. My focus is on time-use. In many languages time is central in the word that describes everyday life, and repetition is the basis of the word: *everyday* in English, *alltäglich* in German, *vardaglig* in Swedish. Repetition, although not necessarily routine, then seems to be an important component of day-to-day life. The repetition of time structures is an essential thing in our time-use. We all have roughly the same framework in the use of our time even if we do different things from one day to the next.

The time structure of everyday life is often imposed on us by different social institutions. All social institutions have their own time structures, schedules and deadlines with which the individual has to cope. All these 'times' create varying constraints and conditions for individual time-use. At least the following social time structures can be specified:

- the time of the state: e.g. compulsory education;
- civic time: e.g. the age of retirement;
- labour market time: employer's time, e.g. the length of working hours, when the workday begins and ends, what one is allowed to do during the workday and annual holidays;
- market time: e.g. business hours;
- cultural time: Christmas and other holidays, birthdays and other culturally defined events which require time-bound preparations;
- family time: the work, school and recreation schedules of members of the family;
- domestic time: the cyclical housework tasks, e.g. the time planning needed for cooking;
- individual time: time at one's own disposal.

These time structures differ from each other as some of them apply to the whole lifecycle while others pertain to daily life. Our daily time-use is structured on many different levels and the individual must cope with several times in order to run her/his everyday life (cf. Berger and Luckman, 1972: 40–2). I want to use the image of a screw to illustrate the effects these time structures have. Each 'time' represents one turn of the screw and the more turns there are, the tighter are the time boundaries placed on the individual. Most of these times, for instance labour market time, market time, family time, domestic time and partly also cultural time, are turns on the daily time screw which means that the time screw is tightest on the everyday level.

In the case of homeworkers one of the turns of the time screw, in other words at least some of the time limits set by the labour market, is omitted, which means that homeworkers have less pressure on their time. How do people doing home-based work organise their everyday lives? How do they relate to and put into practice the possibility of planning their day and organising their time-use when they are not bound by the same temporal constraints as people working outside the home? Do they have a better chance of controlling their time-use and, if they do, what do they think and do about it?

It has been contended that the flexibility of home-based work is one of the myths of homeworking. This point is strongly emphasised, for example, by Sheila Allen and Carol Wolkowitz (1987). I use their discussion of the topic as an example of a line of thinking also shared by many other writers (see Bisset and Huws, 1985; Elling, 1984; Lie et al., 1978; Vedel, 1984). Allen and Wolkowitz, on the basis of British data, say that independent decisions on working hours and pace may be possible for the self-employed, but that this is not the case for homeworkers. The Finnish experiences of homeworking, however, shed a different light on flexibility.

THE DAILY LIFE OF HOMEWORKERS[1]

In the mid-1980s homeworkers composed 2.5 per cent of the Finnish labour force. Homeworkers worked in almost as many occupations as people in paid employment outside the home; in other words there were homeworkers in about 300 different occupations. The occupations form a continuum from creative and autonomous occupations needing high education to routine clerical and industrial occupations. One occupational group dominates above all others, namely child minders. They are the largest individual group formed of women who have found their occupation as a part of the daycare system created by the welfare state. They are women who, employed by the local authority, look after groups of young children in their homes. Forty per cent of all homeworkers are child minders. With the exception of child minders, there is no 'typical' homeworker. All other groups are rather small and equal in size: between 3 to 6 per cent of homeworkers are either in planning and consulting, administrative and clerical jobs, business, or work as artists; only 10 per cent of homeworkers have jobs in industry. Apart from child minders, Finnish homeworkers are men as often as they are women. The different occupations are not strictly gender segregated either; instead, relatively balanced numbers of both women and men have 'creative' and 'routine' occupations.[2]

The way the child minders' work takes up their day is largely determined by the children's parents' working hours. The child minders' working day is also organised on the basis of the nature of their work, in other words by the children's mealtimes, outdoor activities and play. Child minders' working hours are thus rather regular.

People who do other kinds of homework have totally different possibilities for organising their days than child minders and they also take advantage of this possibility. The thought of an eight-hour 'nine-to-five' (actually eight-to-four in Finland) normal workday hardly restricts homeworkers. Working begins and ends at different times on different days, and work is done in short periods throughout the day. In most cases the daily working hours differ remarkably from one day to the next.

Yet there are homeworkers who are in favour of regular and 'normal' working hours: a little less than half of the homeworkers keep to roughly the same working hours every day. They begin and end working at the same times as those who work outside the home (that is between 7–8 a.m. and 4–5 p.m.). However, the norm of a 40-hour working week is applied only by a minority of homeworkers. It is rather common to work outside 'normal' working hours, particularly in the evenings and at weekends (Figure 7.1), and those who do this generally regard their exceptional working hours as a good alternative.

The structure of a homeworker's working day varies regardless of the nature of work. However, those who can make autonomous decisions on the content of their work more frequently work in the evenings and at weekends than those who have little influence over the content of their work.

WOMEN'S AND MEN'S DAILY LIFE

Are the different structural preconditions of women's and men's lives then reflected in the way they do home-based work? The structure of women's

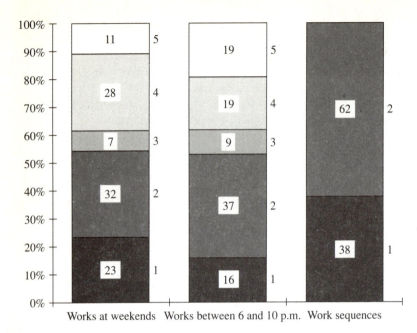

Works at weekends   Works between 6 and 10 p.m.   Work sequences

1. Weekly
2. 2–3 times a month
3. Once a month
4. Sometimes
5. Never

1. Daily
2. 2–3 times a week
3. Once a week
4. 1–3 times a month
5. Never

1. One regularly
2. Several sequences

Figure 7.1   Homeworkers' working times (n = 102, child minders excluded)

and men's days is really rather different. Men, much more often than women, have the same kind of regular schedule as those who work outside the home.

Men begin and end their workdays at the same time, work regularly during a certain period of the day and work the same number of hours each day of the week more often than women (Figure 7.2). Men appear to work more often in the evenings than women, and some women wake up very early in the morning in order to work while men are still sleeping.

Both sexes have the same chances for uninterrupted concentration on their work. It is most usual (40 per cent) that there is no chance whatsoever of concentrating on just waged work. Although both women and men have the same chances of working in peace, they have different ways of putting them into practice. How can this be explained?

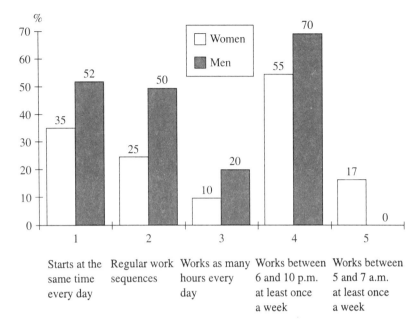

Figure 7.2 Differences in homeworkers' working times between women and men
(n = 102, child minders excluded)

Men's daily work schedules are most often determined by their own choices and the nature of their work, whereas the schedules of the other members of the family have an equal place in women's lives as the constraints imposed by work (Table 7.1). Children's schedules structure women's time-use; it is precisely the time when the children are at school or at day-care that it is possible to work uninterrupted. Inspiration does not structure the time-use of women even in creative work, as a painter puts it:

It is very simple in a family like this, when you have children who go to school, you start working on the dot. I begin when the boys have left for school, and when they come back I must slowly start winding down because they cause too much commotion when they are here and there are always their friends and others . . . [But yes then I, MS] in the evenings I look at them [paintings she is working on, MS] and in a way work with them although I don't do any painting.

Women's and men's own estimates about the factors affecting their overall time-use show even more clearly that although a man works at

Table 7.1   Factors that influence time-use for homeworking women and men a
lot, percentages (n = 102, child minders excluded)

| | Men | | Women | |
	A lot %	Not at all %	A lot %	Not at all %
Daily time-use is defined by:				
Nature of work	61	11	39	17
Employer's instructions	13	57	8	68
Family timetables	17	37	36	23
Own choices	70	3	55	9
Time-use as a whole is:				
Under one's own control	84	6	80	12
Defined by employer's timetables	17	63	15	57
Defined by family needs	12	49	31	33

home, his time-use is seldom determined by what the other family members are doing (Table 7.1). Men can decide on their time-use for themselves, and it is rather often that they decide to structure it according to
a regularly repeated schedule. For women, conforming to the other family
members' schedules is apparently the factor which gets them, or makes
them, more often than men take advantage of the homeworkers' chance of
putting together a varied schedule. If we return to the time screw metaphor, the thread of family time is more pressing on women than it is on
men, but homeworking women are able to ease this pressure by interspers-
ing their waged work with other activities.

The flexibility which a homeworker gains actually happens in the organisation and control of everyday life. Freedom from controlled working
hours and commuting involved in a job outside the home is significant
from the point of view of running everyday life. The opportunity to organise their working hours as they please is the factor which homeworkers
most appreciate in the way they work. The differences between the sexes
are still visible in the things the homeworkers value (Table 7.2). Women
also place equal value on the chance of combining waged work and housework flexibly. Men on the other hand state, as the second most important
advantage of homeworking, the freedom to work at their own pace.

The things women value most have to do with their time-use and their
own decision-making power, and there is also great unanimity about
these advantages. Women consider the same things as the most important

Table 7.2   Experienced advantages in homeworking, percentages (n = 195)

| | Report as an advantage (%) | | |
| | Child | Other occupations | |
Advantages	minders	Men	Women
Chance to organise:			
Working hours to suit oneself	31	88	89
Flexible intertwining of paid work			
and housework	75	55	87
Chance to care for one's own children	81	19	45
Chance to work in peace	41	62	64
Chance to avoid commuting	77	72	76
Independence in work	76	79	85
Compatibility with family life	66	43	59
More time with the family	66	34	51
Chance to decide on pace of work	62	85	85
Working is efficient	22	34	32
Does not have to separate between			
time for family and time for work	43	28	36
n	93	49	53

advantages of homeworking, regardless of whether they do 'creative' or 'routine' work.[3] The same things are valued by people who have been doing this kind of work for both longer and shorter periods, so it is not just a question of 'the honeymoon effect' (Forester, 1988: 232).

If the advantages experienced in homeworking have to do with independent time-use, the same thing can also cause problems. It is difficult for both women and men to separate work from leisure, and almost half of the homeworkers feel that this is a problem. The dilemma of drawing the line between work and leisure is especially acute in the case of both women and men doing 'creative' work. Work also puts pressure in family life on women doing 'creative' work.

The most common problems that women doing 'routine' work face are low income and the lack of colleagues. They, more often than women doing 'creative' work, have the nagging feeling of 'I should be doing', a feeling caused by unfinished work that is constantly before their eyes. It can be said that as 'creative' work is more rewarding, the constant presence of work is not such a strain for the women who do it, even if they do have trouble separating work from leisure. In their case the pressure to separate work from leisure seems to come from the family.

The fact that it is women doing 'creative' work who feel that their work puts more pressure on family life is even more significant if we take into account that they live in families with children less often (54 per cent) than women doing 'routine' work (70 per cent). This can possibly be linked with the idea of women's work orientation. Women who do 'creative' work identify more strongly with their work, and possibly this is why they also feel a greater need to draw the line between their work and their families in view of time-use. The case studies conducted by Kathleen Christensen (1988) indicate that homeworking women must have a rather strong professional identity before they consciously start to establish the limits between work and family.[4]

As we saw above, the family influences the shape men's everyday life takes clearly less than women's. In addition to the differences in factors that control time-use, the same differences are also obvious in the advantages and disadvantages perceived in homeworking. The chance of combining waged work and housework is at the bottom of men's lists of advantages, well behind no commuting and the chance of working in peace. Men also less frequently state compatibility with family life or the fact that time does not have to be compartmentalised into working life and family life as an advantage in homeworking. Family's insignificance also becomes evident the other way round. Men feel clearly less often than women that their homeworking puts pressures on their family lives, and child minding hardly hampers men in their work.

It is thus evident that men's homeworking is not to any great extent affected by the fact that their workplace is also the family home. For women, however, homeworking means combining waged work with caring for the family in a unique way in Finnish society, although their role as homemakers has little to do with their choice of workplace.

So the possibility of shaping everyday life is of crucial importance to women. Time is not free of gender; there is men's time and women's time. Women's time structures, unlike those of men, are essentially defined by the family: '[. . .] a woman lives [. . .] her family's rhythm. Women's particular sphere of life in the gender divided society is that of the family [. . .].' Time has a special nature for women: 'Usually time is conceived of as an individual and undivided resource. From women's point of view it is important to recognise the collective nature of time, the unit of which is not the individual but the family' (Julkunen, 1985: 301–2; see also Davies, 1989, and Liljeström, 1981).

Combining the different rhythms and demands of waged work and the family creates the basic conflict of women's everyday lives. Tora Friberg from Sweden has interviewed women about the things that they find most problematic in organising their everyday lives. Some aspects came up repeatedly in the answers and were common to women in different groups: how to find the time and strength to do all the necessary things and how to be sure that the children are safe and happy (Friberg, 1989: 13). Laura Balbo, a long-standing Italian member of the European parliament, sums up European women's experience with a metaphor of quilting: women's everyday life consists of innumerable colourful patches which they then have to try to sew up into a heat-retaining quilt (Balbo, 1987; see also Ipsen, 1984). The patchwork quilt of homeworking women consists of slightly larger patches because they are, to an extent, able to control the time with which they put the quilt together and some of the patches of everyday life are left out. The number of seams is thus also smaller, and the seams are not quite so prominent.

FLEXIBILITY IN HOMEWORKING – MYTH OR REALITY?

British sociologists Sheila Allen and Carol Wolkowitz, who regard the flexibility of homeworking as a myth, write that of the 90 women they interviewed only 30 said that the possibility of working at one's own pace is an advantage in homeworking. The rest of the women either named no advantages or mentioned other aspects. Problems with time-use were mentioned more often than advantages. They conclude that a homeworker can continue working until she drops and that, all things considered, homeworking is more straining than working outside the home. In their opinion this is caused by the fact that both waged work and unpaid domestic labour are done in the same place, the work is always before one's eyes (Allen and Wolkowitz, 1987: 124–5).

The Finnish results do not give such a grim picture of the homeworker's situation either regarding the workers' views on the autonomy of work or in view of the advantages or problems they mentioned. Homeworker women think that they can especially influence their daily pace of work, and the majority can also have considerable influence on the order in which they perform the work tasks and their scheduling of the tasks. They mention problems in homeworking clearly less often than advantages.

The reasons for the differences between the British and Finnish results can be looked for in at least two directions. First, Allen and Wolkowitz included in their research only women who do industrial piecework. The autonomy of women doing 'routine' work is not less than the autonomy of the other groups in the Finnish research – quite the opposite – so reasons must be searched for elsewhere besides the differences in the nature of work. Another influential factor seems to be that the British data included substantially more women with young children (over half of the data) than the Finnish data (only 20 per cent had children under school age). This does not of course mean that the Finnish homeworking women would be free from the division of labour between the sexes in their families, but it means, however, that most of them have already passed the most binding stage of family life.

For Allen and Wolkowitz, homeworkers are not just anybody doing paid labour at home. They define homeworkers as women engaged in waged labour on a piecework basis. For these women the quantity, type and pace of work, deadlines and even the way in which they perform the work are all dictated by the company who has commissioned the work. This, they say, concerns even clerical work.[5] According to Allen and Wolkowitz, the crucial thing in the situation of homeworkers is the relationship between the worker and the supplier of work, and therefore homework should be defined on the basis of this relationship:

> Given the increasing recognition of paid work done at or from home and the wide range of possible contractual arrangements [. . .], it is imperative that a definition of homework specifies the relationship between those performing the work and those who supply it, in order to differentiate it from other forms of home-based work. Such relationships have very practical outcomes.
>
> (Allen and Wolkowitz, 1987: 47–8)

To place such an emphasis on this issue is, I am sure, appropriate in countries like Britain where industrial homeworking constitutes a large part of all home-based work, although not the major part, as Allen and Wolkowitz argue. Catherine Hakim has estimated that between 25 and 33 per cent of home-based work in Britain is industrial piecework (Hakim, 1987).

The structure of home-based work is different in Finland. Only 10 per cent of all homeworkers have industrial jobs, and a great number of homeworkers are craftspeople or artisans with small enterprises, most often employing only themselves. As few as 2 per cent of Finnish homeworkers have jobs which could be classified as 'sweated labour'.

Women's position in the labour market in Finland is also quite different from that of British women. It is self-evident for Finnish women to work full-time outside the home. This includes also mothers of young children.

Today, three out of four women with children under school age are in the labour market. Women's full-time employment is possible because there is a rather well functioning public day-care system. Thus, home-based work is much more seldom the only alternative for women in Finland than it is in Britain. Homeworking is also an ethnic problem in Britain. According to Cynthia Cockburn, 'disproportionate numbers of Asian women [. . .] are homeworkers. They are confined to this work in part by the dictate of male heads of family, in part by the white racism that renders the outside world a dangerous place for women of ethnic minorities' (Cockburn, 1991: 82).

Does Allen and Wolkowitz's argument, that the relationship between the worker and the supplier of the work is crucial in home-based work, mean that it is misleading to study all kinds of homeworkers at the same time, as I have done? Will I in so doing obscure that which is important in the connection between the flexibility and independence of work? At least a partial answer to this question can be found by analysing, according to employment status, the opportunities to decide on one's working hours and other aspects of work autonomy.

There are no big differences between the Finnish self-employed and wage-earner homeworkers in how they can influence their daily pace of work, the order of tasks, work methods or even timetables. The over-whelming majority of wage earners say that they have a great deal of influence, especially concerning the daily pace of work. Most of them can also decide on the timetable for performing a task. Only one in five wage earners says that orders from the employer are decisive in view of their daily timetables. Others decide on their timetables themselves. Wage earners are less independent than the self-employed only in decisions that concern the content of their work tasks. These results do not support Allen and Wolkowitz's thesis that wage earners' autonomy in time-use is only an illusion.

However, flexibility in homeworking does not only concern the arrangements of the work itself. Allen and Wolkowitz's main point, in declaring the flexibility of homework a myth, is not, after all, the degree of autonomy in work organisation and performance. They stress that:

> constraints associated with the wage labour contract are only one form through which control over labour is organised. When women's work is examined, we also have to consider other limitations on women's autonomy in setting their hours and pace of work. These are limitations imposed by the sexual division of labour.
>
> (Allen and Wolkowitz, 1987: 122–3)

And they continue:

> The ability to realise those advantages which men often seek in self-employment, like the capacity to set one's own hours and pace of work [. . .] rests in part on men's position as men. Homeworkers *share with other women* controls over their use of their own labour which men experience much more rarely.
>
> (Allen and Wolkowitz, 1987: 123, my emphasis)

This is true, of course, as we saw when discussing the influence of the family on women's time-use. But, as the emphasised words above indicate, the constraints laid on homeworking women do not concern only them, but, under the present sexual division of labour, most other women as well. The division of labour in the family is a structural social pattern which sets limits for women irrespective of the site of their work. Whether the woman works at home or outside it, she first has to become aware of her situation within this division of labour, and then negotiate, or fight, to change it. Thus, working at home does not, in itself, create gendered patterns in the family, even though it can have a role in reinforcing them and make it more difficult for the woman to change these patterns.

Even given the current situation where women do most of the unpaid domestic labour, I still claim that working at home can offer women chances of flexibility in coping with their different kinds of work. As the image of the time screw showed, home-based work gives the woman more freedom in her everyday life even though she has other obligations besides those defined by wage labour. She can merge her different activities in a way which is impossible for a factory worker. Even the time spared from commuting is for many women a crucial help in organising their day (Christensen, 1988: 45 and 135).

Allen and Wolkowitz also point out that a homeworker's work goes on 'until she drops' and often leads to very long days. But is not this also the experience of women working outside the home who do their domestic work after the working day in the evenings? Homeworkers can also do domestic work during the day although they then often do paid work in the evenings. However, I want to stress again that the women in my study who actually 'extended their working day into unsocial hours', as Allen and Wolkowitz put it, found this a good alternative. In Allen and Wolkowitz's own material only one third of the women worked at 'unsocial' hours. (Allen and Wolkowitz, 1987: 123–7).

There is, however, one group of Finnish homeworking women who do not regard flexibility in arranging their working hours as the best part of home-based work, and these are the child minders. As we saw, their working hours and rhythm are, obviously, tied to the schedules of the children and their parents. Accordingly, their working time is even less independent than that of people doing piecework because children cannot be put aside for a while in the same way as other 'work objects'. In spite of the relatively bound working hours, the majority of child minders see the chance to control their pace of work as an advantage (see Table 7.2 above). Also, child minders' work includes tasks in which it is possible, to some extent, to combine paid work and domestic work. So a child minder does not have to do all her domestic work on top of her paid work and in this way she gets more time for herself. It is not surprising, then, that while only a third of the child minders think they can arrange their working hours to suit themselves, a great majority think that the chance to flexibly intertwine paid and unpaid work is a positive side to working at home.

FLEXIBILITY AND THE CONTROL OF EVERYDAY LIFE

Thus, what is important in autonomy is not so much the independence in the work itself, but the autonomy in putting together the different pieces of everyday life and coping with the different daily time patterns. More freedom in this difficult process can be an important aspect of women's feeling of independence in homeworking. This independence is not only about freedom to choose the working methods, hours or pace of work, but, and most importantly, it is about better chances to form the structure of one's everyday activities oneself.

These chances of flexibility and autonomy may seem trivial. But if we consider them from the point of view of controlling everyday life, we can see that the chance to do the seemingly small and unimportant things when one feels like it means precisely that there is less external control over daily time-use. To be able to do these things is crucial in order for developing a sense of self-realisation and control of daily life. In fact, 'holding a dialogue with time' is the very basis of self-realisation, because it is the essential condition of achieving satisfaction at any given moment – of living life to the full', as Anthony Giddens (1991: 71) puts it. What at first seems trivial actually goes deep into our existence as active subjects who control our own lives. No wonder that the homeworkers attach special value to their chances of structuring their time-use.

As I have been looking at home-based work from this kind of an everyday perspective, I find it difficult to digest the argument that flexibility in homework is only an illusion. This thesis seems to imply an understatement of 'the trivialities of everyday life'. This line of thought leads directly back to the philosophy which states that we cannot be conscious actors in everyday life itself, but only if we step above or outside it.

A hint of this philosophy can be read from the critique of homeworking which many researchers have presented. There is often an emphasis on the negative aspects of home-based work. Homeworker women appear as more or less passive counterparts in the relationships of their lives. They seem to be left at the mercy of the labour market, the supplier of the work, and also the husband and his demands and opinions about what is proper work for women. The negative attitude to homeworking has been the 'politically correct' one regardless of what the homeworker women themselves have thought of their situation.[6] However, as I see it, the important thing is not to moralise about the negativity of home-based work. The important thing is how much women themselves can have a say in how the totality of their lives is formed.

This must not, however, lead to the conclusion that home-based work is an alternative which could be recommended to all. First, the Finnish study indicates that home-based work has been chosen as a permanent way of working by those who find it suitable for themselves. This has been possible because, at least up until the 1990s' recession, there have, in most cases, been other alternatives for women to work outside the home. Secondly, that which can be a good individual solution acquires completely different dimensions as socially organised labour. Here we enter the debate of the 'flexibility' of work organisation and the question of whether this has happened only on production's terms without the workers having any say in their work.

The conclusion, which should be drawn from the freedom home-based work offers and the easing off of putting together everyday life, is that there is a lot to be improved upon in standard waged work. The flexibility needed in work organisation is found specifically in increasing the workers' room for manoeuvre. The way waged labour is presently organised, which takes no account of the fact that workers have other lives besides their working life and in which most people have no chance of combining the activities in different spheres of life or of controlling their time-use and what they do, is really in need of change.

A case in point in the discussion of 'flexible' work organisation in the first mentioned sense is the position of homeworking in the production and market system and the homeworkers' insufficient social security. If homework has a clear market of its own outside of which the homeworking women cannot move, because of their life situation or their husbands' or their own values, or because they cannot find other work, the situation of homeworkers is not fair and a little flexibility in everyday life will not make it much better. Also the Finnish results show that the economic and social position of homeworkers is weaker than that of people who do similar kinds of work outside the home as well as the fact that low income is especially women's problem. Many homeworkers also suffer because they have no colleagues and their work is undervalued. In other words the comparison between the British and Finnish experience also brings up similarities.

But above all the comparison reveals that the gendered practices in homeworking can be different in different countries, which they naturally are, given the different starting points. In the case of home-based work, its female domination and the polarity between men's creative well paid jobs and women's routine, badly paid jobs have been a taken for granted, universally applicable gendered practice. This presupposition is not supported in this study as these practices do not exist in Finnish homeworking. The absence of certain gendered practices does not mean, however, that there are not other kinds of gendered practices because, among other things, homework is not done only, or mostly, by women. The obvious gendered quality of time-use in home-based work gives rise to the question of how deeply embedded gendered practices can indeed be. The structures of time-use conform to gendered patterns although the way these people work would offer the opportunity of doing things differently. This is because it is a question of practices which are connected to even more profound gendering. Some gendered practices connected with the structuration of time are deeply ingrained and change only very slowly because they are intertwined with the fundamental divisions between the sexes, such as the division of labour and the position of the sexes in the gender system.

NOTES

1.   This study is based on two kinds of data. I compiled statistical information from the 1985 Census by tabulating all people except farmers who identified their workplace as the home. This statistical overview provides numbers, kinds of work and social background. In addition, I surveyed home-based workers in 1986 in conjunction with a larger (n = 12 000) survey on living conditions which included a question about the site of work. The respondents who said that they worked in their own homes received a special questionnaire on homeworking which included questions on work history, reasons for working at home, the structure of time-use, feelings about working at home, social contacts on the job and outside it, and the positive and

negative aspects of homeworking. The sample (n = 195) included people
who work at home at least half of their working time. Although the sample
is rather small it is representative. The structure of the survey material
corresponds fairly well to that of the total population of homeworkers both
as regards numbers, occupational structure and status, type of work, education and gender division. The living conditions survey allowed me to re-
trieve the everyday lives of homeworkers. (More about the methods of the
study may be found in Salmi (1995).)

2.   On the structure of home-based work in Finland and its differences compared to many other countries see Salmi (1995).

3.   When talking about the nature of work I have put the words 'creative' and
'routine' in quotation marks in order to indicate that such definitions of the
type of work are very ambiguous and problematic. Most work includes both
creative and routine tasks.

4.   I have inferred women's work and family orientation from their answers to
the question which is frequently used in different studies: 'Which of the
following spheres of life, work, leisure outside the home, home and the
family, gives you the most satisfaction at present?' How reasonable is this
kind of juxtaposing on the whole? How many parents who do 'creative'
work and have young children would be able to put those 'spheres' of their
life in order of importance? The juxtaposition seems especially ill-founded
in the case of homeworkers in whose lives those two 'centres of life' overlap to the extent that it seems rather fruitless to enquire about their order of
importance as a source of satisfaction.

5.   As to clerical work, this generalisation is put to question by the results of
Robin Leidner (1988) and Monika Goldmann and Gudrun Richter. They
show that women who do word processing work place high value on their
chance to have flexible working hours irrespective of the problems they
have with childcare. These problems varied according to the children's age,
the type of work and the number of working hours. These women wanted
to take care of their children themselves and compared their situation to
working outside the home (Leidner, 1988: 88; Goldmann and Richter, n.d.:
14).

6.   As, for example, in the case of the Vermont knitters (see Boris, 1987: 111).

Part Four
Defining Subjectivities in Working Life

Introduction
Marja Vehviläinen and Hannele Varsa

Cassandra at the Lion Gates:

> Apollo the Prophet
> introduced me to his gift. [. . .]
> Even then I told my people all the grief to come. [. . .]
> Once I betrayed him [Apollo] I could never be believed.
> (Aeschylus, 1977: 150–1)

Apollo to Orestes who had killed his mother:

> Never surrender, never brood on the labour.
> And once you reach the citadel of Pallas, kneel
> and embrace her ancient idol in your arms and there,
> with judges of your case, with a magic spell –
> with words – we will devise the master-stroke
> that sets you free from torment once for all.
> I persuaded you to take your mother's life.
> (Aeschylus, 1977: 234)

In *The Oresteia*, written by Aeschylus in 458 BC, Orestes kills his mother in order to punish her for his father's death and to fulfil Apollo's wish. Apollo later sends Orestes to Pallas Athena who, he knows, can find favourable 'judges of your case'. Athena arranges the first court ever held for human beings. When Orestes is accused of the murder of his own blood, Apollo himself serves as a witness: 'The woman you call a mother of the child is not a parent, just a nurse to the seed' (p. 260), and Orestes can go free, 'cleared of the charge of blood' (p. 265). In Orestes' case Apollo consciously creates social order, textuality, 'with the magic spell – with words', in order to guide people's activities. The judgement of Orestes will be used as a rule-giving example in later struggles between women and men. Orestes goes free and can feel 'not guilty'. The textuality of the judgement intervenes in the subjectivity of human beings. Textualities are powerful and shape even the deepest moral judgements made by people, women and men.

Cassandra was a priestess of Troy. Apollo fell in love with her, but she deceived him and forbade him her love. She was given the skill of seeing and fought to create a voice of her own. Cassandra foresaw the defeat of

Troy in the war with the Greeks, but nobody listened to her. She, like Apollo, saw the order of events taking place in Greece and Troy, but in contrast to Apollo, Cassandra was unable to set the location or the judges for her words. Her voice was lost and she had to go to the Lion Gates of Mycenae to die. But Apollo's words have remained in textuality, in the social order of human societies. Thus textualities are built with both words and power relations.

In present-day societies and working life textualities are involved in all people's activities. Textualities include legal systems, newspapers, statistics and information systems as well as the processes which produce and interpret them. People, women and men, create the textualities, but the textualities also intertwine with their thinking, acting, practices and their subjectivities, parallel to the case of Oresteia.

In feminist discourse, several writers have pointed out that subjectivities are processes. Donna Haraway (1991) speaks about cyborgs, Kathy Ferguson (1993) about mobile subjectivities and Rosi Braidotti (1994) about nomadic subjectivities. All these metaphors emphasise the textual and processual nature of human subjectivities. Cyborgs are built by humans connected to textuality and animals, and there is a space for change. Mobile subjectivities and nomads are, as a rule, both moving. With these metaphors feminist researchers are not only challenging essentialist womanhood, an understanding that there must be something similar in all women, but they are also opening up the social in each subjectivity. There is no one subjectivity in a human being, but subjectivities constantly meet the social and textual world, making subjectivities a process which is always on the move.

Yet, Braidotti's nomads have desires and Haraway's cyborgs have their human and animal sides, their bodies and historical locations. If the subjectivities are on the move, the move is not boundless. Although textualities intervene in the desires and meanings of bodies (see also Butler, 1993), desires take their time, and bodies have histories and biologies. People have commitments. Textualities live textual times of their own and exist without individual people yet they get their meanings only when actual people in local settings use them, interpret and produce new pieces of them (Smith, 1990b). Subjectivities can be open, social and on the move, but they are also very much located in their 'host' bodies and the concrete social relations of their societies.

Talking about women's voices is far from old-fashioned in the era of textualities; it is as relevant as it was to Cassandra. Women need to fight for their own voices from the starting point of their own concrete bodies and experiences and historical locations. Women need to create textualities that correspond to their starting points in order to struggle for their own subjectivities and their own lives.

Women live their lives through everyday practices, do their jobs and are a part of their work organisations (see Parts Two and Three above). They work within more or less hierarchical relations and divisions of labour. They get paid according to the agreements made between labour unions and employers built on the basis of job classifications. They have individual rights which follow the lines of the state's laws and regulations. And they use computer systems built all over the world.

These social relations and textualities take part in women's activities and thinking, in women's subjectivities, but women also actively define them. Women create their own practices and, through the practices, they also participate in the formation of hierarchies and divisions of labour. Through labour unions women have their say on their own wages. They defend their rights in courts of law. Women have not got the powerful position of the god Apollo and cannot exclusively determine the textualities themselves, but neither are they totally excluded.

In this part we explore women's own definitions of their social and textual practices and their subjectivities by starting with two empirical cases, one concerning sexual harassment and the other information systems development. Both cases describe a process of change in which women's practices and subjectivities enter a process of transformation. In the case of sexual harassment women have been insulted in ways that deeply touch their subjectivities. Information systems intertwine with the tasks and control of work processes as well as with the concepts women use in their daily work. In both cases women need to reorganise their thinking and their activities. They need to define their practices and subjectivities in relation to the new situations. We follow the definitions and examine the social and textual construction of the definition processes in order to understand the complex relationship between subjectivity and the socially and textually organised practices of working life.

On the one hand we make room for women's own voices which are based on their bodily experiences. Following Dorothy Smith's methodological ideas (Smith, 1990b) we take the standpoint of particular Finnish women and explore the social organisation embedded in women's accounts and practices as well as locate ourselves as researchers and political actors in the process of women's definitions. On the other hand we take seriously the more postmodern feminist thinking, for example that of Teresa de Lauretis (1987, 1989), Donna Haraway (1991) and Kathy Ferguson (1993), in which subjectivities are textually and discursively constructed and women's own definitions on working life and their subjectivities need to be located in textual contexts. Struggles for women's own definitions are also struggles over meanings and textuality.

Women's own definitions of their subjectivities and working life processes are politically important. It has been difficult for women even to name the insult that they have faced in the form of sexual harassment. Nor have women been able to develop their own information systems in their workplaces; instead information technology in the 1990s is getting more male-dominated. Women need to find their own voices and make their own definitions in working life. If women are not struggling for their own definitions others are making the definitions and gaining control over women's subjectivities.

The problematic of women's own definitions and textuality is very complex. Textualities have references to other textualities, and power relations are embedded in all of them. The processes of interpretation and production of textualities are meeting points for local and historical embodied voices and the social world of textualities. One's 'own' definitions are possible only in relation to the 'strange' (cf. Kristeva, 1992). Women should take into account the construction of textualities and develop their political activities accordingly, including women's mutual support, in order to prevent their bodily and situated subjectivities from disappearing within the textualities and in order to make a balance between experiences and texts on their own terms. Through these two cases we try to understand the possibilities for women's self-definitions within the social and textual practices of modern organisations, and we give examples of women's politics in working life, examples where both women in the workplaces as well as ourselves, as researchers, have been active subjects.

We try to open the 'magic spell – with words' as set up by the judges of Athena and Apollo in order to make room for women now and in the future so that they can be heard.

8 Anne's Story: Sexual Harassment as a Process
Hannele Varsa

RESEARCH ORIENTATIONS

The research on sexual harassment contains three relatively separate but coexisting research orientations (Mankkinen, 1994). These orientations are connected with different groups of societies and the issues defined in them (cf. Varsa, 1993b and Mankkinen, 1994).

The first research orientation is mainly located in the United States and it is based on the use of survey methods and related to the human rights debate. The aim in this tradition has often been to map out how common sexual harassment is. Sexual harassment is defined as the expression of unwanted sexual demands in an unequal power relationship (e.g. Mac-Kinnon, 1979; Gutek et al., 1980; US Merit Systems Protection Board, 1981; Gruber and Bjorn, 1982; Benson and Thomson, 1982; Loy and Stewart, 1984; Gruber, 1989; *Journal of Vocational Behavior*, 1993).

The second research orientation, which makes use of both quantitative and qualitative methods, can be found in Western and Central Europe. It stems from social policy debates (for example, Plogstedt and Bode, 1984; Rubenstein, 1988; Braszeit et al., 1988; Schneble and Domsch, 1989). Sexual harassment includes all kinds of unwanted and intrusive behaviour by men towards women with the aim to show women 'their proper place'. Sexual harassment is seen as a transformational phenomenon which escapes definition and which can only be described in each context. Women are still seen as the primary targets of sexual harassment because of their subordinate social position. However, women are no longer regarded as passive and adapting to incidents of harassment. Instead, the focus is now on women's active awareness and control of these situations, on the dialectics of control (Giddens, 1989).

The third research orientation emphasises qualitative data. This kind of research is localised especially in the Nordic countries in the 1990s and it is a part of the welfare state debate, particularly that on occupational safety and health. The third tradition has clarified the distinction between positive and negative sexuality and sexual harassment. It emphasises the intertwining of social and individual levels and the historical context

(Sørensen, 1992; Brantsæter and Widerberg, 1992; Varsa, 1993b; Mankkinen, 1994).

Mankkinen (1994) has introduced the idea of different conceptions of power into this categorisation by combining the micro and macro levels in each orientation. Research orientations are thus based on power conceptions. In the first tradition power is regarded as institutional (Goffman, 1961), structural and static. The focus is on laws and regulations (e.g. Paetzold and O'Leary-Kelly, 1994). In the second research tradition power is analysed as interaction and it is present in all action. Power is a process which endlessly contends and adapts itself, changes and is reinforced. Power is all encompassing because it is created everywhere (Foucault, 1978; cf. Katajisto, 1982, 1983). According to the second research orientation, sexual harassment is not about achieving sexual advantages. It is an expression of domination instead. Sexuality is a means whereby sexual harassment takes place. Women's subordination is sexualised (Wise and Stanley, 1987; Acker, 1992).

The third power conception examines institutional and interactional power as a synthesis which is crystallised in the sexualisation of the female body (Haug, 1987). The control and resistance of the body connect the body to the prevalent mechanisms of power (Foucault, 1991). Redefinitions of power also produce a mobile definition of sexual harassment. Sexual harassment is seen as elastic (cf. Järvinen, 1993), as a continuum formed by earlier life and work experience and it changes its shape. The focus is on interpersonal relationships and the culture in which the people live. Sexual harassment is also a way of keeping up a certain image of women's and men's sexuality. It reproduces sexual stereotypes. Experience is an important part of personal history and social position (Foucault, 1978; Holter, 1992; Mankkinen, 1994). My research belongs to the third research orientation on sexual harassment.

CONCEPTUAL FRAMEWORK

In this study I will analyse sexual harassment through one key narrative, Anne's story, which I tell from her own standpoint. Anne's story is also a story about working life, workplace power structures and the workplace organisation where the sexual harassment takes place. My starting point is thus the Smithian standpoint-cum-social relations approach (Smith, 1990a).

I will examine what Anne's experience means to her labour market position. I will also look at how textuality is connected to Anne's story of sexual harassment (Smith, 1990a). What emerges as essential are Anne's ideas about the relationships between the sexes and sexuality in general, and also about her own sexuality and herself, her self definitions (Ferguson, 1993). In other words I analyse subjectivity as a process.

During this whole sequence I have been strongly present as a researcher, both in creating the definition of sexual harassment in Finnish society[1] and as a participant in Anne's story (Smith, 1990a). I will also relate Anne's story to the other data I have collected.[2]

ANNE CALLS

Anne phoned me in 1989 after reading an article on sexual harassment in a women's magazine. The article was an interview with me as a researcher of sexual harassment, a phenomenon which until then had no established name to describe it in Finnish, in contrast to many other countries, for instance the USA where it is a common term. At the end of the article there was a request asking people who had been submitted to this phenomenon to take part in my study on sexual harassment by contacting me either by a letter describing their experiences or by making an appointment for an interview. When Anne phoned we arranged to meet at my workplace in the Equality Office. The last time I interviewed Anne was in autumn 1993.

A SEXUAL HARASSMENT PROCESS BEGINS

Anne's story on sexual harassment starts at the end of the 1980s in a small Finnish municipality where the production plant in which the harassment takes place is an important employer and taxpayer. Both Anne and the harasser have moved to this rural area from another – much larger – town because they got good jobs. They both hold high positions in the company.

Anne has been recruited into the firm to do marketing work, later as the marketing director. She has a university degree. Anne is under 30 years old, single and heterosexual. Harry, the harasser, is the company's new managing director. He is in his forties, married, has two children and is also heterosexual.

Anne had been a few weeks on sick leave from her workplace. She had read the article on my research on sexual harassment during her leave and told me later that when she was reading the article she thought that it was like the story of her life. However, at that stage she had yet no idea of all the things that were about to happen.

On the first day Anne was back to work, Harry fired her without any warning or discussion. As the official grounds for firing her Harry stated productive and financial reasons. However, Anne herself thinks that the only reason was sexual harassment.

Anne's harassment story started, also in her own later interpretation, long before her being fired, although it was only then that she first defined what had happened to her as sexual harassment. She had had an affair with Harry, her immediate superior and the company's managing director, and ended the affair on her own initiative. As a consequence, Harry started to systematically undermine her position in the firm, and finally fired her.

Harassment which begins as a result of rejection often entails threats or promises. 'If you won't yield you may find yourself on the next lay-off list' or 'If our "cooperation" goes smoothly we may then consider that new job.' Anne said in the interview:

It all began on the day we got a new managing director in the company where I was working. After two days he walked into my office in the middle of the day and said very casually that he had wanted me immediately, the moment he first laid his eyes on me. I was flabbergasted.

Harry's behaviour broke a lot of the unwritten rules of white-collar workplaces. Sexuality is quite hidden at workplaces and it is not usually talked about so directly (Hearn and Parkin, 1987). Nevertheless, both physical locales and episodes which may be connected with sexuality can be found at workplaces (Burrell, 1992): workplace Christmas parties serve as an example of this. However, Harry came to Anne's office in the middle of the workday on his second day in the company.

Sexual harassment is sometimes a question of desire, but always a question of power. Power relationships at workplaces are particularly evident in who can express his/her desire and who can reject the overtures. This is especially obvious in the secretary–manager setting when the relationship is seen as archetypal (cf. Pringle, 1989). But women often have to encounter secretary–manager stereotypes at workplaces even when they are actually not secretaries. This was what happened to Anne who was in charge of the company's marketing.

Anne continues her description of how things developed:

After a couple of weeks we made a business trip abroad and on the trip he invited me to his room for a nightcap. I went to his room where he tore my tights off. On that occasion I said let's just keep this a business affair and went back to my own room.

Many of the women I interviewed said that business trips were especially difficult. Sexual passes and proposals were more common and much grosser than in ordinary work settings. On a business trip people are away from the social control of their immediate milieu. Business trips also clearly reveal the male power in harassment, since the harassers often worked on the same or a lower hierarchic position in another company than the harassed women.

Anne continues her story:

> During the next couple of months Harry now and then mentioned at the workplace that he had certain intentions regarding me. A couple of times after our board meetings we went out to have a few beers and once, at the end of such a pub evening, he suggested we continue the party in the nearby town. I agreed to this after a few beers and he went on buying me drinks. And in the end, after I had so much alcohol in my blood I don't even know, I agreed to go to his room and that is how our sexual relationship began.

In Anne's words 'some kind of a relationship' lasted for about a year. Anne felt that she had received a number of advantages as a result of her relationship with her immediate superior, the company's managing director. She got, for example, the job title of marketing director which her boss had promised and a 100 per cent salary increase within the year. In the beginning their cooperation proceeded splendidly, Harry worked energetically in favour of Anne's organisational development suggestions and pushed them all through – power at workplaces is multidimensional. Even the power entailed in harassment is not always just a one-way misuse of position by the harasser against the harassed. Instead, power is often a tangled skein.

But does even a mutual relationship give the one in the subordinate position advantages in the long run? The possible benefits derived from the relationship are by no means unequivocal. If the relationship between the superior and the subordinate becomes common knowledge at the workplace it often creates many kinds of mistrust. It had happened to some of the women I interviewed that people at their workplace started to regard all the worker's achievements as if they were only based on the sexual relationship. The other men and women at the workplace easily disregarded the professional role of the woman involved in an affair and looked at everything she did only through the relationship perspective.

At this stage Anne did not expect Harry to divorce his wife or to get married to her, but she expected a deepening emotional relationship. When in her opinion their relationship did not seem to be developing at all, Anne wanted to end it. Harry refused to talk about the situation, and whenever Anne tried to broach the subject he avoided the question. After having had enough of the dead-end situation Anne made it very clear during a business trip that the sexual relationship between them was now over.

When they returned home, Harry's behaviour had changed. Even on their way home from the airport Anne asked him: 'Are you now going to kick me out of the company?' To this the manager said: 'You'll soon find out.'

When the sexual relationship ended on Anne's initiative she was ousted from her job. The boss himself said that it had been his practice to get rid of people whom he thought inconvenient in the organisation. Anne tells about the situation after her discharge:

> I was instinctively prepared for something like this and I was able to be perfectly calm in that situation [when she was fired, HV]. My coolness baffled Harry and he spontaneously said something like 'What's the matter, I've done this before, you know.' And this made me even more certain and convinced that if this is the reason for which I'm being fired, it won't rest here.

If the relationship between two people working in the same organisation ends or is cut short the position of the person on the lower rungs of the hierarchy is awkward almost without exception. For a woman it is often very hard to find support from anywhere. The processual nature of sexual harassment came out in all the interviews I made. At this stage of the process colleagues often unwillingly or unknowingly participate in driving somebody out. When people start paying negative attention to what a person does or does not do, the process soon becomes self-perpetuating. As in cases of mobbing, when somebody is being expelled from her or his job because of sexual harassment, the work community starts to emphasise her or his failures and often also personal characteristics.

Anne's discharge is an epitome of the processual nature. She was isolated from her colleagues and other relationships essential to her work.

> After this trip to the trade fair and after I had ended the relationship I was over a couple of months gradually and imperceptibly isolated from my colleagues and all the significant contacts outside the company. This was paradoxical because I was still the company's marketing director.

The fact that the harasser can continue his actions for a very long time until the victim of harassment knows what to do reveals the secrecy characteristic of sexual harassment. A small community where everyone knows everyone else's position makes it even more difficult to make harassment public. Anne, for example, told me that she had felt some kind of a solidarity with the harasser's wife 'since she could not help the matter'. The shame often connected with harassment also tends to keep the issue a secret.

All this time, for over a year, I never told anyone of our relationship which perhaps helped him to act as he did. And on the other hand this rapid change in the situation from a well functioning work relationship into nightmarish threats and persecution was so confusing that I was unable to react fast enough or in any way at all.

Anne's story also shows how both positive and negative sexuality is a difficult issue at workplaces. People are not allowed to or they do not know how to deal with it. Sexuality is seen to belong in the private sphere whereas workplaces are in the public sphere. This combination largely epitomises the secrecy of harassment and the shameful feelings it arouses.

THE FIRST STAGE – WHAT IS MY POSITION AS A WOMAN IN THE BUSINESS WORLD?

Anne tells about her situation just before the harassment process started to accelerate:

I am at that stage of my working life and career when I am just about to become known among the clientele. People are fond of me and regard me as a professional, active person and especially that I am an inspiring person to have around.

Even right after her dismissal Anne was still very sure about her own rights, her position and herself.

The sexual harassment Anne experienced was also felt in the whole workplace atmosphere. That she was fired after the good results the company had achieved created confusion. Even the municipality had given them a prize for making the town better known. At this stage Anne decided to tell her closest colleagues the real reason for her dismissal. Anne deliberated about making the issue public at the workplace also from the perspective of power. She concludes that in order for power to be effective it has to be invisible:

And since sexual harassment is a question of power, by making the issue visible, in other words talking about it, also means making the use of power visible. Would the power then be negated in that way?

When Anne had told the real reason for her discharge the first reaction at the workplace was almost one of relief. Knowledge about the forbidden subject, that Anne had had an affair with her married boss as people had suspected, seemed to clear the atmosphere. Perhaps it even explained some things that people had been wondering about at the workplace.[3]

The day after she was fired Anne contacted the corporation president, and they met two days afterwards. Anne showed him the women's magazine article on sexual harassment.[4] She heard from him that the corporation board of directors was going to have a meeting on reorganisation in their companies but that no decisions had yet been made. This too indicated to Anne that her boss Harry was 'in a frenzy to get rid of me'.

Next day the corporation president had come to the factory. Harry had admitted that he and Anne had had an affair. At the following weekend the president invited Anne and Harry to come and talk about the situation with him. Anne said to Harry: 'We are both going to be a part of the business life one way or another for the next 20 years or so. And so that you don't totally lose face in front of me could you now in this situation repeat the grounds you have for firing me.' Harry did not answer. He was totally silent and then he started to cry.

According to Anne the corporation president was irritated at this point. Her boss is crying in front of Anne whose discharge on Harry's suggestion has recently been authorised by the president's own signature.

Anne's opinion about the situation was that the only reason for her discharge was that she had been sexually exploited by her boss. At the end of the discussion the president said: 'I'm not so sure about this exploitation thing. You're both adults and as adults you should know how to fix this between yourselves.'

The following week Anne phoned the secretary of the corporation president and also some of the supervisors in the factory about what had happened. She kept in constant touch with her own secretary. She received understanding and encouragement from all the people she talked with, and this is contrary to what normally happens in harassment cases. The women I interviewed said that at first hardly anyone understood them when they brought up their experiences.

Anne's interpretation was that Harry's career had suffered a severe blow. The president had seen what was going on. It also came up that he had himself six months earlier asked Harry what was going on between him and Anne, and Harry had lied that they were just colleagues.

At this stage Anne still thought that she would lose nothing. She even thought that she might herself be promoted to the company's managing director. She added, however, that she would only do it if her colleagues suggested it and asked her to. Anne knew that the company had been successfully run for some time on her ideas. In Anne's opinion this fact was now also known among her closest colleagues. Anne had also had some talks about export jobs in the branch and she remarked laughing that she was now able to tailor a job that would really suit herself. She even told me that she had been toying with the idea that she could become an assistant researcher in my research project on sexual harassment, while she had been promised six months' salary if she would not take the issue any further.

However, some male supervisors warned Anne already at this stage that Harry would never publicly admit the real reason behind her discharge. Anne's understanding of the first stage of her harassment process is best described by her remark that no matter how awful life can be, it is still always fair in some ways.

THE SECOND STAGE – ANNE'S COLLISION WITH TEXTUALITY

When the president signed Anne's discharge the whole corporation was committed to stand behind it. This became clearly evident after Anne took legal action.

Besides being in touch with her colleagues Anne contacted her union lawyer and me on the day she was fired. She also contacted the Equality Ombudsman. By her union Anne was advised to contact a woman lawyer who, however, dropped the case after about six months without letting her client know. Anne learned about this only after she had contacted the lawyer to enquire how things were proceeding. Anne changed lawyers and on the recommendation of her new (male) lawyer sued the company only for unlawful discharge and breach of the Act on Codetermination in Companies.[5] Since Anne had been fired on productive and financial grounds she and her counsel now attempted to prove in court that no such grounds existed.

Also Anne's second lawyer was unwilling to bring up sexual harassment. He may have felt this way because he knew the Finnish legal system well enough to realise that broaching the subject in a lower court of justice in a small town would not lead to the desired result. At that time Finnish legislation did not mention sexual harassment explicitly, although it was possible to take action on the basis of several other laws including labour and equality legislation.[6] However, Anne herself wanted to bring up sexual harassment which she thought was the real reason for her discharge. In court Anne requested leave to speak and read aloud a statement which she had written beforehand and which dealt with her harassment process. She describes the setting and her feelings in the courtroom:

> All the jurors and the judge were men. The jurors were about 50 or 60 years old and the judge was a junior lawyer. There were two competent male lawyers and the defendant was our corporation president and his counsel. [. . .] When I entered the courtroom I was convinced that I would get justice for myself. But very soon after the hearing started I realised or got the feeling as if I had already been cast a role. I understood that I had been categorised as a frivolous and wanton woman who had no grounds for her appeal, but who was appealing nevertheless.

Anne felt it very important to bring up the issue of sexual harassment in court. She wanted it to be mentioned in the record of the hearing, she wanted to see her experience in writing, so that she would be able to prove with this public document that she had not been fired on grounds of incompetence. Here, too, Anne places great emphasis on her professional role.

Sexual harassment was dealt with in the hearing on Anne's initiative, and she was in the exceptional position that her former boss admitted that they had had an affair and that he also partly owned up to sexual harassment – but in spite of all this no mention whatsoever about harassment was included in the official record of the hearing. Of all the things that are talked about in the courtroom only the things that the judge decides to state, considers important or understands end up in the official record. Anne had to experience the impossibility in legal praxis of introducing new issues into the language known by power – into texts – and the difficulty of bringing in issues that were foreign to the judicial language of the legal profession.

Although sexual harassment and everything that had to do with sexuality was expunged during the legal process, the role cast for Anne in the court hearing was first and foremost based on sexuality and gender. In cases of sexual harassment women often remain prisoners of a manifold sexuality. On the one hand there is a tendency to deny and curb sexuality in the public domain. On the other hand, women are often regarded at the workplace first as representatives of their gender and of sexuality and their professional roles come only second (e.g. MacKinnon, 1979). The women I interviewed felt that the most difficult thing related to sexual harassment was that their professional roles were disparaged or even totally denied. The situation was hardest on women who were harassed by their own bosses from whom they had expected support instead of the undue emphasis on sexuality.[7]

Anne tried to create space for her own definition of the situation in the legal system but she collided with its gendered practices. She lost her case of unlawful discharge. The defendant's evidence of productive and financial reasons was found to be valid in court. For the breach of the Act on Codetermination in Companies Anne's employer was made to pay her two month's salary. This verdict remained unchanged in the Court of Appeal where Anne next took her case. Sexual harassment was completely ignored in the legal process. Issues such as sexual harassment 'disappear' in the court hearings unless they are the subject of a separate lawsuit.

Anne describes her situation after the legal process:

> I must admit that I was beaten up real bad. And it was not very pleasant. [. . .] In my own life the legal process perhaps resulted in some sort of a two-year shadowboxing about my overall position as a woman in business life. My immediate reaction or thought was that I shall never again work for anybody else which is a kind of a crazy decision as such. But that was my conviction when I left the business world and now I work in a completely different field.

THE THIRD STAGE – REDEFINING ONE'S OWN LIFE

The sexual harassment Anne experienced had a crucial impact on her labour market position. What seemed a secure upwardly mobile career in business life was entirely broken at least for the time being. She took up a job in a quite different field and she still works there. According to Anne's own estimation this is not necessarily a worse option, although her financial standing is now totally different from what it was when she was a young businesswoman with a relatively good salary, her own car and so on. What is essential, however, is that the sexual harassment Anne experienced had an impact on this radical change of lifestyles.

Apart from the physical and mental consequences Anne experienced, the fact that her own bodily experience was repudiated and ignored when she tried to plead her cause through the official channels, in particular the support organisations of Finnish working life, created some specific repercussions. This experience of repudiation, a new process, may have more far-reaching and longstanding effects for the person who is subjected to sexual harassment (cf. Widerberg, 1992) than the actual sexual advances in harassment. It had an effect on Anne's self-definition and the way she understood her own sexuality.

Throughout the legal process and even after it Anne sifted through her own experiences. She talked about what had happened with both the people she met in connection with her work, for instance she brought the issue up in interviews for new jobs, and with her friends and acquaintances. She found it surprising that there still was little serious public discussion on sexual harassment although the phenomenon was so familiar to the people with whom she brought it up.

Regardless of the threat of stigma Anne wanted to broach the subject with the businessmen she knew. After recovering from their initial shock a few managing directors had asked her 'to join the gang where we talk man to man' because of her experience of harassment.

Anne also received understanding from men who had been harassers themselves. They of course recognised the situation immediately and Anne did not have to waste her energy on proving what had happened. Some men even told Anne how they had fired their female employees in a similar situation.

Anne found it easier to talk about sexual harassment with homosexual men. According to her they were able to see the situation from the point of view of the harassed woman whereas heterosexual men often adopted the harasser's standpoint and started to defend him.

On the other hand Anne also talked about her experiences with a man who, 'because of the principle of the matter', was at that time suing his drunkard bricklayer. The man wondered why Anne had not accepted the offer for money because in his opinion in her case no principles were involved. Anne was outraged and said: 'No principles involved! So I'm just a five-penny hooker with a university degree, fluent knowledge of seven languages and so on. What principles?'

In autumn 1993 a woman who had been subjected to sexual harassment came to see me, and her situation was not unlike the one in which Anne had found herself almost four years earlier. This woman had also just been fired because she was not 'cooperative enough' and she was about to sue her employer. She even had the same lawyer that Anne had. I asked whether she would be willing to meet a woman who had been in a similar situation and taken legal action. We arranged a meeting for the three of us.

Anne talked about her self-reproach, depression and crying for hours ... She compared her feelings to the 'post-traumatic disorders' experienced by the North American soldiers after Vietnam, and to reactions women have after being raped. Anne emphasised the importance of building the legal case explicitly on sexual harassment on the basis of the Equality Act. Without harassment there would not have been a discharge, salary claims from the company and so on. On the other hand Anne felt that it was important that women bring up and talk about their experiences, that they make their own self-definitions also in the public domain. They need to do this not only for themselves, but for other women in similar situations and because 'just maybe lawyers and the whole legal system will start to realise the extent and diversity of these cases'. Anne said:

It is an extremely tough process but as it is in any case going to affect your future employment and your life I can't see any reason why you shouldn't do it exactly the way you feel right.

What happened will stay in the harassed person's experiences: 'you cannot bury it because it's in you'. Anne talks about being subjected to sexual harassment and how it comes up in her relationship to men in general and how one has to encounter the harassment experience when one is about to start a new intimate relationship:

The traces that remain after such a terrible experience have not so much to do with sex itself, but with all the other things involved which can then afterwards be in some ways triggered and activated by anything sexual. And in this way the experience becomes a kind of a bizarre lump.

Anne talks about the dangers to oneself when one as the victim of harassment is blamed for it. She says that one should not deny one's heterosexual orientation.

This now gets in the area of what is your own sexuality, your own understanding of your sexuality. And after you have gone through harassment in all its stages long enough in your own mind, you're still able to see yourself as an attractive person who can be interested in men and there's nothing wrong with that.

At the end of the conversation Anne remarks that as a by-product of going through the process one is not so easily startled by every small thing. One also learns to know oneself and has to deliberate one's own values.

THE PROCESS CONTINUES

Anne had given a name to sexual harassment even before its most active stage had begun. Most of the people I interviewed were only able to give a name to their unwanted experiences long after they had taken place, after considerable delay. In Anne's case the timing of the magazine article and my research were just right. When she was fired she immediately recalled the article she had read and contacted me on the same day. This enabled the two of us to go together through her harassment experiences at that time and later, after she sued the company, also through the legal process.

Anne's case of sexual harassment sums up some of the gendered practices in working life and legal system (Acker, 1989b; Heiskanen et al., 1990). In her case the organisation and the management sided with the harasser. The case makes very clear how the almost total absence of the concept of harassment from official texts (from legislation and from workplace equality programmes) still made even bringing up the phenomenon extremely difficult. As is the case with sexuality in working life in general (e.g. Hearn and Parkin, 1987), harassment may disappear even when it is explicitly brought up.

The sexual harassment Anne experienced and her attempts to find justice and to have her experience named and stated as a text in the official record of the court hearing show how difficult it is to translate a new concept into the language of power. The court proceedings repeated the concepts already known to the system: financial and productive reasons. The whole legal process was infused with male power of definition.

The sexual harassment Anne experienced and the legal action she took instigated a process which resulted in a radical change in her labour market position. She had to reconsider her attitude to sexuality and her conception of herself, so that her self-definition changed (Ferguson, 1993).

Anne's case has differences and similarities with many other harassment cases. When she constantly analyses her situation and goes back and forth in her story she is doing something many others I interviewed did. Anne is, however, exceptional in that she very energetically takes action. Anne also makes her experience public. Many women in my research told me that they never came out with their stories because they thought that in this way they might preserve their dignity (Harre, 1979; Oksanen, 1993). The unique features of Anne's story make even more clear how many visible and invisible obstacles have to be conquered when one starts to process one's experience of sexual harassment in public.

The stories told to me by Anne and the other women I interviewed could be crystallised in just one word: a process. First, the course of events of sexual harassment is above all a process. If singular events are separated from the whole sequence, from the atmosphere in which the harassed person lives, their meaning is not easily conveyed to outsiders. It is therefore understandable that when the harassed person brings up the issue with an outsider she most often encounters bafflement, disparagement and pacification, even blame. This happens with both friends, professional counsellors and the support persons in working life (superiors, shop stewards,[8] labour protection and occupational health service personnel)[9].

So, what takes place when harassment is going on is best understood as a process. But secondly, a completely new process begins if one attempts to broach the subject and to find a solution. A tendency to ignore and deny these physical and mental ordeals experienced by women has very far-reaching effects and ultimately it affects the women's self-definitions. It provokes and speeds up the subjectivity's transformation process. Also on the social level the consequences of sexual harassment are longstanding. Anne's harassment process is still going on.

NOTES

1. During the research project 51 articles on sexual harassment were published which were directly related to this research (Varsa, 1993b).
2. The data consisted of 18 letters, 39 interviews with individual people and five group interviews.
3. The descriptions of the workplace atmosphere are based on Anne's discussions with her former colleagues. She was in touch with them for a rather long time even after her discharge.
4. Anne later sent the corporation president the report on sexual harassment at workplaces published by the Council for Equality which I had given her.
5. According to the Act on Codetermination in Companies discharges and layoffs that are based on financial and productive reasons have to be negotiated with the personnel's representatives beforehand, and the discharged person has to be notified of the impending discharge.
6. Sexual harassment is explicitly mentioned in the updated Equality Law, which took effect on 1 March 1995. The employer is there made responsible that the employee is not exposed to sexual harassment at the workplace.
7. About the phenomenon of 'sexual spillover', see Gutek and Cohen (1992).
8. The rate of unionisation is high in Finland (see Rantalaiho, Chapter 2, above).
9. In Finland many employers organise health services for their employees. The larger workplaces have their own clinics whereas smaller workplaces use the services of private medical centres.

9 One's 'Own' Information Systems
Marja Vehviläinen

It would be good to be interested in computing. I must confess that I am not. But when I realised that it is essential for my current work, I wanted to get to the bottom of it. I am not making it a voluntary hobby, those are in more human areas. But it (interest in computing) is like a marriage of reason.

(Satu, an office worker, 46)

At the moment, it is regrettable that women work with terminals and men have the more demanding design jobs. Office people's work content could be changed quite radically through this new technology [. . .], I have learned to be active myself. Already before anybody talked about (computing) equipment, I said that if I had such an apparatus I would do this and that.

(Maikki, an office worker, 39)

The above extracts are interview accounts given by two office workers who participated in an office workers' information systems study circle in a Finnish governmental bureau (Vehviläinen, 1991). Satu worked mostly with a word processor, without a voice of her own in systems selection and development projects. Maikki devoted a lot of her energy and time to the development of her departmental information systems, in addition to her normal daily duties in project administration. Their situations and possibilities in computing were very different, but they both understood that information systems were crucially intertwining with their work, with their own ways of acting and thinking, with their well-being and subjectivities. They both wanted to take part in systems development in order to have a say in their work content and less suppressive relations between women and men, between office workers and experts – in their work setting.

Information systems are constructed from not only technical artefacts, most importantly computers, but also of knowledge and socially organised 'doing', the concrete practices of people working in actual organisations (Wajcman, 1991; Scarbrough and Corbett, 1992). Artefacts, knowledge and practices intertwine with each other, and the struggle between office

138

workers and information systems experts, of expertise in information systems use and development, can only be understood if seen as interaction between these three elements. Knowledge of information technology is not only related to technical artefacts but also to 'doing' and practices. Hierarchic Tayloristic organisational practices are often connected to an understanding of knowledge as objective, that is experts are able to handle knowledge by themselves. But the more flexible work design strategies come closer to situated knowledge (Suchman, 1994), to an understanding that office workers have their own position, a voice distinct from that of experts, in the realm of knowledge. Similarly, as Webster (1993; also Hofmann, 1994) shows in the case of word processing, artefacts correspond to specific 'doing', namely work practices. All three, artefacts, knowledge and 'doing', have been constructed within social and historical (military and economic) processes. It is in these processes where the gendering of information technology is also embedded (Wajcman, 1991).

In all Western countries, gendering processes (Acker, 1992; Harding, 1986) have shaped information technology into a male dominated domain, especially during the 1990s 'backlash'. In hierarchies and divisions of work women are mostly excluded from information technology development and are rather located in the low hierarchy positions of computer users (Kirkup, 1992; Schelhowe, 1993). At the symbolic level information technology is constructed by a military, male rhetoric (Edwards, 1990; van Oost, 1992; Truckenbrod, 1993), and the information technology discourse has had difficulties in integrating any understanding of gender or other social relations into itself (Vehviläinen, 1994b). The image of identity in information technology is masculine (Wajcman, 1991) and the image of subjectivity very much resembles that of the Hegelian male subjectivity (cf. Ferguson, 1993).

In the overall picture of information technology, gendering takes concrete forms in concrete situations and practices. Gender divisions have varied from organisation to organisation, from time to time within one country, as well as from country to country (Blomqvist et al., 1994). Women have also been able to use information technology for their own purposes and in their own ways (Mörtberg, 1994; Vehviläinen, 1994a; Wajcman, 1991; Zuboff, 1988). Communication systems originally designed for the US military now serve as women's networks and strengthen women's voices and mutual support in different universities and large organisations.

Several studies from the English speaking countries (Probert and Wilson, 1993a) as well as from the Netherlands (Tijdens, 1994) show that information technology is male (expert) dominated and the domination intervenes in the daily practices and subjectivities of a growing number of women in working life. In 1990, 45 per cent of women in paid work in Finland used computers (Lehto, 1992: 101). Yet, computing presents possibilities for women in concrete situations (Wagner, 1994). Women should struggle to make their own definitions of information technology, as Satu and Maikki at the beginning of this chapter had noticed, in order to maintain a hold over their own lives and their own subjectivities (cf. Cockburn and Ormrod, 1993: 175). Women should challenge the expertise of information tech-nology itself so as to break the 'nexus between experts and technology' (Wajcman, 1991: 165) in order for it to be replaced by a 'located account-ability' of actual people (Suchman, 1994). Women should not only strive to 'deprofessionalise the author' of technology (Spender, 1993) but also to create a 'cyberspace' of their own, as Ebben and Kramarae (1993: 17) suggest. My goals in the office workers' study circle were very similar to these.

Office workers in Finland, like women in low hierarchy positions in organisations everywhere, are mostly excluded from systems development (Lehto, 1992; Korvajärvi, 1989). I, as a feminist researcher and a resource person with computing skills, initiated a study circle which included ten office workers. The group gathered in a large governmental bureau once a week for seven months. In this chapter, I take two of the participants, Maikki and Satu cited at the beginning, by using interview accounts they gave before, during and some months after the study circle, as well as the notes that I made at the study circle meetings. I explore how they faced the organisational practices of information technology and focus on 'do-ing' rather than knowledge or artefacts of information systems expertise. I investigate how they defined their information systems. Through Maikki's and Satu's accounts I take an office workers' standpoint (Smith, 1987) by looking at the social and textual construction of their definitions in the context of the bureau and Finnish society (cf. Vehviläinen, 1994c).

WORK DESIGN PRACTICES AND INFORMATION SYSTEMS

In a working life setting, one's 'own' definition of information systems is connected to organisational practices. Women's groups, as well as other political activities in information systems, need to be located in organisa-tions and organisational work design strategies. While many elements of information systems expertise, namely the idea of objective knowledge and the failure to see the social and gender aspects in computing, for example, have persistently remained the same ever since computer profes-sionals' discourse was born (Vehviläinen, 1994b), the understanding of work design in information systems has changed to some degree and now appears to leave more room for women's own definitions.

Information technology development started as a strictly hierarchic and Tayloristic practice in both North America (Braverman, 1974; Machung, 1983) and Europe (Kirkup, 1992; Webster, 1994), including Finland (Korvajärvi and Rantalaiho, 1984). It gave the computing professionals power over work processes and excluded workers, especially women, from systems development. However, since the 1970s, information systems practices have been influenced by alternative, more flexible and human-oriented managerial theories (Scarbrough and Corbett, 1992; Probert and Wilson, 1993a; Vehviläinen, 1994b). In Britain, Enid Mumford and Don Henshall (1979), for example, applied socio-technical thinking to informa-tion technology, and in Scandinavia working life democracy projects con-nected to labour unions were also introduced in information technology (for example, Ehn, 1988). The women's movements in Britain (Microsyster, 1988; Baines, 1991; Green, Owen and Pain, 1993a), in Denmark (Foged and Sørensen, 1985) and in many other countries (e.g. de Cindio and Simone, 1993) have raised the question of gender and women's own expertise in information technology.

There has not been any labour union or women's movement projects in information technology in Finland, but one of the alternative theories that has had an impact on systems development, in particular in state admin-istration, has been the developmental work research approach (Engeström, 1985 and 1991) based on the activity theories of Vygotsky and Leont'ev. It emphasises the workers' own analysis of their work as well as the workers' participation in the development of their own work but, similarly to the gender and physics project described by Leila Räsänen (in Chapter 10), this alternative was taken up as a top-down rather than a bottom-up project in the state administration. The approach was used in a govern-mental committee which developed vocational education in information technology. There was a major effort in the committee to move the power over information technology development from computer experts to pro-fessionals in work processes (Vehviläinen, 1994a). Although there was no discussion about gender or special support for women, the developmental work research approach made room for my study which was to advance women's mutual support practices to enable them to do system develop-ment in a governmental bureau.

From the bureau's point of view I was giving free education in infor-mation technology at a point when they were strongly introducing new information systems and were lacking appropriate education. According to the bureau's long-term information systems plan, influenced by the developmental work research thinking, the bureau's whole personnel needed knowledge of their work and information processing. In addition, a wider information systems training on systems development was planned for a good 10 per cent of the personnel. There was no computer department in the bureau, but with its long-term plan the bureau tried to make people already working in the bureau develop skills and knowledge of information systems. The bureau's plan defined information systems as something that everybody had to deal with in their everyday work rather than as special expertise.

The bureau's educational expert, as many other educational experts in Finland, had become acquainted with the developmental work research approach through the courses of the state institute of vocational education (the Administrative Development Agency). She wanted to organise her bureau's education so that everybody could learn enough to develop her or his work and she stated that the development would include information systems, too. Her educational plan, parallel to the bureau's long-term plan, almost invited experiments. Maybe I was organising the study circle with a group that was not 'meant' to be educated in the long-term plan, but since the plan did not explicitly name any particular people or groups, my proposal was accepted. The developmental work research approach, as an alternative to strict Tayloristic and Weberian divisions of expertise, built space for office workers' information systems definitions both in organisational practices and by legitimising the study circle. The space was full of contradictions but it contained elements of working life democracy.

MAKING USE OF WORKING LIFE DEMOCRACY

Maikki, one of the study circle participants, worked as a department secretary. In cooperation with one expert level official she supervised the money orders and schedules of the 200 projects that were carried out in her department, made project agreements between the bureau and other organisations and participated in customer service and information.

Maikki said that her department manager supported the workers' own activity. They arranged weekly department meetings and the office workers were also used to taking the floor in these meetings. The division of labour between office workers and upper-level officials was flexible. All the workers, mostly women in this rather small department, sometimes got together and had parties. Maikki emphasised the fact that their workplace atmosphere was free and supportive.

Information systems were discussed and developed together. However, this had happened only recently. Maikki had already suggested five years earlier that they get a computer system for project administration, but all they got then was a word processor which was not suitable for the job. At that point the managers and computer experts did not realise that they should have asked the users themselves, but now they all realised that computer systems had to be developed together. The whole department had gathered for a development day to analyse the work processes in the department's project administration and to plan a new system. Everybody, including Maikki, was able to list their expectations and needs. The system itself was technically planned and programmed outside the department, but Maikki kept in touch with the programmers and also supervised the process of transforming the project documents to an electronic form by partly doing it herself and by partly guiding temporary workers in keying. The times had changed as Maikki put it. The discourse on participatory systems design (Mumford and Henshall, 1979; in Finland, Järvinen and Tyllilä, 1980) and the new alternative work development theories (for example, Engeström, 1981) had reached experts and managers who were willing to give room to the workers. Maikki's manager had created practices that allowed Maikki and the others to be active and develop their own as well as the department's work and information systems. Maikki used this opportunity, and as she said 'had learned to be active herself'.

During the study circle the programmers delivered the project administration program and Maikki started to test and develop it according to her daily work. It turned out that the program still had mistakes that needed to be corrected by the programmers. The program interfaces also contained information that she never used, and she had to go through series of screens in order to collect the pieces she needed in her job. The program had been built on the basis of the plans made in the department information systems meeting, which meant that the interfaces had information for everybody's needs. Maikki studied the technical details of the system and, in the study circle work analysis, started to look for her own perspective to the 'general' department work processes. By letting information systems intervene in her thinking and by exploring her own work she was able to choose the necessary information and create a new design on the screens. She herself defined the information systems textuality which would intertwine with her thinking and her daily practices. She was defining her textual subjectivity.

By developing the project administration system Maikki also developed her department work processes. The new system stored all the project information handled in the department in one place so that the department workers could easily access it through an enquiry in case they needed it to answer customers' questions by telephone. Before the system was introduced experts and managers used to rush to Maikki's or other office workers' rooms to ask for the details in the project documents. Because of the new system office workers were thought to have fewer interruptions, and the division of labour as well as the hierarchy between experts and office workers was to be reorganised. Maikki was defining her own work by information systems development which meant defining her own activities and thinking and also her relation to her co-workers. She was defining the division of labour and hierarchies which are two of the central elements of gendering processes (cf. Acker, 1992; Connell, 1987). By her information systems development she was defining her subjectivity as well as the working life relations to which she belonged.

AUTHORITARIAN DEMOCRACY

I have analysed Maikki's activities and accounts in order to examine how working life democracy and developmental work research discourse embedded in organisational practices and in information systems plans, in a local textuality, made room for Maikki's information systems definitions. However, it is not easy for office workers to define their own work. I interviewed Maikki again after the study circle had finished and she had been developing her new system for some months. The overall picture is quite different now.

Maikki described her development work by saying:

I do feel a bit annoyed. When I sit in front of the machine, people always think that I rest or shirk my duties. Someone is constantly interrupting, coming to ask or say something. It is not thought of as work that requires concentration. [. . .] They do not see that when you stop to sort out the program mistakes, you have to concentrate. [. . .] You can postpone the implementation of computer systems but these daily things cannot be postponed. People expect to get their money and the agreements move from person to person and manuscripts must be prepared and delivered. They cannot be left to wait for a moment when you happen to have time.

The development work had to wait but it remained as a niggling feeling of an unfinished job. Maikki hoped to have fewer interruptions when the system was ready but she could not avoid them during the system development. She was stressed and her blood pressure was high.

Maikki continued: 'I cannot stand the situation any more. I have lately consciously turned away from taking responsibility, since I do not have any authority or power, and I also told this to my superior.' Because of the hierarchy, the office workers were unable to implement the development completely by themselves. Maikki did not have the authority to leave the normal everyday tasks aside, but she was able to do development only by doing two people's jobs in a very contradictory situation.

The bureau's managers or experts did not recognise the office workers' development work. They did not provide proper resources and authority, as Maikki's case illustrates, but they also forgot to inform the office workers adequately and did not include them on mailing lists. The study circle participants learnt about the bureau's information systems plans only by inviting experts to the study circle. The bureau arranged once or twice a year personnel meetings for its workers, but that was not enough to keep the office workers up to date.

One of the study group members said in a later interview:

Although they tried to make democratic decisions in the bureau, there is still a tendency to consider the office workers as a 'performing level'. It does not show in any striking ways, yet it comes up in many people's opinions, and in particular the educational expert is a walking example of this. The expert says aloud 'performing level' with the kind of a tone that one does not quite know if one is a human being at all, without a university degree.

Satu thought that the study circles would also be forgotten after we finished since the educational expert and the bureau in general were only interested in the upper-level officials' education.

The democratic principles of information systems development did not apply to office workers very well. The bureau's long-term plan promised information technology education to all workers but allowed only a limited group to have extensive education in information systems development. Although the plan did not explicitly say that it was managers and experts who were going to have the education, it became quite clear that within the hierarchical situation of the bureau, that was the case. Within the small numbers there was little room for office workers. Although the bureau did not build up a special expertise for information systems, it seemed to strengthen the division between experts and office workers within the information systems development. Office workers like Maikki faced a hierarchical form of working life democracy in information systems development. In contrast to human-oriented information systems practices taken up in most other countries, for example in socio-technical participatory design practices developed by Mumford and Henshall (1979), the practices and textualities of the bureau did not give the power and responsibility to technical experts in computing, but emphasised the responsibility of the workers themselves. Yet, it turned out that the hierarchies within the workers' organisation were not questioned. It was still the experts, those in high positions in the hierarchy in work organisation, that were supposed to arrange the development and create the definitions of the information systems.

The hierarchic form of working life democracy was no coincidence in this Finnish governmental bureau. The initiators of the developmental work research approach, for example Engeström, came from the 1970s' socialist political movements, which in Finland took hierarchic rather than grassroots democracy forms (Hyvärinen, 1994). The work development theory repeats the rhetoric of these politics in both its democratic and authoritarian elements.

The bureau where the study circle took place was also itself a conventional hierarchic bureaucracy. Satu worked as a typist in a department next to Maikki's. In her department office workers did not do any information systems development, but Satu often had to work all day at her word processor. She said in an interview: 'I have no need to think myself. I used to produce texts in my previous work. Now I doubt whether I could write anymore. I just type other people's texts.' In the department she was considered as a part of the bureau machinery itself (Reimer, 1987) and not as a worker who could have a voice of her own.

In the study circle Satu studied and evaluated programs and systems, made a meticulous work analysis and was always in favour of extending the study circle work. She wanted to learn more and had interest and skills to do different tasks and to develop her work, but the practices of her superior limited her activities to a monotonous use of the information system. A Weberian bureaucracy with its gendered hierarchy and division of work shaped her possibilities of using the competence gained in the study circle, and no doubt, in a similar manner, it intervened in all efforts for working life democracy and flexible work design (cf. Appelbaum, 1993; Green, 1994) taken in the bureau.

OFFICE WORKERS' GROUP AND RELATIONS OF ENTRUSTMENT – FEMINIST PRACTICES IN WORKING LIFE

If I had taken an expert's standpoint I could have concluded that the bureau complied with an equality policy on information systems, that is all the employees were supposed to learn skills in information technology. From the office workers' standpoint the situation looked quite different. The hierarchy got very involved in their information systems activities and definitions both through organisational practices and through information systems policy. For the most part the hierarchy excluded women office workers from systems development, although it did provide some space. It became clear that it is especially women in low hierarchy positions that need special support for their own information systems definitions. Maikki might have done her development work without the study circle but for most other participants it was the study circle, a small group combined with expert resources, that made their own definitions possible and made them aware of the small spaces available for the development of information systems in the bureau.

In the first study circle meeting the participants were unable to discuss computing, nor could they think about developing information systems. 'At least in our department, it was impossible to have any influence on it,' responded one participant. Only Maikki had examples of concrete development work. However, little by little, one after another they started to give accounts about initiatives and development work that they had been doing. In the third series of interviews almost everybody reported that they had been active in development work, maybe not always in information systems, but in some other issues concerning their work.

Maikki had taken several (user) courses in computing and done information systems development. In the study circle meetings she shared her experiences with the others. Maikki also cared about the other members' work and drew conclusions for the group. In an interview after the study circle she thought that she had especially learnt evaluation skills and a way of being critical, but she was also able to make use of the other participants' experiences. The other women said that the study circle was good since they had learnt how computers function and what (equipment) was available. Other participants' experiences of working with computers in the office such as Maikki's helped them to see how information systems could be used in their own work.

Within the study group the office workers were able to let the information systems' language intervene in their thinking. They could do it by starting from their own situation and their own work. The other participants' experiences intermediated between office work and technical language, and each participant was able to build her own definitions by grounding them in her work. In previous computing courses they had been unable to let the information systems' concepts take over their language but through group mediation they were able to allow that to happen. They were able to control the process themselves and build their own definitions of information systems.

For Satu in her typist's job preoccupied with computer terminal work, the group mainly provided encouragement in taking advantage of small opportunities in concrete situations. She taught another office worker word processing and she asked for an opportunity to have microcomputer education. With group support she was able to develop her work discreetly, by herself and in the office workers' group. Information systems definitions as well as the group support were very situational and related to each member's concrete settings and practices.

There were also contradictions in the group. Some thought that some of the other members were on 'lower levels' in the organisational hierarchy which disturbed the mutual trust. Some were afraid that rumours of their departmental difficulties would spread through the study circle. Maybe the one man we had in the group prevented topics concerning sexual difference from appearing, although he was quiet and had experienced discrimination himself. Nevertheless, the participants seemed to appreciate group support and were looking forward to something similar in the future. Maikki, for example, was planning a program user group with another woman. They were conscious of the lack of experts and thought that the mutual support in a user group was the best alternative they could develop. Even a restricted group support helped in information systems definitions.

I also actively and consciously supported the group and its members. I helped the office workers to learn to evaluate information technology, to conduct critical discussions about it and persuaded them to analyse their work. Without my support the office workers would not have analysed their work or evaluated information systems critically, which means that they would not have developed information systems definitions from their own standpoints. Instead they would have selected options made available to them by the bureau experts (Vehviläinen, 1994c).

It is possible to define information systems suitable to one's own work and to one's own situation only if one knows both information technology and one's own work. In information systems we have to let others, living experts or at least textual guidebooks, supervise us in order to acquire the skills of definition. Politically this means that women need to build mutual support within expert relations. Women need relations of entrustment that the Italian women's movement (Libreria delle Donne di Milano, 1991) has emphasised, namely women with computing expertise could support others in order for them to develop their own definitions. In the relations of entrustment, the supporting woman is not only in a sisterly relationship to the other women, as women in small women's groups are, but she also has authority over the other women, she has something to give, and she makes room for the other women's voices and definitions.

Modern organisations and societies are complex. Various textualities, not only information systems but also, for example, long- and short-term plans, laws, rules or work analysis and evaluation methods, intervene in the workers' everyday situations (see also Korvajärvi in Chapter 5). In many cases the combination of women's small groups and relations of entrustment is the only way of both giving value to women's own ways and of challenging the gender boundaries embedded in modern textualities (Blum, 1991). What women should question, though, is the form employees' and experts' relationships take. Maybe workers should listen to experts only in small groups. There are contradictions in expert relations, problems that are related to authority, hierarchic positions and gender. The contradictions cannot be avoided but they should be discussed in the group otherwise women's support practices also repeat the hierarchies and recreate the authoritarian democracy described in this chapter rather than encourage women's own voices.

ONE'S 'OWN' DEFINITION – SITUATED POLITICS

In the interview accounts presented at the beginning of this chapter, both Maikki and Satu said that it was important for them to be aware of information technology issues, and especially Maikki emphasised the importance of one's own activities in systems development. They both thought that information systems were an integral part of their work. By defining information systems they defined their own work and gendering relations in work processes as well as their own activities, practices, concepts and thinking, in other words their own subjectivity. Subjectivity consists of many other elements, for example bodies, emotions and family commitments, but the working life practices and textualities also make an inseparable blending with it, especially in Finland where work careers and work days occupy a major part of women's active time.

Making one's 'own' definitions of information technology means connecting one's subjectivity to information technology artefacts and knowledge as well as to practices of technology. In this chapter I have explored organisational practices, especially the work design aspects of information systems, in order to understand the social and textual construction of office workers' information systems definitions. A Finnish developmental work approach based on activity theory, which is an alternative to Taylorism, had reached some of the bureau's experts and department managers. It was built in the bureau's information systems plan (local textuality) and the managerial practices and made room for the office workers' own definitions of work processes and the gendering relations in these.

The workers gained responsibility for information systems development, instead of computing experts having it, as for example in participatory design approaches in both Britain and Scandinavia, and indeed made definitions of their 'own' by starting from their own work and locations in their organisation. Yet, the hierarchy among employees remained and that restricted the office workers' development. The politics of technology and expertise should also challenge the expertise among employees, women and men, in order to make space for women on the lowest levels of hierarchies and their definitions of information systems.

In the organisational setting, the study circle group, as well as my own support, intervened in the office workers' definitions by encouraging the office workers to find their own voices and by giving them the means of using their voices in the context of information systems. By discussing together information systems developed in other continents and the organisational settings controlled by experts and managers they were able to connect the information systems (textuality) to their own language and actions, to their subjectivities. They examined the situational interplay of textually and socially constructed practices in their offices and their society. With the study group support they created situated politics on information technology.

Women's politics on technology have global goals, namely breaking the nexus of expertise and technology, and making room for women's own definitions. In relation to these goals there are often gains from women's small groups and relations of entrustment. Yet women's politics can take its concrete forms only in local historical and social settings. It was in this particular Finnish context where I was able to arrange for an office workers' study circle in a workplace within the actual work practices during the office hours. It was in this particular bureau context where the office workers made the definitions described in this chapter. In women's politics of technology the local and global should intertwine with each other.

After the study circle, all of the office workers said that they had done something to develop their work and information systems. They had defined information systems and had not let information systems defined by others freely intervene in their subjectivities. They had gained strategies for handling and defining information systems textuality in their own ways. They had gained ways of intertwining 'the strange' with their 'own' in their subjectivities. Also, since they gathered together in the workplace, they had gained possibilities for challenging the gendering relations which appear through and within technology and in concrete practices. They travelled the area connected to masculinity without becoming 'one of the guys' and they broke strict divisions of gender in their subjectivities and practices.

Part Five
Changing Gendered Practices

Introduction
Tuula Heiskanen and Leila Räsänen

Feminist research and practical gender politics have a close, sometimes tense relationship. The interests of understanding and changing are closely intertwined in feminist research. The intellectual purpose of research has been characterised by emancipative projects – by a wish to improve women's position in society. Feminist research has been part of the discursive field where policy questions are formulated, ideas taken for granted or natural are questioned and the invisible is made visible. Social movements and strategies for change, on the other hand, have been a challenging field of cooperation for research by setting strict demands of relevance on the knowledge produced by research.

The intensive 'equality versus difference' debate in feminist literature offers graphic glimpses of the relationships between understanding and changing, between theory and politics. The concept of equality has functioned as the central organising principle in national and international political action for improving women's position. The idea that girls and boys, women and men deserve equal treatment in schools, working life and before the law is recognised worldwide. International agreements and national laws have been drafted to implement this idea. However, many supporters of feminist movements have found these measures insufficient for women's emancipation. Both the concept of equality itself and actions guided by it have met with criticism. The point of the critique has been that the needs, interests and qualities especially typical for women are ignored; the difference between women and men is suppressed in an attempt to achieve sameness.

From the perspective of research on political action 'equality versus difference' has appeared to be a conceptual trap in need of a constructive solution. Some would abandon the concept of equality altogether; others maintain that the solution is to reformulate the concept. For instance, Scott (1988a,b) thinks that the trap is created by the dichotomous way of reading concepts, and the solution is thus to overcome the dichotomy. According to her, equality is not the elimination of difference, and difference does not preclude equality. Equality versus difference is a fruitless way to structure political choices. Scott thinks that the political notion of equality includes, even depends on, an acknowledgement of the existence of difference. She says that equality might well be defined as deliberate indifference to specified differences (1988b: 44). Cockburn (1991) clarifies her own point of view by using parallel concepts to transcend the contradiction of equality. She thinks that women are not actually looking for equality but equivalence, not sameness for individual women and men, but parity for women as a sex, or for groups of women in their specificity (p. 11).

From the Nordic perspective the equality versus difference debate is based on North American practice. In the Nordic political practice the concept of equality includes the politics aiming to improve women's position since the middle of the 1960s. It is based on the demand to equalise the gender division of labour in all life areas: working life, family life and politics. The understanding in Nordic countries has been that this presupposes strong official support. The state and the municipalities have been required to organise day-care for children, care for the elderly, and many other kinds of social services so that women have the possibility to enter the labour market and to study. The concept of equality has covered campaigns for day-care, maternity, paternity and parenthood leaves, as well as for anti-discrimination legislation and for equal pay and comparable worth. The equality demand has meant both equal treatment and a strong demand for material equity. It is the latter point which differentiates the Nordic equality practice from the North American. One explanation is that the issue of gender equality has achieved its place on the agenda of various countries from within their differing historical perspectives: in the Nordic countries gender equality has been promoted through practices formed in class struggles, whereas in the USA the framework has been the civil rights movement and its demand for equal treatment for individuals and groups.

The equality versus difference dimension in the Nordic equality policy thus has substantial features and backgrounds of 'sameness'. The Nordic equality laws set the goal of equal gender division of labour, both horizontally and vertically, but the means used to achieve this goal, however, have not been legislative to the extent they are in the USA, and have therefore not raised the same conflicts and debates. The strategies to get women into men's jobs have created debate also in the Nordic countries.

The perspectives of gender sameness and gender difference can both be used to demand equalisation of gender structures. Actually, both arguments may be used simultaneously; the experiment described by Leila Räsänen is an example of that. She tells of a project with a politically given starting point to equalise gender structures in working life and education. This project, however, set an open goal: the 'correct' gender distribution can neither be known nor defined beforehand. But whenever there are substantial differences in the gender (distributions of) positions in education or working life, we have to ask how these differences are created, and whether they are based on discriminatory practices. Teaching practices and working life practices were studied from this viewpoint. The research used participative methods, so that teachers, personnel managers and shop stewards studied their own activity, asking how that produces the observed gender differences. This is a demanding approach, because it presupposes a questioning of your own work practices and established ways of thinking.

The case Leila Räsänen describes is specifically connected to the forms of equality work that have emerged in the Nordic context, where government promotion of equality and feminist research are intertwined. The second case reported by Tuula Heiskanen is about the comparable worth strategy, and closely connected to an international debate on the same issue.

The comparable worth strategy made a breakthrough in the USA and Canada, and has since then also gained ground in other countries. Affirmative action programmes for gender equality in the North American scene had paved the way for the comparable worth strategy, and it emerged partly as their critique, but at the same time taking advantage of their achievements. The comparable worth strategy focuses attention on the wage gap between men's and women's jobs. On a pragmatic level it aims at redistribution rather than equality as such. In that respect it does not conspicuously depend on the interpretations of the concept of equality, as the affirmative equality programmes do. On an ideological level, however, through the social legitimation of the strategy, there is a strong tie to the gender equality discourse in a society. The comparable worth debate has brought along to the equality discourse one possible vision of what an equality which acknowledges gender difference would mean on the practical level. Job re-evaluation, the critical examination of the valuation and undervaluation of women's jobs, needs as a starting point the recognition of gender differences (e.g. Blum, 1991).

Tuula Heiskanen presents a comparable worth case where a national model was developed on the basis of an international strategy. The central roles as change agents and actors shaping the discursive field are played by the labour market parties and the media. The description focuses especially on the role of research and expertise in a process where the aim is to develop a job evaluation method for the requirements of labour market parties.

To study change processes involves sorting out the skein of preconditions and consequences. In these two empirical cases, special attention is paid both to the conceptual frame guiding action and formed in action, and to actor positions. Because of the nature of the change processes the frame is in both cases multilayered; its material comes from the everyday experiences of gendered practices of the people involved in the process, from the equality policy discourse at the level of the society, and from the theoretical commitments guiding the projects.

Research on change processes produces knowledge of the course and preconditions of the processes, and also of the phenomenon targeted for change. These cases open up two parallel windows into the phenomenon we have called gendered practices. The experiments aimed at breaking gender segregation show that lack of knowledge and esteem of the values, skills and interests characteristic of women's areas in the division of labour contribute to segregational processes. The same things are encountered in the comparable worth strategy where these factors can be found in the underlying structures of wage determination.

10 Desegregation – How to Climb Invisible Walls
Leila Räsänen

Had you paid any attention before the Project to the fact that some subjects favour one sex rather than the other?

Very little. I have noticed in my work that the textbooks on physics are written on men's terms entirely. The exercises and examples are taken from men's lives. There is room for improvement in the books. In lessons one can also easily offend the girls with unintended comments. Now I constantly think that the girls are present so that I would not put them down or mock them. [. . .] An interesting fact became apparent in the final exams; girls used to leave the physics questions unanswered, but now, after this experiment, they solved a lot of physics problems.

(A 50-year-old male physics teacher)

Tuesday: We studied the basics of electricity and there was a lot of familiar stuff too but more things that were unfamiliar. Recognising different components was quite easy. But then we started working on blinking lights. Almost all thought that it was not going to work, but in the end it did, it worked real fine for everybody.

(Tanja, 9th grade comprehensive school, 16 years old)

These are extracts from the Nordic BRYT-project and both tell about change. The physics teacher has become more sensitive to recognising gender difference in textbooks and the teacher–pupil interaction and he has started to behave in a more gender inclusive way. The girls who study physics have also changed. They have started to answer physics questions in the school-leaving exams. They have more confidence and their performance has gone beyond their expectations. The aim of the project was to give the girls experience of succeeding in learning new skills and, as a result, to enable them to adopt a positive attitude towards their abilities to learn about technology. Since the 1970s Nordic equality policies have included breaking up occupational segregation and hierarchies. In order to strengthen this objective the Nordic Council of Minister's Commission for Equality founded the BRYT-project (1985–89). The task of the project was to develop and test methods for breaking up gender divisions in the labour markets. Experiments were launched in one locality in each Nordic

159

country. The aim was to improve and expand women's access to education and guarantee women's employment by influencing both the education system and working life.

Many kinds of measures have been developed for breaking up segregation. Anti-discrimination legislation prohibits differential treatment on the basis of sex in employment and education. It forbids segregative acts, but it is activated only by individual complaint, in other words after the segregative act has already taken place. Positive or affirmative measures have been used, for instance, in the USA and European Union countries in the attempt to change working life practices and structures. They are proactive and aimed at groups instead of individuals. In most Nordic countries the school and the employer are obligated to promote gender equality, including evening out imbalanced gender structures, but it is a long way from formal obligation to concrete practice.

This chapter is based on my experiences of the BRYT-project, which I examine from its launch to the application of its results. My point of view is that of an equality adviser working in the central administration and I want to know what can be done for desegregation. Interest in the project was mainly focused on organisational and professional practices. Workers had to re-evaluate their work practices and goals and their way of thinking. This kind of an approach requires internalised contribution of the cooperative partners. It is important to ask how the commitment is created. In my experience this is by no means a simple problem. 'Developing methods' includes not only professional practices but also the creation of preconditions for the desired cooperation. The aim of all methods to be developed was to expand women's areas within the division of labour both vertically and horizontally to the traditional male areas, especially technical fields. Thus BRYT is linked with numerous projects set up for crossing the gender boundaries of 'traditional' careers and occupational choices.

Such projects may also touch an overall concern for women's access to science and technology, which form a central part of the modern world. One of the most well-known actors in the field is the GASAT Association (the acronym originally stood for 'Girls and Science and Technology' but was later changed to 'Gender and Science and Technology'). The active members of the GASAT Association are professionals working in the area of science and technology education all over the world. GASAT has evolved from an informal network to an international forum that has organised large biannual conferences in the Netherlands, Norway, the UK, the USA, Israel, Australia, Canada and India (see Contributions to GASAT Conferences).

These projects have also been criticised for accommodating women to the men's world and for underestimating women's fields. For example,

Blum (1991: 19) writes on the basis of the experiences of women in the USA: 'Affirmative action attempts to push women into male fields, and in so doing it implicitly accepts the devaluation of women's work and reinforces the greater social esteem accorded male activity' (see also Hirdman, 1990b). BRYT's goal was to challenge both women and men to observe and question segregation in their environment and as a result to re-evaluate their goals and actions. Women's self-definitions were given room by increasing cooperation among them, for example by creating women's groups. For instance, young women studying for degrees in engineering and women entrepreneurs took advantage of women's groups in order to clarify the position in their lives of professional goals and the diverse needs of private life.

PRELIMINARY COMMITMENT?

The experiment was placed in suitable administrative structures in each Nordic country: labour administration in Finland and Sweden, research institutes in Denmark and Norway, and a town board in Iceland. The Finnish Ministry of Labour had previous experience in desegregation projects, and for choosing the experimental localities its regional administration was useful.

In all Nordic countries the central administration chose the area where the experiment took place. In Finland the representative of the Ministry of Labour looked in its regional administrative areas for a locality which had a varied educational and industrial structure. An area was chosen which included a small town and two rural communes and had a population of 24 000. The representatives of the Ministry of Labour presented the project proposal to the town council and the rural communes were left outside. The town accepted the proposal but did not make any concrete commitment. It had been said in the town council meeting that 'the project can come here as long as it does not cost us anything'. In short, BRYT was set up from the top down, pushed through by officials in the central government. The chosen locality was interested not in the aims of the experiment, but in the accompanying publicity and possibilities of influence. The selection process of participants did not favour commitment to aims, but left the building of commitment to the researcher. On the other hand, 'just an ordinary' attitudinal milieu was sought for the project.

Since segregation has extensive roots in many areas of life, a group of small experiments was set up. In schools giving liberal education, careers advice and working life training a course in cooperation was organised with vocational schools plus approximately one hundred workplaces, in addition to the development of physics teaching in comprehensive and upper secondary schools. In vocational schools the project started the development of teaching female students in technical courses, and cooperation between girls studying in technical courses. Other experiments included a course for women entrepreneurs and careers and education counselling for unemployed women in vocational adult education, and an experiment of expanding women's career prospects in a paper mill and organising the education of equal opportunities managers for labour administration.

Is segregation a social problem?

The experiments were meant to be set up in schools and workplaces. Here I concentrate on the experiences from schools. There were two comprehensive schools in the area, two upper secondary schools, two vocational schools giving training in technical occupations, an employment office and about 5–10 bigger enterprises, such as factories and printing houses, with technical jobs.

I started my negotiations in the comprehensive and upper secondary schools. The teachers were given written material about the experiment and teachers' meetings and discussions were held. I tried to point out that school upheld and produced gender divisions and hierarchies and in this way it acted against the set learning and equality goals. I also emphasised the school's role in girls' lower self-esteem. I suggested that all teachers participate in the experiment in order to improve the girls' self-image. Thinking of the horizontal differences in the division of labour between women and men I explained how school in practice, although not in principle, differentiates between textile and technical crafts according to gender. In upper secondary school there are huge differences in how girls and boys choose courses in mathematics and physics, which reduces the girls chances for further education in science and technology. In order to reduce the differences in how the pupils choose their subjects I suggested that the experiment should be taken up especially in careers guidance, crafts and science, and mathematics. I expected that the contradiction between equality goals and practical gender differences would arouse moral indignation in the teachers.

I expected them to be astounded by the contradiction and motivated to investigate the creation of difference in their teaching. I also assumed that they would not accept the production of sex-based difference and that they would want to change the learning environment and the way they teach in order to reduce the differences. There was something wrong with my assumptions because the teachers hardly even reacted to the moral dilemma I proposed. They opposed the experiment and asked questions about completely different things.

- Why of all the places had their town been chosen for the experiment?
- Why had the town council not heard the teachers during its negotiations with the Ministry of Labour?
- Why is there no compensation for the extra work caused by the experiment?

The teachers felt that the way the town council had acted at the launch of the project was an infringement on their autonomy. It seemed that starting the project from top down as a given duty would jeopardise the experiment. Although members of the town council and headmasters were aware of the teachers' annoyance and reluctance to take on the experiment, they did nothing to facilitate the launch of the project. This proved the researcher's suspicion that the town council had accepted the experiment without commitment to its aims. The situation was different in the rural communities, where the municipal councils had taken no stand towards the experiment. The teachers there had the power to decide on participation. They were not interested in the project and decided against participation.

The negative attitude that the liberal education teachers had to the project was thus not caused by their position in the negotiations because, regardless of position, they were all against it. The answer had to be sought in the consciousness of the teachers. Among other things the teachers brought up in the discussions was the fact that the division of labour between women and men is natural and biologically determined. It is impossible to change it and the teachers do not even have the moral right to do it. Changing it would cause problems for women and family life. On the other hand, the teachers regarded women who had done well in male dominated fields as proof of equality and individual freedom of choice. Neither did the teachers believe in their own or the educational system's influence in gendered educational and occupational choices. They thought that the trendsetters are to be found in the labour market, in the family, among peers and in the media.

The conclusion from the teachers' attitudes is that they do not regard occupational segregation as a social problem and find no contradiction between the equality goals of the educational system and the gendered subject choices at school. In their mind gender equality already exists in educational opportunities, curricula and the practices in schools. Gender differences are caused by individual choices which must be respected.

The attitudes of the vocational guidance counsellors towards the experiment were different from those of the other teachers. Why then were the guidance counsellors in all four schools in favour of the experiment? The guidance counsellors' awareness of the problems in gendered labour markets develops in their careers advising job. They talk about occupational and educational choices with pupils. Many pupils hold more stereotypical views than the guidance counsellors and the counsellors think that these restrict the pupils' choices in an irrational way. Guidance counsellors also gather information about the gender divisions in the labour market and estimate the importance of these in view of their pupils' future. As they repeatedly encounter different points of view, guidance counsellors become aware of the significance of gender stereotypes in career choices. It is paradoxical that it is guidance counsellors who are often blamed for the persistence of gender stereotypes in educational and occupational choices. I suspect that it is the position the guidance counsellors have in career choices that generates more criticism than their supposed prejudices. Guidance counsellors act as informers and advisers when pupils choose between different courses and options for further education, and it is at this stage that the gender divisions seem to be produced in schools. Because it is the guidance counsellors' task to promote rational occupational choices, the persistence of gender stereotypical choices is readily explained by saying that guidance counsellors have failed in their job. The self-generative power of the existing gender divisions is simultaneously forgotten as are the other teachers' conservative attitudes.

Work experience in segregated labour and educational markets increases awareness

I suggested to the two vocational schools in the area that they organise a technology course for the girls in comprehensive schools as a part of their working life training course. The project initiative was at first news to the teachers of technical subjects and they did not know what to think about it. They were not enthusiastic but they did not turn the offer down either. Their positive initial attitude was somewhere between the attitudes of vocational guidance counsellors and the teachers in comprehensive and upper secondary schools. This was surprising because the teachers in technical subjects were all men and the tradition in these studies is highly masculine. The majority of teachers in liberal education were women and the teaching tradition was more feminine.

Why do the vocational school teachers have a more positive attitude to desegregation than the liberal education teachers? The teachers' own work experience has a significance in expanding their perspective on the issue of gendering in education. Gender divisions are sharp and plain in vocational schools. Technical courses are strongly male dominated everywhere, whereas textile, care, cleaning, beauty and also hairdressing courses in Northern Europe are strongly female dominated. Only in catering courses, although they too are female dominated, are there more equal numbers of male and female students. Gender divisions in education are thus an everyday reality to teachers in vocational schools. These two groups of teachers also have different labour market experiences. Experience in the field in which they teach is usually required of vocational school teachers. So they have first-hand knowledge of the gender divisions in workplaces in technical fields. In Finnish industry women also work in the so called blue-collar jobs. The women's tasks are more monotonous than the men's, they have less autonomy in their work, the work may be physically strenuous and they have lower pay and worse career advancement prospects than men. Not many women in blue-collar industrial occupations have vocational training in the field, although they may have vocational training in some female dominated field, for instance in catering or hairdressing.

Based on their experience, teachers in technical courses are aware of the discrepancy between young women's educational choices and their job opportunities in later life. It was easy for them to find reasons why young women's interest in technical education should be increased. These male teachers thought, however, that women had to have special personal characteristics in order to cope and get ahead in male dominated workplaces and, because of this, they were reluctant to advertise technical education as an easy choice suitable for all women.

In conclusion I would say that the teachers' readiness to participate in an experiment designed for breaking occupational segregation was determined on the basis of how aware they were of the significance of segregation to women's position in working life. There were several ways of achieving the necessary awareness. Guidance counsellors had gained their knowledge in their job. Vocational teachers had plenty of experience of segregation in schools and labour markets. They weighed their own experiences against the goals of the experiment and became more conscious of segregation and their attitudes to it. Teachers in liberal education are recruited straight from teacher training courses or universities and so they usually do not have work experience from the labour markets outside the educational system. The teacher's profession is one of the few in which there are equal numbers of women and men. They lack personal experience of segregated labour markets which means that to them occupational segregation and desegregation are extraneous and even abstract questions.

A CLOSE-UP OF THE CHANGES IN TEACHING PHYSICS – THE MESSY PRACTICE

The study of physics is the bottleneck in broadening women's occupational choice towards the natural sciences. Only one in five girls, but every second boy in gymnasium (i.e. high school upper grades leading to university) chooses the extensive physics curriculum which is the precondition of many university programmes in science and technology. After two months of negotiations, four comprehensive school and one upper secondary school physics teacher joined the experiment; three of them were male and two of them female. They had about 20–30 years' experience as physics teachers. Persistent negotiations, support from one comprehensive school headmaster who also worked as a guidance counsellor, and the friendships between guidance counsellors and physics teachers all had an effect on their decision to participate. The teachers and I formed a group which got together about once a month to talk about the special problems included in teaching physics to female students. The discussion was generally based on things that the teachers brought up. I loosely organised the group's work, kept the goal in mind, asked questions, discussed, made practical suggestions and related the experiences of development projects in other countries.

Even in the first two-hour meeting there was a lively discussion on the topic of girls and physics. For instance, the following were well-known themes and arguments: 'Girls are less interested in physics than boys.' 'Studying physics requires basic knowledge and experience of technology which girls have less than boys.' 'Girls read a lot, they even learn things by heart, boys do more experiments.' 'Girls have no self-confidence.' 'Teachers take the girls' lack of interest for granted.' 'Boys, and even teachers, can intimidate girls, for instance when they do demonstrations in electricity', etc. The teachers' conceptions were basically concurrent with the research results published in the field (e.g. Contributions to GASAT Conferences; Lie and Sjøberg, 1984; Whyte, 1986).

On the one hand I found this reassuring because we were on the right track. On the other, I was nonplussed. The teachers 'had known' all this but they were not interested in the experiment and did not know how to increase the girls' interest or help their learning. What was all this? The problem was both visible and invisible; people were aware of it and it was still unclear. It often felt like we were going in circles in the discussions. I had expected that a research question could have been outlined from the teachers' work. This did not happen, however. Donald Schön (1987) writes that the 'problems of real-world practice do not present themselves to practitioners as well-formed structures. Indeed they tend not to present themselves as problems at all but as messy indeterminate situations' (p. 4). We were precisely in this kind of a situation during the first few months.

New attentiveness, problem setting and experiment

At first the teachers felt ambiguous about the development task. The question of what they were supposed to do frequently came up in the discussions and it troubled them. In his theory of learning by expanding Engeström (1987) discusses the aggravating need state of an individual in a compelling situation where she/he has to learn new ways of thinking and acting. The old thinking and acting patterns are not sufficient for the demands of the situation. The individual understands and feels the inner contradictions within the old activity as well as between the old activity and the new societal demands, i.e. in this case the demand on increasing girls' interest in physics. The teachers felt these contradictions and at times they were so disheartened that some of them wanted to get out of the project. However, the compelling need to find new ways and the social interaction and support within the group of teachers brought about some new openings in a relatively short time.The first effect I noticed after a decision of the experiment was made was a change in the teachers' attentiveness.

I've started to pay attention to girls. (w)

I've started to notice girls in a different way. (m)

I've calculated both girls' and boys' average test results. (m)

Attention or wonder is an interesting form of consciousness. The teacher concentrates her attention on the pupil in order to receive both verbal and non-verbal messages. She delays interpreting the information and leaves room for new questions. The teachers' perceptions changed and girls became visible and interesting in a new way. Teaching girls became problematic.

Paying attention to girls resulted in the girls' improved visibility. The teachers observed what the girls were interested in and thought about what the girls were familiar with and planned their teaching accordingly.

Now I've noticed how closely physics is connected with everyday practices.

The teachers started to involve the girls more in their teaching. Girls did demonstrations and presented their lab results in other classes. Visits to industrial laboratories were organised for them.

[. . .] I usually always had some boy set up the equipment and knew he'd do it just right, but now I've had girls do the same thing.

Teachers told about classroom banter. A woman teacher said that there were no longer so many jokes about girls, and that even encouragement might previously have included a touch of scorn. A male teacher had changed his use of humour and said that physics is a subject in which a teacher can make learning very unpleasant for girls. According to him some women are even displeased with the words 'physics' or 'technology', and technology is still a male domain.

And, let's think about the lessons next, I, and I'm sure a lot of other people, very easily get such misogynist thoughts in their minds – jokes are meant to make the lessons more fun, it gives something extra – the guys then have all the fun, but girls or in a way the whole of woman-kind, is made a laughingstock.

The experiment's goals included increasing the girls' confidence and the removal of teaching situations that create insecurity. Research had shown that a pupil's positive visibility increases self-confidence. These things were much talked about in the teachers' group. The teachers also increased the amount of positive feedback, but only where it was due. They especially tried to support the girls' participation in classroom discussions, give room for their comments and value their thoughts.

In the second year of the experiment the number of girls choosing the extensive course in physics increased by one third. The experimenters were both astonished and encouraged by such an outstanding effect. The upper secondary school physics teacher thought that it was now important that the girls should do well in their studies. He paid attention to the quiet girls who did not participate in discussions. The teacher tried to make the classroom atmosphere more free so that all the pupils would have the courage to talk. He improved his personal contacts with the girls. At the beginning of the school year the teacher interviewed each girl in order to create confidence in both learning and themselves. After the interviews most quiet girls became more active in class, they became happier and more sociable. The girls had said that they were, for instance, afraid of 'making a blunder' in class. When the girls started to become more active, the teacher also had to change his own conduct, for instance always finding something right in 'wrong' answers.

This has an impact on the overall performance in the subject. A positive attitude to pupils is the cornerstone of all teaching. I have also tried to encourage them with good grades. I haven't criticised anybody. In spite of this they have studied extremely well.

Girls' interest in physics grew

The results of the experiment can be evaluated from many different viewpoints. The task of the project was to create methods for desegregation. How did the project succeed in this? The proportion of girls studying the extensive physics course grew in the school which participated in the experiment. Before the experiment 33 per cent of the girls in upper secondary schooling had chosen the extensive physics course. After the first year their share was 46 per cent and after the second year 61 per cent. At the same time the boys' share grew from 65 to 86 per cent. So the gender division between girls and boys was somewhat reduced, but the differences now occurred at a new level. The numbers of girls choosing physics in the other schools in the area with which these figures were compared grew from 18 to 22 per cent and the numbers of boys increased from 53 to 58 per cent. The success of the girls choosing extensive physics was followed throughout upper secondary school, and their drop-out rate in physics was not greater than average. The girls in the experiment answered physics questions in the final exams much more frequently and their performance was of the national average. One can conclude that the girls now had a wider choice in male dominated further education, for example in technology, which was one of the aims in the project.

What was the method produced? From the point of view of teaching physics it was the development of professional practices. If practice is understood as ordinary, conventional action and praxis as enlightened action committed to social and societal values (Carr and Kemmis, 1986) one can say that gender sensitive or gender inclusive praxis was developed in physics teaching. Girls' interests, hopes and experiences were used as a starting point. Making gender difference visible required highlighting difference, and the project talked considerably about girls and boys in general and the differences between them. Classroom practices were aimed at recognising individuals and finding methods and attitudes which took account of individual characteristics. The project created a framework for the teacher's personal learning process. The development of the teacher's gender consciousness and her or his innovations in teaching methods were each other's consequences and conditions. The experiment showed that it is possible to develop a new kind of gender sensitive praxis in physics teaching in a regular school environment. Expert advice, cooperation between teachers, commitment to developing one's own work and time are all needed. It is essential that the teachers are guided to the start of a new kind of work process. The method would seem to be a very suitable element for teachers' in-service training as well as for their basic education.

The experiment showed that teachers are not just at the mercy of the available material such as textbooks but that the selection, addition and interpretation they do themselves is of crucial importance. Equality does not require perfection as much as perhaps an honest effort by people aware of the limitations and shortcomings entailed.

The increase in the numbers of girls choosing physics was caused not only by improvements in teaching. It was the joint result of several interventions. The fact that girls do not choose science subjects and mathematics derives from a number of interwoven factors (Sørensen, 1990). Projects promoting change must correspond to the multifariousness in the phenomenon and create many simultaneous processes. The same girls whose teachers were developing physics teaching participated in an extensive careers counselling project directed by their vocational guidance counsellors and vocational school teachers. All pupils spent one or two weeks at the workplaces in the town getting to know female and male dominated occupations. Some girls participated in one-week technology courses organised by the vocational school sections leading to technical occupations. The courses had a dramatic effect. At first many girls were very much against the course, but as they gained more experience, they changed their opinion and thought that the technology courses were a welcome experience with regard to further education and career choice. The change in girls' attitudes also increased their interest in studying physics. The teachers' positive attitude to the girls' studies and the effort they made for improving the quality of teaching made the girls carry out their intended choices of physics courses in practice.

Although teachers were the cooperative partners in the experiment, it is possible to say that the experiment offered girls varied and recurring opportunities to redefine their relationship to the sciences and technology:

- Girls were taken into account and they were appreciated as students of physics.
- The girls got the chance to study technology for one week in a course especially designed for them and led by competent and enthusiastic teachers. They got the personal experience of studying technology as well as reassurance in their ability to learn technical things. The importance of studying physics in order to qualify for technical jobs also became more tangible.
- Studying technology happened in all-girl groups whose live interaction was a part of the redefinition process.

- Female professionals in technology and the sciences visited careers advisory classes and this offered a chance for redefinitions in relation to adult women who had chosen technical occupations.
- Families were encouraged to discuss gender divisions in career choice. The experiment was talked about in PTA meetings. Parents showed pupils their workplaces. Pupils interviewed their parents on occupa-tional choices and this was used as the basis for an exhibition present-ing the mothers' and fathers' career and life histories. The exhibition included gender analysis.
- The experiment got both local and national publicity, for instance at conferences and in relation to the Minister of Education's and Nordic visits. This gave the girls the chance to see and hear about the experi-ment in the media and have their share of the positive publicity thus gained.

MAKING USE OF THE RESULTS

The four-year experiment conducted by the BRYT project consisted of over 30 subprojects in the five Nordic countries. It employed 17 people and produced over 30 reports and a final report in which all the results were summarised. The results were presented in a Nordic conference in Reykjavik in December 1989. How were the results disseminated among wider audiences?

The school experiments belonged to the area of educational administra-tion. The project had formed contacts with educational administration, and the purpose of these was to secure information exchange and the applica-tion of results. I had established personal relationships with the educa-tional authorities, invited them to get to know the project, sent them material and so on. The school experiments had also been accepted as 'official experiments' which the Ministry of Education followed and supported financially. It first seemed that all my efforts to use the physics experiment were in vain. One official in the National Board of Education held the responsibility for physics teaching and, despite my attempts, did not com-bine the results of the project with the mainstream of educational develop-ment. The results were published in a few articles and they were presented in educational forums. They gave rise to some discussion but had no effect on teacher training or research.

I had imagined that the 'good' results would interest the people devel-oping physics teaching, but it was not that simple. The authorities and academic circles who influenced physics teaching were unanimous that there were great problems in teaching physics at school, problems which were reflected, for instance, in a lack of interest to study physics and declining numbers of pupils. That was a situation where the project results would conceivably have been relevant. Nonetheless, the experts of physics teaching defined the problems involved as gender neutral and did that in a way that gave no chance of making gender problematic. The results of the project were in a way disregarded as something irrelevant, as if they were some sort of a distraction outside the right paradigm. The attempts of the project to achieve fruitful interaction with the activist developers of physics teaching did not succeed.

The feminist perspective on physics teaching has also aroused interest. Because of its novelty and perhaps also its critical point of view, people have wanted to hear about the project in many conferences, working groups and seminars. The project has nurtured experts whose cooperation has continued after the termination of the project. A network of feminist experts has been formed, and its task is to endorse women's standpoint in the teaching of technology and the sciences. So one result of the project is the empowerment of proponents and authorities. Changes in the national curriculum, new development projects, publications, etc. have resulted from the cooperation. Public knowledge of the problem has spread within a few years. As elaborated above, recognising phenomena as social problems is the precondition for development, and in this sense the preconditions have improved. Extending awareness also creates new challenges current at the time of writing this article. As new tasks are taken on and the number of actors grows, expertise should also deepen and expand. If this does not happen, failures ensue and as a result reform efforts can be rejected as superficial fads.

These BRYT experiences show that the dissemination of results has taken place via personal contacts. Many of the people who have made use of and spread the results have already been involved in the first project. The project has presented them with the opportunity to undertake a new kind of action which they have taken further in new contexts after the project. The disseminators of these innovations are mainly feminist professionals who have enough expertise to apply the results in their jobs and who have the positions and power to take new initiatives. Few have distributed the results of the project by simply reading reports. Reports are tools for actors who are already otherwise motivated.

Hierarchic systems produce both possibilities and obstacles to desegregation. Political commitment is needed at the top levels of administration, and useful decision-making presupposes that the phenomenon is understood in its entirety. Each position has to see its connection to the social relations that maintain segregation. The professionals who have immediate contacts with pupils, clients or patients can dismantle segregation in their work. Professions are connected to the large organisations in which they are practised. They also have solid links with scientific research on whose results they have to take a stand. Both organisations and research have to unravel the connections between segregation and the dominant paradigms. However, the work is slow because segregation has to be separately broken down at every place.

To a great extent desegregation is a question of the power relations between women and men. That is evident even in the fact that innovations are undertaken by feminist professionals. The male dominated top administration is also especially reluctant to promote desegregative actions. What was characteristic of this project, however, was that great numbers of men – teachers, trade union activists, authorities and personnel managers – worked for expanding women's educational and career opportunities in technology and the sciences. Men's interests cannot be defined in advance nor unambiguously. The task of this project was not to investigate interests as such, but to study what can be done and what can be changed. This kind of research throws light on the available avenues, the feasible alliances and the matters in which success is possible.

11 Comparable Worth as Social Problem-Solving

Tuula Heiskanen

The discussion about the wage gap between women and men is a hot issue in which opinions are emotionally charged. Wage differentials as such are a social problem, and its solving is filled with expectations and pressures. At the same time the wage gap is just the tip of the iceberg, a reflection of women's problems in working life and society in general.

Comparable worth is an international strategy and its basic principle can be expressed briefly: equal pay for jobs of comparable worth. The strategy has special significance because its legitimacy is supported by national and international laws and regulations which are simultaneously a concrete result of the strategy. Concrete examples of comparable worth come mainly from the United States. There are well documented descriptions of its implementation in different states (e.g. Acker, 1989a; Evans and Nelson, 1989; Blum, 1991). The equality legislation in Canada has also proved interesting in view of the strategy. European countries can learn from these experiences when they consider how the principle of equal pay for equal value, which has been included, for instance, in the European Union directives, can be put into practice (e.g. Cockburn, 1991: 16–45; Flynn, 1993; Rubery, Fagan and Grimshaw, 1993).

Although improving wage systems is the aim, comparable worth strategy and the discussions surrounding it are deeply embedded in the underlying issues concerned with women's position in society. Joan Acker (1989a) has remarked that the lower level of women's wages is based on historical models of division which are inbuilt in the structural processes of organisations and often remain invisible. Research on the implementation of this strategy gives an insight into the structures and practices which maintain women's inferior position and a scope to the rules for achieving changes.

Comparable worth strategy regards discriminatory practices against women as the reason for the wage gap between women and men, and it is these practices the strategy aims to eradicate. Special attention has been paid to the contents of work and the fact that women's work is undervalued. Women do not receive the same compensation as men for comparable skills and job requirements. Sex segregation, the existence of female and male dominated sectors of employment, has been seen as the main reason for the lower esteem of women's work, but there are also other reasons such as the structure of wage systems as well as job placement and hiring processes. Those in favour of the strategy support explicit wage policies whose most essential method is job evaluation. In order to rectify the wage bias it is thought that the contents and requirements of work should be acknowledged as the key issues which determine wages and that these should be assessed with a reliable evaluation method.

Evidence and reasons for arguments and counter-arguments are sought from different sources in this ongoing debate. The strategy has received more understanding in the writings of sociologists and psychologists than, for example, in economists' texts, although the dividing line is not unambiguously situated between these disciplines (e.g. England, 1992). Many economists maintain the view that the idea of wage discrimination, which underlies comparable worth thinking, is against the economic theories they have adopted in which market forces and laws of supply and demand define the right wage level in each sector (e.g. O'Neill, 1985; Becker, 1957). If and when differences between women and men can be found, they are attributed to differences in human capital, in other words that employees have real differences in qualifications.

The supporters of the strategy tell us to take a closer look at both how employers evaluate and reward different jobs within organisations (e.g. England and Dunn, 1988) and what kind of processes influence the fact that women hold the positions they now have (e.g. Wittig and Lowe, 1989). Barbara Bergman (1989), herself an economist, remarks that economists' ideas of how wages are determined are based on an abstract model which takes no account whatsoever of the psychological and social aspects of economic relations. Most economists implicitly assume that social relations, habits and prejudices have no relevance in the treatment of women and men. However, making decisions which concern the labour force is inescapably different from making decisions on, for example, marketable goods. Bergman concludes that cultural attitudes are the most likely reason for the fact that jobs continue to be earmarked as either 'men's jobs' or 'women's jobs'.

Comparable worth strategy is an element in the international feminist movement, and consequently the philosophy behind it is sensitive to the currents within feminist discourse. The strategy works within a field of power in which the powers of both ideas and politics are continuously tested. In its justifications the strategy appeals to the fairness and equity of compensation which is a widely accepted principle in industrial societies. Yet the supporters as well as the opponents of the strategy know that the rhetoric of fairness can serve both sides of the argument. The views of fairness depend on what is being compared to what. According to Hegtvedt (1989) the paradox of fairness is that the actual beliefs about fairness are intimately related to social positions and power, although the normative views of fairness emphasise impartiality. There may be marked differences in the concept of fair wages depending on the perspective adopted, namely that of the job, employee or some subgroup. Comparable worth strategy suggests that the characteristics of the job should be used as the basis for comparison. The assumption is that in both the evaluations concerning the worker's qualifications and the comparisons between different subgroups, gender tends to operate in some subtle way as a reward-relevant criterion. The role of job evaluation could be characterised as a tool used to penetrate the entrenched practices. Explicit attention to relevant job contributions reveals the situations in which women's jobs have been evaluated below their real requirements and so forces us to face the practices, ways of thinking and discourses which maintain the underrating of women and their work (e.g. Cockburn, 1991: 128–31). This confrontation has repeatedly resulted in the discovery that some of the skills women use in their work remain invisible and get no official recognition in organisational practices and that this invisibility is also actively supported.

Since a variety of scientific endeavours have contributed to the comparable worth debate, the discursive field can with good reason be characterised as diverse, rich in nuances and having internal tensions. It is open to reformulations and new conceptual developments. One of the strategy's characteristics is that research has been intertwined with discussions and practical solutions. Comparable worth strategy has gained support among many researchers. Researchers have participated in framing the questions (e.g. Hartmann, 1985) and estimating the practical solutions, and they have offered help in the development of job evaluation methods (e.g. Wittig and Turner, 1988).

The cooperation of science and politics in the concrete cases of comparable worth has given the strategy a reflexive and regenerative nature. Paradoxically the relationship of science and politics can also rob the strategy of its impetus. The relationship did not materialise out of a mere wish for reflexivity; instead the strategy depends on expertise which comes from the fields of science and research. Some researchers have been concerned about the significance technical expertise has gained within the strategy, and they fear that the results of the comparable worth movement are limited to technocratic reforms (e.g. Evans and Nelson, 1989; Blum, 1991).

My empirical case gives a good opportunity to examine the relationship between expertise and politics. What has been typical of the practical application of comparable worth is that job evaluation has been assigned to consultants who have used existing job evaluation methods. However, in the project I examined the method did not exist but had to be developed. The development process exposes the underlying assumptions and forces decision-makers, in this case the representatives of labour market organisations, to face them.

Apart from creating a new method the case is a process aimed at both preparing the conceptual ground and adapting the political preconditions for the eventual implementation of a new policy. I talk about 'the Finnish case' because the process had nationwide effects. The chain of events had many actors and levels of publicity. A special emphasis is placed on the role of research, namely what its contribution has been and how research could be fruitfully contributive on the practical level. The data consist of public documents, such as committee and research reports and newspaper and magazine articles, interviews with people who have been actively involved in the process, and group discussions in which I participated in my role as researcher. The process took place between 1988 and 1994.

THE ARRIVAL OF COMPARABLE WORTH STRATEGY – DISCUSSION AND POLITICS

Comparable worth strategy in Finland has aimed at creating a model based on international experiences. The strategy's roots are clearly and identifiably in international discussions and experiences. However, the aim has been to create a unique model which would suit the special characteristics of the labour market system.

Labour union and equal rights activists as well as researchers have made a significant contribution in preparing the conceptual ground for the idea of equal worth. At the initial stage the strategy was clearly a women's project. Contacts between Finnish women in labour unions and the state's equal rights administration with women in other countries, where the strategy had already been implemented, were the most important channel for the new way of thinking. The legislation in the provinces of Canada, especially in Ontario (Pay Equity Act 1987), aroused interest. The Canadian experiences were considered relevant because the Pay Equity strategy had there been applied not only to the public sector – which had been the pioneer in the USA – but also to the private sector, and the strategy integrated into the collective bargaining process (Gunderson, 1989). Because of these contacts the activists became convinced that the strategy was feasible and could be used to obliterate the wage gap and that concrete results could be achieved.

An important event in increasing the interest was a seminar organised jointly by the Office of the Equality Ombudsman, a work research centre and the feminist researchers' national network. The aim of the seminar was to present current research topics and to discuss the equal rights policies in working life. The participants were civil servants dealing with equality issues, trade union activists, members of political parties, members of parliament, journalists and researchers. The women's project had aroused some interest among men too: eight of the 83 participants were men. The Equality Ombudsman, a male lawyer, called for action in many arenas and levels in order to achieve equal wages for women and men. He suggested that law reforms, the incomes policy negotiations and more fair job evaluation would be suitable methods of action. Margaret Hallock and Joan Acker talked about the equal worth project in Oregon, USA. Their message encouraged action, although it also entailed critical viewpoints. The route they sketched was by no means an easy one. The measures would presuppose technical problem-solving which would call for professional assistance. It would also unavoidably entail competing interests. Hallock's advice to trade union activists was that the political nature of comparable worth strategy should be confronted right at the beginning. The unsolved conflicts of interest would surface in any case at some later stage.

Political processes promoting the idea were in progress in different arenas. The blue-collar and white-collar central unions had appointed a joint working group whose task was to set targets for the solving of equal rights issues in working life. The group's report emphasised the development of job evaluation practices as a means of promoting equality. Women chairs in some female dominated unions as well as in some central unions formed new networks between the unions which previously jealously guarded their own turf. The women chairs' group appearance worked as a form of pressure and helped to promote the equal rights question. That was historically important. Equal pay had naturally been talked about in Finland earlier (for instance by MP Leivo-Larsson in 1951), because a large proportion of Finnish women has traditionally been in paid employment and also active in politics. But what is notable in this situation is the determination and unanimity with which blue-collar and white-collar women workers from all educational levels joined together for a common goal.

FROM THE TOPIC OF SEMINARS TO A NATIONWIDE ISSUE

In May 1990 the central unions appointed the Job Evaluation Committee and the status of comparable worth changed overnight: it became a nationwide labour market issue. The unions had agreed to appoint the committee at the incomes policy negotiations.

The consensus, which prevailed at the time the decision to found the committee was made, was put to the test for the first time at the selection of committee members. The committee was supposed to have members from all central unions, from both employers' and workers' organisations in the private as well as the public sector, a few experts and be chaired by someone from the outside. Finding a chair with whom all parties concerned would be happy was especially time-consuming. In the end, the newly appointed Equality Ombudsman was elected as the chair. She was a lawyer who had previously been a conservative MP and worked as a bank manager.

The committee's tasks were defined as follows: (1) to find out more about the existing job evaluation systems; (2) to make suggestions as to how these could be developed further with special attention to female dominated sectors and jobs; and (3) to think of ways of how job evaluation comparisons could be made across sectors of employment. The committee was supposed to complete its work by the end of 1991, but this deadline was later extended as it turned out that the work was more difficult and more open to different interpretations than anticipated.

RESEARCH AND EXPERIMENTS IN THE SPOTLIGHT OF PUBLICITY

Who does the research?

The setting up of the Job Evaluation Committee was prominently reported by newspapers. Trade union papers had published articles on equal pay since the beginning of the year. News of the committee work was enthusiastically received by these papers with the following headlines: 'Women's Hopes are High. Job Evaluation Ends Wages Gap' and 'Women's Hope Lies in Job Evaluation'. Employer organisation newspapers were more reserved. The chair of the committee said that the preconditions for development would seem to exist. According to her the labour market parties seemed determined to start evaluating jobs in a new way and a kind of a *détente* seemed to prevail. In spite of this the differences in points of departure were evident in public. The committee chair tried to cool down the overheated expectations by emphasising that this was only groundwork for further development. She remarked that the moment of truth will come when the committee's work is completed and when the theory is put into practice.

Research was the way to get answers to the three questions defined at the onset of the committee work and, because research had such a prominent role, the question of who would do the research became crucial. At the first stage the committee wanted information on the existing job evaluation systems in both public and private sectors, and it gave a three or four months' time limit for this part of the study. The committee divided the research task into two and a university of technology was assigned to carry out the part concerning the private sector. Research on the public sector created conflicts within the committee. Many female committee members wanted to assign this part of the research to the Work Research Centre with which they had already had contacts at the above mentioned equal rights seminar. The Work Research Centre had concentrated on the quality of work in their research and carried out research on female dominated sectors. The employers' representative in the committee had already made initial contacts with a professor of corporate analysis who had shown interest in job evaluation. The women members did not want to delay the process right at the beginning. They agreed to the employers' candidate doing the research on the condition that they would be able to choose the place where the next stage of the study would be conducted. It was also decided that the research would have a supporting group of experts and a representative from the Work Research Centre was invited to join this group. As the research proceeded the committee also consulted 15 experts in different areas of research, education and evaluation.

Research processes and results were reported to the committee, and these gave rise to some debate. But from the point of view of the committee's job as a whole the data remained 'separate background information', and the next research stage was not built upon these.

The committee wanted research-based information on the main factors giving the most representative picture of job requirements and to find feasible indicators with which this could be done. This part of the research was given a six to eight months' time limit and corresponding with the deal made within the committee the job was offered to the Work Research Centre where it was met with serious discussion. It was felt that the project would give a good opportunity for a dialogue around an important social problem. However, the assignment and the schedule were so tightly set that they would not have allowed the necessary freedom needed in academic research. As a representative of the Centre I answered that we were unable to take on this project. This was a disappointment to the women activists, who had hoped that the committee would gradually reach the more fundamental issues.

Newspaper articles

The trade union newspapers kept up their members' interest in job evaluation issues. The papers wrote about international experiences in the development of job evaluation. Union leaders and committee members gave interviews on the wages gap and possible solutions. Explanations for the wage gap were brought up both in researcher interviews and in the unions' reports. The blue-collar workers' union organised an equality forum at its representative assembly, and other seminars and discussions, including a Nordic seminar (Sigurardóttir, 1992) were organised around the job evaluation issue. Reports were written on the different experiments and plans.

A lot of attention was paid to a job evaluation experiment which was initiated in one city at the same time but independent of the Job Evaluation Committee. The experiment was influenced by Canadian thinking (e.g. Armstrong and Cornish, 1992). The city wanted to develop a job evaluation system which would apply to all of the 10 000 jobs in the city and be used as the basis for new job classifications. Also the employee organisations in banking had started a research and development programme, and these experiences were reported in the newspapers.

Although the contents, style and ways of presenting arguments varied between individual articles, certain differences in profile could be observed between the papers. The blue-collar workers' paper and the paper representing the female dominated white-collar union were the keenest to place the question in the framework of equality issues. The articles brought up known and invisible reasons for women's lower wages, and fairness was called for in order to improve the situation. Job evaluation was argued to be a realistic way of solving the problem: 'Women Already Reap the Benefits of Job Evaluation – Canada as a Pioneer' (headline). The paper representing female-dominated sectors emphasised the possibilities of job evaluation in bringing up women's hidden, unrecognised skills and expertise with headlines like: 'Who Puts a Price on Hidden Skills?', 'Are Men's Jobs Really More Demanding?' and 'Making Women's Skills Visible'.

The employers' papers wrote primarily about segregated labour markets which were recognised as a problem as such. The importance of achieving equality was not denied: 'Employers Benefit from Equality', 'Efficiency Depends on Fair Wages' (headlines), but it seems that the members of the employer organisations needed different arguments than the ones derived from the equal rights framework. For instance, in one employer newspaper interview the committee chair emphasised the benefits of job evaluation in developing working life in both male and female dominated sectors.

A start – for what?

Based on the research the committee had done, it designed a job evaluation frame which would be used as an information base for the adaptation of job evaluation for different fields. The frame included four main requirement categories: know-how, responsibility, stress and working conditions. The committee outlined factors which would be taken into account in each main requirement category, but it did not yet decide how the different requirement factors would be graded. The question whether a general evaluation method enabling comparisons between work in different sectors could be found remained unanswered.

According to the committee's recommendations job requirements should be of central importance when wages are graded and developed in each sector. The committee also recommended that the labour market parties should undertake actions to promote the creation of job requirement evaluation systems and their practice in each collective agreement sector and that they should see to it that all cooperation and education on job evaluation issues happened on equal terms. The committee further recommended that the state and the central trade unions and employee organisations should cooperate in increasing research on job requirement evaluation. The committee was unanimous on basic issues, although the final report contained one opinion which disagreed on the specific contents of job requirement factors.

The report was published in a spirit of official optimism. Trade union and employee organisation leaders gave their blessing to the basic idea that work demands should be the most important basis for wage determination and that this should be better taken into account. However, several commentators expressed doubts about the possibility of comparisons across sectors. For instance one committee member representing the male-dominated white-collar technical union said in their trade paper that he had had doubts about this goal right from the beginning. He said that if such a measure could be found it would deserve the Nobel Peace Prize as it would once and for all end all wage conflicts in the country.

Behind the official optimism hidden pessimism grew among the women activists which they analysed in their meeting with the researchers. There was a gap between expectations and what had so far been achieved. It had been surprisingly quick and easy to reach the decision about founding the committee and starting the development work. This had created expectations about swift progress and concrete wage changes, and these expectations had been communicated to trade union members.

Two years ago the expectations were very concrete but also very unproblematic. We imagined that this would be a much quicker and easier way. We were unable to anticipate, for instance, what difficulties would be entailed in finding the key characteristics of work in job descriptions.

(A committee member)

All agreed that the committee needed more time. The aim was, with the help of research, to continue outlining job analyses and testing the requirement frame by using different weights. The goal was to achieve generalisable results which would require a large research sample. In addition, the committee aimed at gathering information on the application of the requirement frame in comparisons across the boundaries between workplaces, sectors and hierarchies. The same consultant who had been responsible for the earlier part of the research was chosen to carry out this stage of the research.

What had been characteristic of the committee work was that all polarisation of interests between employers and employees and men and women had intentionally been avoided. The women activists were becoming concerned about the disappearance of the initial goals of job evaluation. They could no longer be sure that the committee would reach the essence of the undervaluing of women's work. This concern was further amplified when they noticed that the male employees did not appear to support the women's demands of making the starting point clear. When the research goals, samples and methods were discussed the situation was further exacerbated to a point that at one stage the whole work of the committee was jeopardised. The dispute concerned the depth and representativeness of research. The female committee members would have been happy with research which would have concentrated on just a few workplaces and described the process completely, but those in favour of representativeness won the dispute.

The consultant doing the research and the women activists had different views also on how to guarantee equality in the job evaluation process. The consultant maintained that this was not a problem since the research project included both women's jobs and men's jobs, female and male dominated sectors and sectors where there were both men and women. The women in the committee demanded that a special guarantee should be made in the research so that the frames would measure the key characteristics of women's work, and that women workers would be allowed to express their ideas about job requirements. Feminist scholars (Åstrand and Anttalainen,

1993) later criticised the research because it did not give a concrete enough picture of how the evaluation groups reached their evaluation at the workplaces or what lay behind the scores the groups gave.

The committee achieved a unanimous final report in which it recommended that analytic job evaluation systems should be widely implemented when wage systems are developed. The report did not advocate one coherent system for all sectors, but recommended that evaluation systems should have similar information bases and starting points. Because the method question was left open, the committee recognised the importance of ongoing research and development and suggested that a follow-up group should be founded which would support both research and the implementation of evaluation systems. Trade union and employer organisation chairs and leading officials agreed with the report's recommendations. More than one of them said that old attitudes had changed during the process. The ball was set rolling from the committee table to the central organisations and unions.

The process as interactive social problem-solving

The Finnish case of comparable worth was a multilayered process. The committee and its work has made the process significant and visible. The discursive field, within which the expectations towards the committee work have also been formulated, has been wide. The actors in the process included the committee members and the organisations they represent, women activists from the trade unions and the Council for Equality, researchers and journalists. The weight of the centralised collective bargaining system helped to make comparable worth into a nationwide issue. In this respect the structural preconditions of the discourse were decisively dissimilar to those in the USA and Canada, where different bargaining traditions and the federal state structure with its differing legislative provisions have channelled the discussions and experiments. The process has aimed at achieving concrete improvements which justifies calling it social problem-solving (e.g. Lindblom and Cohen, 1979). I examine more closely the preconditions for social problem solving by paying attention to: (1) how the problem was formulated; (2) what information was valid; and (3) whether there was room for social learning in the process.

The decision to set up the committee included a formulation of the problem the committee was initially to solve. Wages were not mentioned in this context, but the underlying common starting point was that job requirements were accepted as a significant factor in the wage determination process. On the other hand, this starting point did not predetermine the members' opinions on the extent to which job requirements are important.

The understanding of the research and development function varied within the committee and among its members' interest groups. Some members regarded this task as relatively technical: for them it belonged to the area of remuneration techniques and involved the development and testing of instruments with calculation mechanisms as essential in establishing the job requirement levels. Some members thought that the committee's job involved the production of systematic information on job evaluation and its possibilities. For women activists this involved the expectation that systematic information would reveal the lower esteem of women's jobs. Some members and their interest groups expected the group to produce a directly applicable method which would obliterate the wage gap caused by the undervaluing of women's jobs.

These different views of committee work became apparent both inside the committee and in public discussions, but their importance was not systematically examined from the point of view of problem formulation. The differences in starting points were dealt with in connection with other questions, for example by making a big issue out of who was going to carry out the research. So there were no common clear-cut criteria for estimating success because the criteria were tied up with the formulation of the problem. In view of the official aims, the committee conducted its business quickly and professionally. The women activists' disappointment with the process was connected to the hidden formulation of the problem. Their expectations went one step further than the official formulations.

Research and expertise had a strong social demand in the job evaluation process. In a politically sensitive and conflict ridden area all parties wanted to base their arguments on 'objective information'. Discussion was kept up by research. The proceeding of committee work was associated with the research process and the conflicts within the committee were dealt with through the problems involved in research questions and methods. The research supporting the committee work was started as a 'contract' which meant that it had a limited scope for formulating the problem. Simultaneously it meant that the researchers taking on the task lacked information on the different expectations. They got the information 'the hard way' as the research proceeded.

The committee gave the research preconditions that suited clear-cut technically oriented research tasks but were not good, for example, for examining the bases used in the formulation of the problem or for searching for new perspectives. Strict time limits were set for each subproject and it was the committee's opinion that different researchers could be employed at each stage. The fact that researchers changed wasted the opportunity for learning and deeper information.

The research had to confront a variety of hidden formulations of the problem at different stages, but as they remained undealt with in the discussions within the committee they were not dealt with in the research. The consultant who was hired to take on the development of the job evaluation method was a capable researcher, but when he started the job he was not familiar with the comparable worth debate. A first reminder of this came out when the research outline for the preliminary research was evaluated. The research outline had as its starting point the idea of beginning with existing job evaluation systems and testing them in a limited number of workplaces. One expert pointed out the often repeated fact within the comparable worth debate that the existing methods are not necessarily free of gender bias. The neutrality that the researcher was aiming to achieve could well have been false neutrality. Another reminder to the consultant of his insensitivity to the aspect of gender came in the second stage of the research from the female committee members and temporarily put the committee work into crisis. The reminder had to do with the process: not only could the methods involve a gender bias, but the whole job evaluation process could be biased.

Provided the widely used job evaluation methods are the best methods so far to illustrate job requirements, and that when they are implemented it is primarily a question of being careful and systematic, the research outlines were good professional social enquiries. These presuppositions satisfied some committee members but not all. The women activists called in question both working life practices and research which produces information on working life. The assumption that both could include a gender bias made the research outlines look less satisfactory.

The international debate on comparable worth was important to the onset of the process in two ways. On the one hand, the debate on legislation created the need to find out whether it would be necessary in Finland to adapt laws especially to the European Community legislation. On the other, international experiences were encouraging. The female trade union chairs' collective appearance added momentum to the concrete measures. All parties involved acknowledged the need for discussions and development, but the starting point was tension-filled. The *détente* between the labour market parties, which the committee chair had talked about, was a relative *détente*. Maintaining the social process required vigilance.

Research was designated the function of keeping up the process. Research was resorted to without stopping to think whether the questions which interested the committee were in the end those that could be answered by professional knowledge. Although the subjective elements and historicity in job evaluation were talked about in several commentaries within the committee, in newspapers and in research reports, the relevance of everyday knowledge was denied. For example, at one stage the women activists who had criticised the research had to answer the question of their fellow committee members: 'What is your competence to criticise research?' An emphatically non-normative approach was chosen when highly normative issues were dealt with (e.g. Pilalis, 1986).

Despite the tensions caused by the underlying conflicts of interest the comparable worth process offered a chance for social learning. There was a considerable amount of public discussion within the committee, in the media, in seminars and in meetings with researchers. The meetings with women activists and researchers were aimed at reflecting on the process and its critical points. Although they had different basic orientations and points of view, the debaters focused their interest on the same problematic area. This made it necessary for all parties to clarify their arguments.

The shared lesson from committee work was that the process is long and that sooner or later one must encounter questions of value. That is the very same lesson about which Joan Acker and Margaret Hallock – on the basis of their experiences in Oregon, USA – had warned their Finnish audience in the beginning. Despite the fact that the debate on comparable worth was initiated around the question of the wage gap between women and men, gender remained a sensitive issue. Questions of gender were approached indirectly rather than directly. For instance, the women activists said that both the domestic and international recession at the turn of the 1990s has made equality and women's issues less significant. This also made them justify their cause by fairness in general rather than by the need to resolve the question of women's wages as such.

Another lesson was that the different aspects involved in job requirements became more distinct. The job requirement factors in women's work, a part of which tends to remain unrecognised, gained visibility during the process. It remains to be seen what the practical consequences of this will be. After all, it was not the committee's job to negotiate on what will be the importance given to job requirements in the overall development of wage systems.

The learning process created contradictions for the committee members. Especially the female dominated trade unions expected a lot from committee work. It was the job of the female committee members to assure both the female trade union chairs and the union members that keeping up the work was worthwhile although there would not be concrete results for a while yet. It was a victory that the committee set the ball rolling and that the labour market leaders officially took up the game. An important result altogether was the understanding that the process would be long and had to be supported. However, that left the need to explain that it indeed had been a victory.

Part Six
Concluding Discussion

... she is outside, she gets herself a key and
a front door where she can come and go, she
can do as she pleases, she can smile and talk,
meet other people, there is air and possibilities
and only now is the house behind the walls a
shelter, not a prison to Little Red Riding Hood.

The Wolf does not like this at all, he
retaliates, he threatens, but it is a question
of Little Red Riding Hood's life and she can
not care about the Wolf's threats, and when
Wolf notices it has no effect he falls silent.

So unnecessary. So unnecessary to quarrel
about a little bit of air.
Thinks Little Red Riding Hood.

(Tikkanen, 1986: 279–80)

12 Persistence and Change of Gendered Practices

Tuula Heiskanen and Liisa Rantalaiho

Our book has tried to make several aspects visible: the practices that maintain gendering processes at workplaces and in society at large, the practices of living and acting in gendered social relations, the potential or actual breaking points in established practices and structures, and the difficulties people may face trying to change gendered practices. We have introduced cases which may seem either encouraging or discouraging examples, depending on the reader's frame of reference. The cases point both to great durability and to a potential for change in gendered practices.

The empirical cases started with the problems of hierarchy. Quite often 'gendered' means the common hierarchical difference between men and women, between the masculine and the feminine, with men and masculinity in the dominant position. This difference is quite strong in working life all over the world, and also in a context where gender equality is an acknowledged ideology.

The importance of gender in workplace power relations varied quite a lot between the different workplaces in our studies. But we never found a workplace where women's and men's tasks and positions were not differentiated, or where the organisation's own goal would have been the deconstruction of gendered hierarchies. And yet, the picture is not one of a uniformly gloomy gender repression either.

Gendered hierarchies are not always visible or audible at the workplace level. It is rather rare in the present Western part of the globe that a researcher can point to open and conscious discrimination of women. Instead, the prevailing construction of women's hierarchically lower positions is a delicate practice in which women and men mostly do not intentionally indulge. Gender is constructed at the workplace in the daily work process and it is involved in solutions about how to organise the work. Some jobs and tasks almost unnoticeably become defined as feminine and others as masculine.

The definition of qualifications are central to the process of construction and maintenance of all working life hierarchies, including gender hierarchies. We could see deep cultural roots in the definitions of women's and men's work and women's and men's action spaces. However, the

191

consequences for professional autonomy are dramatically different depending on whether the gender distinctions are flexible or strictly dichotomous. When women in organisations acquire their own professional space, gender hierarchies do not feel strong to them. Women see and appreciate autonomy and the possibilities of developing their own work, even when that is not reflected in their wages. But when work is organised or managed so that men control women's work, gender hierarchies are also experienced as strong and the situation is open for conflicts.

Gendered practices may be global, as for instance some management ideologies or uses of information techonology, and they may be simultaneously local and situational. A typical feature of hierarchical gender differentiating practices is an intertwining of several factors rather than a simple cause–effect relation. So, for example, the relation between statistical categories, collective agreement practices and workplace action is circular – but undeterministic. The circular process includes both mutually reinforcing process links and unpredictable points. Therefore a strictly gendered hierarchical 'iron cage' may coexist together with an easy indifference towards it.

We have considered work as one area in the everyday totality. This fits together with women's common experience but contrasts with the prevailing organisational ideal of an abstract worker. But neither women's nor men's life in the context of our studies is limited to just working life or to just family. Nobody, or rather no body, lives exclusively within one 'sphere'. Working life and family overlap in people's experience, and it is time they should overlap also in both theoretical and organisational thinking.

We have talked about a person's life totality in the sense that it is something she actively constructs, 'quilts together' as Laura Balbo has expressed it (1987), so that the fragments of her life make a pattern. However, she does that in an inherently tense situation, constrained on the one hand by this organisational ideal of an abstract worker, on the other hand by the realities of her everyday life which demand practical solutions. Whatever their occupation or branch of employment, women encounter this tension more often than men when they try to reconcile the demands of work and family. The division of labour between men and women in the families has long traditions, and changes are slow in this area – but changes take place.

We also found that motherhood and fatherhood at work give women and men differing premises to construct their everyday pattern, since organisations in working life recognise parenthood in a varying degree. Workplaces differed in how much flexibility and understanding of family demands they exhibited and how great a burden the combining of work and family therefore made for the workers. Both women and men made femininity in general visible at the workplaces, women with a greater cultural freedom and imagination, and men often quite stereotypically. Masculinity, instead, was seldom discussed, except when a man broke the usual pattern of action, for instance taking his part of the parental leave.

A special impulse to focus on gendered practices was given by our wish to see how the existence of gendered divisions can be as fixed as it seems to be. Are there no breaking points in the persistency? One central difficulty is that change in itself may contribute to the persistency of gendered hierarchies. Working life is constantly changing before our eyes: new technological practices appear, organisational structures are reorganised, employment relations diversify. But does gender change? We are now 'doing gender' differently from our mothers, but are we still doing basically the same kind of gender?

Many visible gender relations in working life have indeed changed – and yet remain basically the same. For example, a profession may become feminised and all the while a new gendered division of labour and prestige develops within its frame. Women have learned to master information technology but that does not alleviate the masculine closure of its expert culture. When new criteria for qualifications and wages are collectively adopted in female branches, men's wages at the branch are increasingly paid on individual criteria. 'The more things change, the more they stay the same', and like the Red Queen in Alice's adventures, women have to run hard to stay in the same place.

We have also analysed how the problems created by gendered practices are recognised and become objects of reform, from the perspective of both collective and individual social actors. Many of our interviewees recognised gender discriminatory practices and inequality, for instance wage inequality, only in society at large, but not in their own workplace. Some thought that the well-known gender differences of social positions are natural, or consequences of individual choice, not a social issue. The daily practices which result in differing treatment and different positions for women and men were not recognised.

The Nordic countries have had a pioneering role in many legislative and social policy measures which unquestionably have improved the social position of women. The ideology of equality is strong – in a way everybody supports it. Considering this, it may seem paradoxical how difficult it was in our case studies to take up equality as a practical problem in the workplaces. This had many aspects: sometimes the problems had to do with power, sometimes with a lack of language.

In the case of comparable worth, a tentative understanding of the problem area was achieved relatively easily, but in the process of a closer definition of the problem, the situation turned into a power struggle. The arguments of women activists based on women's interests in a 'gender frame' were not as acceptable to the men in power as a 'general justice' frame. In the school the researcher had difficulties convincing the teachers that any gender problem existed: the idea that their teaching could have any connection with labour market gender segregation seemed abstract and alien to them.

The researcher's participative role was an important element in several of our studies. In some of them the researchers held key roles as change agents, they kept the discussion up and brought to it concepts that could be used to analyse the situation. In the case of sexual harassment, the victim could analyse her problem only after it was given a name; she would have been lonelier and more confused with her experienced indignity without the researcher's concept that connected her to the group of other harassed women. The researchers' own expertise was an indispensable part of the change projects. The development and use of the job evaluation method, a basic tool of the comparable worth strategy, requires a certain technical expertise, and so does the teaching of computer programs. In the information technology study circle, the situation could be analysed when the researcher gave the keys to an unfamiliar language. In the schools, the change project would hardly have started without an outside impulse, considering the defensive orientation of the teachers towards the project's ideas.

The relationship between expertise and the grassroot level has its problems. That is the case even when the researcher herself may be ideologically committed to women's empowerment as in the information technology study circle, or to opening a door for new action possibilities as in the desegregation project. We could get a glimpse from the other side of the situation. In the school the project was introduced top-down through an outside command and its basic ideas seemed contradictory to the teachers' own thinking. The teachers' opposition to the change project was twisted around the question: whose project is this? The researcher had quite a task to convince them that it could also be their own project.

The comparable worth project was in its starting phase emphatically a women's action. It was accommodated to become a project of the labour market parties, with all the concomitant achievements and sacrifices that such an argumentative terrain could give and demand. The backside of the technical expertise which maintained the process was the danger that women activists might lose their own voice to the altar of 'objective knowledge'. The problematic of women's own definitions and textuality in working life organisations is very complex. It seems that women need to develop their mutual support accordingly, to prevent their subjectivities from disappearing within the textualities, to make a balance between experiences and texts, in their own terms.

The local context of gendered practices turns out to be crucially important for change. And here we should count both the macro- and the micro-level of the local. The desegregation project, for instance, showed that if you want to change gendered practices, results are possible, provided you get to the source where the practices emerge – and provided you do it anew in each location. Diffusion of change does not automatically take place even when the macro-level would favour it, because cultural resistance takes place on the micro-level.

Just as it can be difficult to recognise gendered practices when we ourselves live among them, to recognise change also requires systematic attention. It may be easier to look far than close. Looking back a couple of decades, we can often recognise big changes brought about by countless anonymous women and men who decided to live differently, for instance in new family forms. Instead it is hard to put in a proper perspective the changes that are presently taking place – for example, will mass unemployment change gender relations? What will be the relevance of the European Union to gendered practices in the member countries? Whether the practice is rooted in local or global, often textually mediated practices, it is essential for a change project to take into account what meanings and definitions the people involved in the practices attribute to them in the specific context of where they live and act.

Considering the difficulties of intentionally changing gendered practices we could abstract two major problems of cultural definitions. One is the 'naturalisation' of gender and gendered hierarchies, another is the idea of gender neutrality in the spirit of an-already-achieved-equality. In our local cultural and national context those two aspects are closely intertwined. They are often unintentional ways of creating the persistence of gendered hierarchies and a resistance to change them – though of course the naturalisation of gender may also serve as a conscious resistance or backlash strategy.

The construction of gender is entangled in many processes. Persistence in itself is a problem, because all constancies reproduce themselves as 'naturalness', as the unquestioned and unquestionable ways of being. One side of that coin is that you gain cultural competence: you know automatically how to act and react. The other side is being shut inside the invisible walls of your local culture. Naturalisation of gender has the consequence that the cultural walls close up. After that people no longer see any walls.

Are fishes conscious of the water in which they swim? People in organisations quite often are not conscious that their practices are gendered because they take them for granted. What else could be done, how else could they behave? Or they consider gender as a discourse on general social injustice, not something that relates to their own everyday life at work.

The practices which differentiate between women's and men's activities naturalise the gender hierarchy in the world of wage work. But so do the practices which tend to hide the difference. The seeming gender neutrality and the ideology of equality produce the very same hierarchy. The idea of gender neutrality proposes that gender should not be considered in some context because to do so would be either gender partial or detrimental to gender equality, that things 'should have nothing to do with gender', with the implicit argument that equality already prevails between women and men. But actually the neutrality idea is a great obstacle to sensitivity, and produces gendered consequences.

We would like to take the idea of gender neutrality a little further, to introduce the term of 'gender disabilities'. Not, however, in the meaning that it is women as a group or individuals who are the disabled as the subordinated gender category. On the contrary, it is the organisations in working life that have the gender disabilities – gender blindness, gender deafness and gender muteness. Just as the three apes of the story who do not see, hear or speak evil, many people in organisations refuse to see, hear or speak about gender. Organisations and people suffer from gender blindness: they will not see gender where it fills the scene. They suffer from gender deafness: they cannot hear gender where it whispers and shouts. And they suffer from gender muteness: they are unable to speak about the gender they do in their daily practices.

Research on gendered practices demands sensitivity and readiness to make yourself a part of a common learning process with the people you study. From the researchers this has required a conscious effort to see the common cultural walls that enclose them as well as others. Gender neutrality may be a special difficulty in the Nordic cultural context, but certainly not only there. It is connected to the avowed ideology of equality and the belief that our societies already have achieved full gender equality. An important cultural background may also be the common traditional reluctance to make gender a basis of conflict: 'women and men should act together, not oppose each other.' Do not quarrel. Don't be a troublemaker to the male elite is one valid interpretation – but even Little Red Riding Hood cannot understand why her wish to get herself 'a little bit of air' should cause a quarrel. After all, it is a question of her life.

References

Acker, Joan (1980) 'Women and Stratification – A Review of Recent Literature', *Contemporary Sociology*, 10 (9), 25–39.

Acker, Joan (1988) 'Class, Gender, and the Relations of Distribution', *Signs: Journal of Women in Culture and Society*, 13 (3), 473–97.

Acker, Joan (1989a) *Doing Comparable Worth: Gender, Class and Pay Equity*, Temple University Press, Philadelphia.

Acker, Joan (1989b) *Proposal for an Umbrella Perspective for Kvinnotemagruppen*, Draft 4.4.1989, Arbetslivscentrum, Stockholm (unpublished).

Acker, Joan (1990) 'Hierarchies, Jobs, Bodies: A Theory of Gendered Organizations', *Gender & Society*, 2 (4), 139–58.

Acker, Joan (1992) 'Gendering Organizational Theory', in Mills, A.J. and Tancred, P. (eds), 248–60.

Adam, Alison and Owen, Jenny (eds) (1994) *Breaking Old Boundaries: Building New Forms*, Proceedings of the 5th IFIP International Conference on Women, Work and Computerization, UMIST, Manchester, UK.

Adam, Alison, Emms, Judy, Green, Eileen and Owen, Jenny (eds) (1994) *Women, Work and Computerization, Breaking Old Boundaries: Building New Forms*, IFIP Transactions A-57, North-Holland, Amsterdam.

Aeschylus (1977) *The Oresteia*, Penguin Books, Harmondsworth. Translated by Robert Fagles.

Aitta, Ulla (1988) *Miesten ja naisten tasa-arvon toteutuminen akavalaisessa työelämässä*, AKAVA ry, Helsinki.

Alapuro, Risto (1995) 'Structure and Culture: Finnish Sociology 1990–94', *Acta Sociologica*, 38 (2), 167–80.

Alasoini, Tuomo (1990) *Tuotannolliset rationalisoinnit ja teollisuuden työvoiman käyttötapojen muutos: Tutkimus viidestä modernista suomalaisesta konepajateollisuuden, kevyen sähköteollisuuden ja paperiteollisuuden yksiköstä*, Työpoliittinen tutkimus 5, Työministeriö, Helsinki.

Allen, Sheila and Wolkowitz, Carol (1987) *Homeworking: Myths and Realities*, Macmillan, London.

Allén, Tuovi (1989) 'Köyhyyden naisistuminen – tosiasia vai myytti?', *TTT Katsaus*, 17 (1), 86–102.

Allén, Tuovi, Keinänen, Päivi, Laaksonen, Seppo and Ilmakunnas, Seija (1990) *Wage from Work and Gender: A Study on Differentials in Finland in 1985*, Studies 190, Statistics Finland, Helsinki.

Alvesson, Mats and Due Billing, Yvonne (1992) 'Gender and Organization: Towards a Differentiated Understanding', *Organization Studies*, 13 (12), 73–102.

Anttalainen, Marja-Liisa (1986) *Sukupuolen mukaan kahtiajakautuneet työmarkkinat Pohjoismaissa*, Naistutkimusmonisteita 1, Tasa-arvoasiain neuvottelukunta, Helsinki.

Anttonen, Anneli (1994) 'Hyvinvointivaltion naisystävälliset kasvot', in Anttonen, A., Henriksson, L. and Nätkin, R. (eds), 203–22.

Anttonen, Anneli, Henriksson, Lea and Nätkin, Ritva (eds) (1994) *Naisten hyvinvointivaltio*, Vastapaino, Tampere.

Appelbaum, Eileen (1993) 'New Technology and Work Organisation: The Role of Gender Relations', in Probert, Belinda and Wilson, Bruce W. (eds), 60–84.

Armstrong, Pat and Cornish, Mary (1992) *Equal Pay and Job Evaluation: The Ontario Experience*, ETUC/TUC seminar on Equal pay, job evaluation and job classification, Oxford, 2–4 July 1992.

Åstrand, Kaisa and Anttalainen, Marja-Liisa (1993) 'Työn vaativuuden arviointi', *Työelämän tutkimus*, 4 (4), 24–7.

Baines, Susan (1991) 'Personal Computing, Gender and Distance Education', in Eriksson, I.V., Kitchenham, B.A. and Tijdens, K.G. (eds), 267–82.

Balbo, Laura (1987) 'Crazy Quilts: Rethinking the Welfare State Debate from a Woman's Point of View', in Showstack Sassoon, A. (ed.), 45–71.

Baron, J. and Bielby, W. (1984) 'The Organization of Work in a Segmented Economy', *American Sociological Review*, 49 (August), 454–73.

Barrett, Michéle (1980) *Women's Oppression Today*, Verso, London.

Bech Jørgensen, Birte (1988) ' "Hvorfor gør de ikke noget?" – Skitse till en teori om hverdagslivskræfterne og selvfølgelighedens symbolske orden', in Bloch, Charlotte et al., 68–121.

Becker, Gary S. (1957) *The Economics of Discrimination*, University of Chicago Press, Chicago.

Beechey, Veronica and Perkins, Theresa (1987) *A Matter of Hours. Women, Part-Time Work and the Labour Market*, Polity Press, Cambridge.

Benson, Donna and Thomson, Gregg (1982) 'Sexual Harassment on a University Campus: The Confluence of Authority Relations, Sexual Interest and Gender Stratification', *Social Problems*, 29 (3), 236–51.

Bercusson, Brian and Dickens, Linda (1995) *Collective Bargaining and Equal Opportunities in Europe: Concept Report*, Draft.

Berger, Peter and Luckmann, Thomas (1972) *The Social Construction of Reality: A Treatise in the Sociology of Knowledge*, Penguin, Harmondsworth.

Bergholm, Tapio (1991) *Organizing Individualistic Masculinity: The Case of Finnish Dockers*, Departmental Seminar and the Work and Industrial Relations Seminar 30.5.1991, University of Manchester, Department of Sociology (unpublished).

Bergman, Barbara R. (1989) 'What the Common Economic Arguments against Comparable Worth Are Worth', *Journal of Social Issues*, 45 (4), 67–80.

Bhavnani, Kum-Kum (1993) 'Tracing the Contours: Feminist Research and Feminist Objectivity', *Women's Studies International Forum*, 16 (2), 95–104.

Bisset, Liz and Huws, Ursula (1985) *Sweated Labour: Homeworking in Britain Today*, Low Pay Unit, Nottingham.

Bloch, Charlotte (1991) 'I lust och nöd – om vardagsliv och känslor', *Kvinnovetenskaplig tidsskrift*, 12 (2), 31–42.

Bloch, Charlotte et al. (1988) *Hverdagsliv, kultur og subjektivitet*, Akademisk forlag, København.

Blom, Raimo, Kivinen, Markku, Melin, Harri and Rantalaiho, Liisa (1992) *The Scope Logic Approach to Class Analysis – A Study of the Finnish Class Structure*, Avebury, Aldershot.

Blomqvist, Martha, Mackinnon, Alison and Vehviläinen, Marja (1994) '*Exploring the Gender and Technology Boundaries: An International Perspective*', in Eberhart, T. and Wächter, C. (eds), 101–18.

Blum, Linda M. (1991) *Between Feminism and Labour: The Significance of the*

Comparable Worth Movement, University of California Press, Berkeley and Los Angeles.

Bock, Gisela and Thane, Pat (eds) (1992) *Maternity & Gender Policies: Women and the Rise of the European Welfare States 1890s–1950s*, Routledge, London.

Boh, Katja, Bak, Maren, Clason, Cristine, Pankratova, Maja, Qvortrup, Jens, Sgritta, Giovanni B. and Wærness, Kari (eds) (1989) *Changing Patterns of European Family Life. A Comparative Analysis of 14 European Countries*, Routledge, London and New York.

Boman, Ann (1983) *Omsorg och solidaritet – ohållbara argument?*, Arbetsrapport 1983:4, Arbetslivscentrum, Stockholm.

Bono, Paola and Kemp, Sandra (eds) (1991) *Italian Feminist Thought: A Reader*, Basil Blackwell, Oxford.

Boris, Eileen (1987) 'Homework and Women's Rights: The Case of the Vermont Knitters 1980–1985', *Signs: Journal of Women in Culture and Society*, 13 (1), 98–120.

Boris, Eileen and Prugl, Elisabeth (1995) *Homeworkers in Global Perspective: Invisible No More*, Routledge, New York (forthcoming).

Braidotti, Rosi (1994) *Nomadian Subjects – Embodiment and Sexual Difference in Contemporary Feminist Theory*, Columbia University Press, New York.

Brantsæter, Marianne C. and Widerberg, Karin (eds) (1992) *Sex i arbeid(ed) i Norge*, Tiden Norsk Forlag, Oslo.

Braszeit, Anne, Holzbecher, Monika, Muller, Ursula and Plogstedt, Sibylle (1988) *Sexuelle Belästigung am Arbeitsplaz*, Das Landesinstitut Sozialforschungsstelle, Dortmund.

Braverman, Harry (1974) *Labor and Monopoly Capital: The Degradation of Work in the Twentieth Century*, Monthly Review Press, New York and London.

Briskin, Linda and McDermott, Patricia (eds) (1993) *Women Challenging Unions – Feminism, Democracy and Militancy*, University of Toronto Press, Toronto.

Brumlop, Eva (1995) *Collective Bargaining and Equal Opportunities in Europe*, Research Group, Bryssel.

Bryson, Lois (1993) *Working Life and Family Life: Does Policy Make A Difference?*, A Report for the Office of Status of Women Department of Prime Minister and Cabinet, Department of Anthropology and Sociology, The University of Newcastle, Newcastle.

Burrell, Gibson (1992) 'Sex and Organizational Analysis', in Mills, A.J. and Tancred, P. (eds), 71–92.

Buswell, Carol and Jenkins, Sarah (1994) 'Equal Opportunities Policies, Employment and Patriarchy', *Gender, Work and Organization*, 1 (2), 83–93.

Butler, Judith (1993) *Bodies That Matter*, Routledge, London.

Calas, Marta B. (1992) 'An/Other Silent Voice? Representing "Hispanic Woman" in Organizational Texts', in Mills, A.J. and Tancred, P. (eds), 201–21.

Carr, Wilfred and Kemmis, Stephen (1986) *Becoming Critical: Education, Knowledge and Action Research*, Falmer Press, London.

Christensen, Kathleen (1988) *Women and Home-Based Work: The Unspoken Contract*, Henry Holt, New York.

De Cindio, Fiorella and Simone, Carla (1993) 'The Universes of Discourse for Education and Action/Research', in Green, E., Owen, J. and Pain, D. (eds), 173–93.

Cockburn, Cynthia (1983) *Brothers: Male Dominance and Technological Change*, Pluto Press, London.

Cockburn, Cynthia (1985) *Machinery of Dominance: Women, Men and Technical Know-How*, Pluto Press, London.

Cockburn, Cynthia (1991) *In the Way of Women: Men's Resistance to Sex Equality in Organizations*, Macmillan, London.

Cockburn, Cynthia and Ormrod, Susan (1993) *Gender & Technology in the Making*, Sage, London.

Cohen, Theodore F. (1993) 'What do Fathers Provide?', in Hood, Jane C. (ed.), 1–22.

Colling, Trevor and Dickens, Linda (1989) *Equality Bargaining – Why Not?*, Equal Opportunities Commission, HMSO, London.

Collinson, David and Hearn, Jeff (1994) 'Naming Men as Men: Implications for Work Organization and Management', *Gender, Work and Organization*, 1 (1), 2–22.

Connell, Robert W. (1987) *Gender and Power – Society, the Person and Sexual Politics*, Stanford University Press, Stanford, Calif.

Contributions to the Third GASAT Conference (1985) Chelsea College, University of London, London.

Contributions to the Fourth GASAT Conference (1987) University of Michigan Arbor, Ann Arbor.

Contributions to the East and West European GASAT Conference (1992) University of Technology, Eindhoven.

Crompton, Rosemary and Le Feuvre, Nicola (1992) 'Gender and Bureaucracy: Women in Finance in Britain and France', in Savage, M. and Witz, A. (eds), 94–123.

Csikszentmihalyi, Mihaly (1975) *Beyond Boredom and Anxiety*, Jossey-Bass, San Francisco.

Cunnison, Sheila and Stageman, Jane (1993) *Feminizing the Unions – Challenging the Culture of Masculinity*, Avebury, Newcastle upon Tyne.

Dahlström, Edmund (1987) 'Everyday-Life Theories and their Historical and Ideological Contexts', in Himmelstrand, U. (ed.), 93–114.

Davies, Celia (1980) 'Making Sense of the Census in Britain and the USA – The Changing Occupational Classification and the Position of Nurses', *The Sociological Review*, 28 (3), 581–609.

Davies, Karen (1989) *Women and Time – Weaving the Strands of Everyday Life*, Grahns boktrcykeri, Lund.

Demokrati och makt i Sverige (1990) Maktutredningens huvudrapport, SOU 1990:44, Stockholm.

Doeringer, P.B. and Piore, M.J. (1971) *Internal Labor Markets and Manpower Analysis*, D.C. Heath, Lexington, Mass.

Douglas, Mary (1986) *How Institutions Think*, Syracuse University Press, Syracuse, NY.

Ebben, Maureen and Kramarae, Cheris (1993) 'Women and Information Technologies – Creating a Cyberspace of Our Own', in Taylor, H.J., Kramarae, C. and Ebben, M. (eds), 15–27.

Eberhart, Tina and Wächter, Christina (eds) (1994) *Proceedings 2nd European Feminist Research Conference: Feminist Perspectives on Technology, Work and Ecology*, 5–9 July, Graz, Austria.

References 201

Edwards, Paul N. (1990) 'The Army and the Microworld: Computers and the Politics of Gender Identity', *Signs: Journal of Women in Culture and Society*, 16 (1), 102–27.

Ehn, Pelle (1988) *Work-Oriented Design of Computer Artifacts*, Arbetslivscentrum, Stockholm.

Eisenstein, Hester (1991) *Gender Shock: Practising Feminism on Two Continents*, Allen & Unwin, Sydney.

Eisenstein, Zillah (ed.) (1979) *Capitalist Patriarchy and the Case for Socialist Feminism*, Monthly Review Press, New York.

Elias, Norbert (1978) 'Zum Begriff des Alltags', *Kölner Zeitschrift für Soziologie und Sozialpsychologie*, Sonderheft 20, 22–9.

Elling, Monica (1984) *På tröskeln till ett nytt liv?*, Arbetslivscentrum, Stockholm.

Engeström, Yrjö (1981) *Johdatus didaktiikkaan*, Valtion koulutuskeskus, Julkaisusarja B n:o 13, Helsinki.

Engeström, Yrjö (1985) *Toiminnan teoria ja kehittävä työntutkimus*, Helsinki (unpublished).

Engeström, Yrjö (1987) *Learning by Expanding – An Activity-Theoretical Approach to Developmental Research*, Orienta-Konsultit Oy, Helsinki.

Engeström, Yrjö (1991) 'Developmental Work Research: Reconstructing Expertise through Expansive Learning', in Nurminen, M.I., Järvinen, P. and Weir, G. (eds), 124–43.

England, Paula (1992) *Comparable Worth – Theories and Evidence*, Aldine de Gruyter, Hawthorne, New York.

England, Paula and Dunn, Dana (1988) 'Evaluating Work and Comparable Worth', *Annual Review of Sociology*, 14, 227–48.

Eriksson, Inger V., Kitchenham, Barbara A. and Tijdens, Kea G. (eds) (1991), *Women, Work and Computerization: Understanding and Overcoming Bias in Work and Education*, North-Holland, Amsterdam.

Esping-Andersen, Gøsta (1990) *The Three Worlds of Welfare Capitalism*, Princeton, Princeton University Press.

Evans, Sara M. and Nelson, Barbara J. (1989) *Wage Justice – Comparable Worth and the Paradox of Technocratic Reform*, University of Chicago Press, Chicago and London.

Faludi, Susan (1992) *Backlash. The Undeclared War Against Women*, Chatto & Windus, London.

Feldberg, Roslyn L. and Glenn, Evelyn Nakano (1979) 'Male and Female – Job versus Gender Models in the Sociology of Work', *Social Problems*, 26 (5), 524–38.

Ferguson, Kathy E. (1993) *The Man Question. Visions of Subjectivity in Feminist Theory*, University of California Press, Berkeley and Los Angeles.

Fiske, John (1990) *Introduction to Communication Studies*, 2nd edn, Routledge, London.

Flynn, Padraig (1993) *Opening Address – Equal Pay, 36 Years Later: In Search of Excellence*, Brussels, 25–26 October 1993, Belgian presidency of the European Community.

Foged, Britta and Sørensen, Bente (1985) Åben datastue for kvinder, *Den 2. nordiske konference om Kvinder, naturvidenskab og teknologi under temaet Kvinder og teknologisk udvikling*, Aalborg, 193–8.

Forester, Tom (1988) 'The Myth of the Electronic Cottage', *Futures*, 20 (3), 227–40.

202 *References*

Foucault, Michel (1973) *The Order of Things: An Archaeology of the Human Sciences*, Vintage Books, New York.

Foucault, Michel (1978) *The History of Sexuality: Volume 1, An Introduction*, Penguin Books, Harmondsworth.

Foucault, Michel (1991) *Discipline and Punish: The Birth of the Prison*, Penguin Books, London.

Friberg, Tora (1989) *En måndag i september – Om vardagens organisation och kvinnors liv*, Lund (unpublished).

Game, Ann and Pringle, Rosemary (1983) *Gender at Work*, George Allen & Unwin, Sydney.

Gardell, Bertill and Johansson, Gunn (eds) (1981) *Working Life – A Social Science Contribution to Work Reform*, Wiley, Chichester.

Gatens, Moira (1983) 'A Critique of the Sex/Gender Distinction' , in Gunew, S. (ed.), 139–57.

Gherardi, Silvia (1994) 'The Gender We Think, the Gender We Do in Our Everyday Organizational Lives', *Human Relations*, 47 (6), 591–610.

Giddens, Anthony (1984) *The Constitution of Society*, Polity Press, Cambridge.

Giddens, Anthony (1989) *Sociology*, Polity Press, Cambridge.

Giddens, Anthony (1991) *Modernity and Self-Identity – Self and Society in the Late Modern Age*, Polity Press, Oxford.

Goffman, Erving (1961) *Asylums – Essays on the Social Situation of Mental Patients and Other Inmates*, Aldine, Chicago.

Goldmann, Monika and Richter, Gudrun (n.d.) *Telehomework by Women*, Sozialforschungsstelle, Dortmund.

Gonäs, Lena (1989) *En fråga om kön. Kvinnor och män i strukturomvandlingens spår*, Arbetslivscentrum, Stockholm.

Green, Eileen (1994) 'Gender Perspectives, Office Systems and Organizational Change', in Adam, A. et al. (eds), 129–42.

Green, Eileen, Owen, Jenny and Pain, Den (1993a) 'City Libraries: Human-Centred Opportunities for Women?', in Green, E., Owen, J. and Pain, D. (eds), 127–52.

Green, Eileen, Owen, Jenny and Pain, Den (eds) (1993b) *Gendered by Design? Information Technology and Office Systems*, Taylor & Francis, London and Washington, DC.

Gruber, James (1989) *Sexual Harassment Research – Problems and Proposals*, Paper presented at the American Sociological Association Conference, August.

Gruber, James E. and Bjorn, Lars (1982) 'Blue-Collar Blues – The Sexual Harassment of Women Autoworkers', *Work and Occupations*, 9 (3), 271–98.

Gunderson, Morley (1989) 'Implementation of Comparable Worth in Canada', *Journal of Social Issues*, 45 (4), 209–22.

Gunew, Sneja (ed.) (1983) *A Reader in Feminist Knowledge*, Routledge, London.

Gunnarsson, Ewa and Trojer, Lena (eds) (1994) *Feminist Voices on Gender, Technology and Ethics*, Centre for Women's Studies, Luleå Univeristy of Technology, Sweden.

Gutek, Barbara A. and Cohen, Aaron Groff (1992) 'Sex Ratios, Sex Role Over, and Sex at Work: A Comparison of Men's and Women's Experiences', in Mills, A.J. and Tancred, P. (eds), 134–6.

Gutek, Barbara A., Nakamura, Charles Y., Gahart, Martin, Handschumacher, Inger and Russell, Dan (1980) 'Sexuality and the Workplace', *Basic and Applied Social Psychology*, 1 (3), 255–65.

Haastrup, Lisbeth (1993) 'Mad som vor mor lavede den', *Kvinder, køn och forskning*, 2 (2), 62–76.
Haavind, Hanne (1984) 'Love and Power in Marriage', in Holter, H. (ed.), 136–67.
Haavio-Mannila, Elina (1984) 'Perheen ja työn suhde', in Haavio-Mannila, E., Jallinoja, R. and Strandell, H., 184–202.
Haavio-Mannila, Elina (1989) 'Gender Segregation in Paid and Unpaid Work', in Boh, K., Bak, M., Clason, C., Pankratova, M., Qvortrup, J., Sgritta, G.B. and Wærness, K. (eds), 123–40.
Haavio-Mannila, Elina, Jallinoja, Riitta and Strandell, Harriet (1984) *Perhe, työ ja tunteet – Ristiriitoja ja ratkaisuja*, WSOY, Porvoo.
Haavio-Mannila, Elina, Dahlerup, Drude, Eduards, Maud, Gudmundsdóttir, Esther, Halsaa, Beatrice, Hernes, Helga Maria, Hänninen-Salmelin, Eva, Sigmundsdóttir, Bergthora, Sinkkonen, Sirkka and Skard, Torild (eds) (1985) *Unfinished Democracy: Women in Nordic Politics*, Pergamon Press, Oxford.
Hakim, Catherine (1987) *Home-based Work in Britain – A Report on the 1981 National Homeworking Survey and the DE Research Programme on Homework*, Department of Employment Research Paper No. 60, London.
Haraway, Donna (1988) 'Situated Knowledges – The Science Question in Feminism and the Privilege of Partial Perspective', *Feminist Studies*, 14 (3), 575–99.
Haraway, Donna (1991) *Simians, Cyborgs, and Women – The Reinventions of Nature*, Free Associations Books, London.
Harding, Sandra (1986) *The Science Question in Feminism*, Cornell University Press, Ithaca, NY and London.
Harre, Rom (1979) *Social Being*, Basil Blackwell, Oxford.
Hartmann, Heidi (1976) 'Capitalism, Patriarchy and Job Segregation by Sex', *Signs: Journal of Women in Culture and Society*, 2 (1), 137–69.
Hartmann, Heidi J. (ed.) (1985) *Comparable Worth – New Directions for Research*, National Academy Press, Washington, DC.
Haug, Frigga (ed.) (1987) *Female Sexualization: A Collective Work of Memory*, Verso, London.
Hearn, Jeff and Parkin, Wendy (1987) *Sex at Work – The Power and Paradox of Organisation Sexuality*, Mackays of Chatham, Kent.
Hegtvedt, Karen A. (1989) 'Fairness Conceptualizations and Comparable Worth', *Journal of Social Issues*, 45 (4), 81–98.
Heidegger, Martin (1981) *Varat och tiden*, Doxa, Lund.
Heiskanen, Tuula, Hyväri, Susanna, Kivimäki, Riikka, Kinnunen, Merja, Korvajärvi, Päivi, Martikainen, Riitta, Lehto, Anna-Maija, Räsänen, Leila, Salmi, Minna, Varsa, Hannele and Vehviläinen, Marja (1990) *Gendered Practices in Working Life – Projcet Outline*, University of Tampere, Research Institute for Social Sciences, Work Research Centre, Working Paper 17, Tampere.
Heller, Agnes (1984) *Everyday Life*, Routledge, New York.
Henriksson, Lea (1994) 'Ammatillisen sisaruuden uudet jaot – sota terveystyön taitekohtana', in Anttonen, A., Henriksson, L. and Nätkin, R. (eds), 97–127.
Hernes, Helga Maria (1984) 'Women and Welfare State: The Transition from Private to Public Dependence', in Holter, H. (ed.), 26–45.
Hietala, Marjatta and Myllys, Kari (eds) (1982) *Tutkijan tilastolliset tiedonlähteet*, Gaudeamus, Helsinki.
Himmelstrand, Ulf (ed.) (1987) *The Multiparadigmatic Trend in Sociology*, Acta Universitatis Upsaliensis, Uppsala.

Hirdman, Yvonne (1988) 'Genussystemet – reflexioner kring kvinnors sociala underordning', *Kvinnovetenskaplig Tidskrift*, 10 (3), 49–63.

Hirdman, Yvonne (1990a) *Att lägga livet till rätta*, Carlssons, Stockholm.

Hirdman, Yvonne (1990b) 'Genussystemet', in Demokrati och makt i Sverige, 73–116.

Hochschild, Arlie (1983) *The Managed Heart*, University of California Press, Berkeley.

Hofmann, Jeanette (1994) 'Two Versions of the Same – The Text Editor and the Automatic Letter Writer as Contrasting Conceptions of Digital Writing', in Adam, A. et al. (eds), 129–42.

Holli, Anne Maria (1990) 'Why the State? Reflections on the Politics of the Finnish Equality Movement Association 9', in Keränen, M. (ed.), 69–88.

Holli, Anne Maria and Wartiovaara, Katarina (1991) *Kortti puhuu*, Sosiaali- ja terveysministeriö, Tasa-arvojulkaisuja, Sarja A1:1991, Helsinki.

Holter, Harriet (ed.) (1982) *Kvinner og felleskap*, Universitetsforlaget, Oslo.

Holter, Harriet (ed.) (1984) *Patriarchy in a Welfare Society*, Universitetsforlaget, Oslo.

Holter, Harriet (1992) 'Seksuell trakassering – en hersketeknikk i arbeidsorganisasjonen?', in Brantsæfter, M.C. and Widerberg, K. (eds), 130–45.

Hood, Jane C. (ed.) (1993) *Men, Work, and Family*, Sage, Newbury Park, Calif.–London–New Delhi.

Human Development Report (1995) New York, Oxford University Press. Published for the United Nations Development Programme.

Hyvärinen, Matti (1994) *Viimeiset taistot*, Vastapaino, Tampere.

Ipsen, Sanne (1984) 'Tidsstrukturer & fleksibilitet i kvinders hverdagsliv', *Rapport fra kvindeforskningsseminar om kvinder og teknologi*, Roskilde universitetscenter 20.–21.3.1984, 28–39.

Jackson, Pauline Conroy (1990) *The Impact of the Completion of the Internal Market on Women in the European Community*, Commission of the European Communities, Equal Opportunities Unit, Brussels.

Journal of Vocational Behavior (1993) 42 (1).

Julkunen, Raija (1985) 'Naisten aika', *Tiede & edistys*, 10 (4), 295–308.

Julkunen, Raija (1994) 'Suomalainen sukupuolimalli – 1960-luku käänteenä', in Anttonen, A., Henriksson, L. and Nätkin, R. (eds), 179–201.

Järvinen, Margaretha (1993) *Of Vice and Women – Shades of Prostitution*, Scandinavian University Press/The Scandinavian Research Council for Criminology, Oslo.

Järvinen, Pertti and Tyllilä, Pekka (1980) *Erään atk-systeemin käyttöönotto, Toimintatutkimus atk-systeemin vaikutuksista työntekijöiden toimiin*, Tampereen yliopisto, Matemaattisten tieteiden laitos, A 42, Tampere.

Kanter, Rosabeth Moss (1977) *Work and Family in the United States: A Critical Review and Agenda for Research and Policy*. Social Science Frontiers: Occasional Publications Reviewing New Fields of Social Science Development, Russell Sage Foundation, New York.

Katajisto, Heikki (1982) 'Mitä näkee silmä, kuulee korva . . .', *Sosiologia*, 11 (3), 209.

Katajisto, Heikki (1983) 'Asuntolan miehet lähikuvassa', *Sosiologia*, 12 (1), 33–42.

Kauppinen, Timo (1994) *The Transformation of Finnish Labour Relations*, Finnish Labour Relations Association, Publication Number 8, Helsinki.

Kauppinen, Timo and Köykkä, Virpi (1991) *Palkansaajien järjestäytyminen 1989*, Työpoliittinen tutkimus 9, Työministeriö, Helsinki.

Keinänen, Päivi (1994) 'Perheet työelämässä', in Suomalainen perhe, 125–37.

Kelly, Rita M. and Bayes, Jane (eds) (1988) *Comparable Worth, Pay Equity and Public Policy*, Greenwood Press, New York.

Kenrick, J. (1981) 'Politics and the Construction of Women as Second-Class Workers', in Wilkinson, F. (ed.), 167–91.

Keränen, Marja (ed.) (1990) *Finnish 'Undemocracy' – Essays on Gender and Politics*, The Finnish Political Science Association, Gummerus, Jyväskylä.

Kevätsalo, Kimmo (1992) *Eriarvoisuuden arki metalliteollisuuden tehtävissä*, Metallityöväen liitto, Jaarli Oy, Helsinki.

Kinnunen, Merja (1989) *Työt, toimet ja luokittelut*, Sarja T2, Tampereen yliopisto, Yhteiskuntatieteiden tutkimuslaitos, Työelämän tutkimuskeskus, Tampere.

Kirkup, Gill (1992) 'The Social Construction of Computers: Hammers or Harpsichords?', in Kirkup, G. and Keller, L.S. (eds), 267–81.

Kirkup, Gill and Keller, Laurie Smith (eds) (1992) *Inventing Women, Science, Technology and Gender*, Polity Press, Cambridge.

Koistinen, Pertti and Suikkanen, Asko (eds) (1990) *Edessä pysyvä tilapäisyys: Tapaustutkimuksia joukkoirtisanomisista ja niistä suoriutumisesta*, Monisteita 2, Joensuun yliopisto, Karjalan tutkimuslaitos, Joensuu.

Kolehmainen, Sirpa (1995) *Naisten ja miesten työmarkkinat – Segregaatio ja rakennemuutos Suomessa 1970–90*, Sosiaalipolitiikan laitos, Tampere (unpublished).

Korvajärvi, Päivi (1989) 'New Technology and Gendered Division of Labour', in Tijdens, K., Jennings, M., Wagner, I. and Weggelaar, M. (eds), 77–83.

Korvajärvi, Päivi (1990) *Toimistotyöntekijäin yhteisöt ja muutoksen hallinta*, Sarja T6, Tampereen yliopisto, Yhteiskuntatieteen tutkimuslaitos, Työelämän tutkimuskeskus, Tampere.

Korvajärvi, Päivi and Rantalaiho, Liisa (1984) *Toimistoautomaatio ja toimistotyö*, sarja B40, Tampereen yliopisto, Yhteiskuntatieteiden tutkimuslaitos, Tampere.

Korvajärvi, Päivi, Järvinen, Riitta and Kinnunen, Merja (1987) *Työ, toimihenkilöt ja muutokset – väliraportti projektista Pitkäaikaisseuranta työelämän muutoksista toimihenkilöaloilla*, TVK ry, Helsinki.

Korvajärvi, Päivi, Järvinen, Riitta and Kinnunen, Merja (1990) *Muutokset kiireen keskellä – Seurantatutkimus muutoksista toimihenkilöiden työpaikoilla 1980-luvulla*, Sarja T7, Tampereen yliopisto, Yhteiskuntatieteiden tutkimuslaitos, Työelämän tutkimuskeskus, Tampere.

Kosik, Karel (1978) *Det konkretas dialektik*, Röda bokförlaget, Göteborg.

Kristeva, Julia (1992) *Muukalaisia itsellemme*, Gaudeamus, Helsinki.

Kumar, Pradeep (1993) 'Collective Bargaining and Women's Workplace Concerns', in Briskin, L. and McDermott, P. (eds), 207–30.

Kuusipalo, Jaana (1990) 'Finnish Women in Top-level Politics', in Keränen, M. (ed.), 13–36.

Kvande, Elin and Rasmussen, Bente (1993) 'Organisationen, en arena för olika uttryck av kvinnlighet och manlighet', *Kvinnovetenskaplig tidskrift*, 13 (4), 45–56.

Laclau, Ernesto and Mouffe, Chantal (1985) *Hegemony and Socialist Strategy – Towards a Radical Democratic Politics*, Verso, London.

Lane, Christel (1987) 'Capitalism or Culture? A Comparative Analysis of the

Position in the Labour Process and Labour Market of Lower White-Collar Workers in the Financial Services Sector of Britain and the Federal Republic of Germany', *Work, Employment and Society*, 1 (1) 57–83.

Langan, Mary and Ostner, Ilona (1991) 'Gender and Welfare: Towards a Comparative Framework', in Room, Graham (ed.), 1–14.

De Lauretis, Teresa (1987) *Technologies of Gender – Essays on Theory, Film and Fiction*, Indiana University Press, Bloomington and Indianapolis.

De Lauretis, Teresa (1989) 'The Essence of the Triangle or, Taking the Risk of Essentialism Seriously – Feminist Theory in Italy, the U.S., and Britain', *Differences*, 1 (2), 1–37.

Lawrence, Elisabeth (1994) *Gender and Trade Unions*, Taylor & Francis, London.

Lefebvre, Henri (1971) *Everyday Life in the Modern World*, Penguin, London.

Lehto, Anna-Maija (1988) *Naisten ja miesten työolot*, Tutkimuksia 138, Tilastokeskus, Helsinki.

Lehto, Anna-Maija (1992) *Työelämän laatu ja tasa-arvo – naisten ja miesten työolojen muutoksia 1977–1990*, Työolokomitean liiteselvitys, Komiteamietintö 1991:39/Tutkimuksia 189, Tilastokeskus, Valtion painatuskeskus, Helsinki.

Leidner, Robin (1988) 'Home Work – A Study in the Interaction of Work and Family Organization', in Simpson, R.L. and Simpson, I.H. (eds), 69–94.

Leira, Arnlaug (1992) *Welfare States and Working Mothers – The Scandinavian Experience*, Cambridge University Press, Cambridge.

Leivo-Larsson, Tyyne (1951) *Mitä sanotaan samapalkkaisuudesta*, Suomen Ammattiyhdistysten keskusliitto (SAK), Kuopio.

Lévi-Strauss, Claude (1966) *The Savage Mind*, University of Chicago Press, Chicago.

Lewis, Jane (1992) 'Gender and the Development of Welfare Regimes', *Journal of European Social Policy*, 2 (3), 159–74.

Libreria delle Donne di Milano (1991) 'More Women than Men', in Bono, P. and Kemp, S. (eds), 110–22.

Lie, Merete, Berg, Ann-Jorunn, Kvande, Elin and Kvåle, Eli (1978) *Lunnet hjemmearbeid*, Institutt for industriell miljuforskning, Trondheim.

Lie, Svein and Sjøberg, Svein (1984) *'Myke' jenter i 'harde' fag?*, Universitetsforlaget, Lommedalen.

Liljeström, Rita (1981) 'Time Aspects of Production and Reproduction', in Gardell, B. and Johansson, G. (eds), 95–113.

Liljeström, Rita (1983) *Det erotiska kriget*, Stockholm, Liber.

Lillrank, Annika (1991) 'Kvinnors dilemma i välfärdsstaten: att arbeta och sköta sjukt barn', *Naistutkimus*, 4 (1), 7–13.

Lindblom, Charles E. and Cohen, David K. (1979) *Usable Knowledge – Social Science and Social Problem Solving*, Yale University Press, New Haven, Conn.

Loy, Pamela Hewitt and Stewart, Lea P. (1984) 'The Extent and Effects of the Sexual Harassment of Working Women', *Sociological Focus*, 17 (9), 31–43.

Lukes, Steven (1986) *Power – A Radical View*, Macmillan, London.

Lundén Jacoby, Ann and Näsman, Elisabet (1989) *Mamma, pappa, jobb – Föräldrar och barn om arbetets villkor*, Arbetslivscentrum, Stockholm.

Luokkaprojekti (1984) *Suomalaiset luokkakuvassa*, Vastapaino, Tampere.

Machung, Anne (1983) *From Psyche to Technic – Politics of Office Work*, Dissertation, University of Madison, Madison, Wis.

MacKinnon, Catharine (1979) *Sexual Harassment of Working Women – A Case of Sexual Discrimination*, Yale University Press, New Haven and London.

Mankkinen, Teija (1994) *Sukupuolisen häirinnän ja ahdistelun teoreettinen rekonstruktio – Mielisairaalaa koskevan tapausanalyysin valossa*, Helsingin yliopisto, Sosiologian laitos, Helsinki (unpublished).

Manninen, Merja and Setälä, Päivi (eds) (1990) *The Lady with the Bow – The Story of Finnish Women*, Otava, Helsinki.

Martikainen, Riitta and Yli-Pietilä, Päivi (1992) *Työehdot ja sukupuoli – sokeat sopimukset*, Sarja T12, Tampereen yliopisto, Yhteiskuntatieteiden tutkimuslaitos, Työelämän tutkimuskeskus, Tampere.

Martin, Joanne (1990) 'Deconstructing Organizational Taboos – The Suppression of Gender Conflict in Organizations', *Organization Science*, 1 (4), 339–59.

Microsyster (1988) *Not Over Our Heads – Women and Computers in the Office*, Third IFIP Conference on Women, Work and Computerization, Amsterdam, The Netherlands, 27–29 April 1988 (unpublished).

Mikkonen, Eine (1987) *Minäkö SAK:ssa? Tutkimus SAK:n naisjäsenistöstä*, SAK:n järjestötutkimusprojekti, Painokaari, Helsinki.

Mills, Albert J. and Tancred, Peta (eds) (1992) *Gendering Organizational Analysis*, Sage Publications, Newbury Park, Calif.

Mumby, Dennis K. and Putnam, Linda L. (1992) 'The Politics of Emotion – A Feminist Reading of Bounded Rationality', *Academy of Management Review*, 17 (3), 465–86.

Mumford, Enid and Henshall, Don (1979) *A Participative Approach to Computer Systems Design – A Case Study*, Associated Business Press, London.

Mörtberg, Christina (1994) 'Women's Ways of Acting – Possibilities and Obstacles', in Adam, A. and Owen, J. (eds), 374–83.

Naiset ja miehet Suomessa 1994 (1994) Elinolot 1994:2, Tilastokeskus, Helsinki.

Niemi, Iiris (1994) 'Perheiden ajankäyttö', in Suomalainen perhe, 165–75.

Nurminen, M.I., Järvinen, P. and Weir, G. (eds) (1991) *Proceedings of the Conference on Human Jobs and Computer Interfaces*, 26–28 June, Department of Computer Science, University of Tampere, Tampere.

Nätti, Jouko (1989) *Työmarkkinoiden lohkoutuminen: Segmentaatioteoriat, Suomen työmarkkinat ja yritysten työvoimastrategiat*, Jyväskylä Studies in Education, Psychology and Social Research 68, Jyväskylä.

OECD Employment Outlook (1991) OECD, Paris.

Offe, Claus and Wiesenthal, Helmut (1980) 'Two Logics of Collective Action – Theoretical Notes on Social Class and Organizational Form', in Zeitlin, M. (ed.), 67–115.

Oksanen, Merja (1993) *Rom Harren episodianalyysi sukupuolisen häirinnän ja ahdistelun tutkimisessa*, Helsingin yliopisto, Sosiaalipsykologian laitos, Helsinki (unpublished).

O'Neill, June (1985) 'An Argument for the Marketplace', *Society*, 22 (5), 55–60.

Van Oost, Ellen (1992) 'The Masculinization of the Computer – A Historical Reconstruction', in Preprints of International Conference on Gender, Technology and Ethics, Luleå, 1–2 June, 235–44.

Paetzold, Ramona L. and O'Leary-Kelly, Anne M. (1994) 'Hostile Environment Sexual Harassment in the United States – Post-Meritor Developments and Implications', *Gender, Work and Organization*, 1 (1), 50–7.

Pateman, Carole (1988) *The Sexual Contract*, Polity Press, Cambridge.

Pay Equity Act 1987 (1988) Statutes of Ontario, Chapter 34.

Pilalis, Jennie (1986) 'The Integration of Theory and Practice – A Re-examination of a Paradoxical Expectation', *British Journal of Social Work*, 16, 79–96.

Pitkänen, Kari (1982) 'Väestötilastot', in Hietala, M. and Myllys, K. (eds), 103–31.

Pleck, J.-H. (1977) 'The Work–Family Role System', *Social Problems*, 24, 417–27.

Plogstedt, Sibylle and Bode, Kathleen (1984) *Übergriffe – Sexuelle Belästigung in Büros und Betrieben – Eine Dokumentation der Grünen Frauen im Bundestag*, Rowohlt, Reinbek bei Hamburg.

Pohls, Maritta (1990) 'Women's Work in Finland 1870–1940', in M. Manninen and Setälä, P. (eds), 55–73.

Pringle, Rosemary (1989) *Secretaries Talk*, Verso, London.

Probert, Belinda and Wilson, Bruce W. (1993a) 'Gendered Work', in Probert, B. and Wilson, B.W. (eds), 1–19.

Probert, Belinda and Wilson, Bruce W. (eds) (1993b) *Pink Collar Blues, Work, Gender and Technology*, Melbourne University Press, Carlton.

Prokop, Ulrike (1978) *Kvindelig livssammenhæng*, Ethelberg boktryck, Tranehuse.

Rantalaiho, Liisa (1985) 'Kvinnlig arbetsorienteering och kontorsautomation', *Sosiologia*, 14 (1), 23–34.

Rantalaiho, Liisa (ed.) (1986) *Miesten tiede, naisten puuhat*, Vastapaino, Tampere.

Rantalaiho, Liisa (1990) 'Office Work as Women's Work', *The Polish Sociological Bulletin*, No. 2, 64–74.

Rantalaiho, Liisa (1993) 'The Gender Contract', in Varsa, H. (ed.), 1–9.

Rantalaiho, Liisa (1994) 'Sukupuolisopimus ja Suomen malli', in Anttonen, A., Henriksson, L. and Nätkin R. (eds), 9–30.

Rantalaiho, Liisa and Julkunen, Raija (1994) 'Women in Western Europe: Socio-economic Restructuring and Crisis in Gender Contracts', *Journal of Women's History*, 5 (3), 11–29.

Regalia, Ida (1988) 'Democracy and Unions – Towards a Critical Appraisal', *Economic and Industrial Democracy*, 9 (3), 345–75.

Reimer, Marilee (1987) *The Social Organization of the Labour Process – A Case Study of the Documentary Management of Clerical Labour in the Public Sector*, Dissertation, Department of Educational Theory, University of Toronto, Toronto.

Reiter, Rayna (ed.) (1975) *Toward an Anthropology of Women*, Monthly Review Press, New York and London.

Reskin, Barbara and Padavic, Irene (1994) *Women and Men at Work*, Pine Forge Press, Thousand Oaks, Calif.

Rich Adrienne (1980) 'Compulsory Heterosexuality and Lesbian Existence', *Signs: Journal of Women in Culture and Society*, 5 (4), 631–60.

Room, Graham (ed.) (1991) *Towards a European Welfare State?*, SAUS, Bristol.

Rowbotham, Sheila and Mitter, Swasti (eds) (1994) *Dignity and Daily Bread*, Routledge, London.

Rubenstein, Michael (1988) *The Dignity of Women at Work – A Report on the Problem of Sexual Harassment on the Member States of the European Communities*, Office for Official Publications of the European Communities, Luxembourg.

Rubery, Jill, Fagan, Colette and Grimshaw, Damian (1993) *Wage Determination and Sex Segregation in Employment in the European Community – Summary,*

Equal pay, 36 Years Later – In Search of Excellence, Brussels, 25–26 October, Belgian presidency of the European Community.

Rubin, Gayle (1975) 'The Traffic in Women: Notes on the Political Economy of Sex', in Reiter, R. (ed.), 157–210.

Ruostetsaari, Ilkka (1992) *Vallan ytimessä: Tutkimus suomalaisesta valtaeliitistä*, Gaudeamus, Helsinki.

Saarikangas, Kirsi (1993) *Model Houses for Model Families. Gender, Ideology and the Modern Dwelling. The Type-Planned Houses of the 1940s in Finland*, SHS, Helsinki.

Saarinen, Aino (1987) 'Naisten poliittinen kulttuuri ja kamppailu äänioikeudesta – Taustaa ja kysymyksen asetteluja', *Politiikka*, 29 (1), 3–13.

Salmi, Minna (1991) *Ansiotyö kotona – toiveuni vai painajainen? Kotiansiotyö Suomessa työntekijän arkipäivän kannalta*, Tutkimuksia 225, Helsingin yliopisto, Sosiologian laitos, Helsinki.

Salmi, Minna (1995) 'Finland is Another World – The Gendered Time of Homework', in Boris, E. and Prugl, E. (eds) (forthcoming).

Sargent, Lydia (ed.) (1981) *Women and Revolution: A Discussion of the Unhappy Marriage of Marxism and Feminism*, South End Press, Boston.

Savage, Mike and Witz, Anne (eds) (1992) *Gender and Bureaucracy*, Blackwell, Oxford.

Scarbrough, Harry and Corbett, J. Martin (1992) *Technology and Organization: Power, Meaning and Design*, Routledge, London and New York.

Schelhowe, Heidi (1993) 'Gender Symbolism and Changes in Lifeworld Through Information Technology', *AI & Society*, 7 (4), 358–67.

Schneble, Andrea and Domsch, Michel (1989) *Sexuelle Belästigung von Frauen am Arbeitsplatz – Eine Bestandsaufnahme zur Problematik, Bezogen auf den hamburger Öffentlichen Dienst*, Leitstelle Gleichstellung der Frau, Hamburg.

Schunter-Kleeman, Suzanne (1992) 'Wohlfahrtsstaat und Patriachat – Ein Vergleich europäischer Länder', in Schunter-Kleeman, Suzanne (ed.), *Herrenhaus Europa – Geschlechterverhältnisse im Wohlfahrtsstaat*, Edition Sigma, Berlin, 141–328.

Schön, Donald (1987) *Educating the Reflective Practitioners*, Jossey-Bass, San Francisco.

Scott, Joan W. (1988a) *Gender and the Politics of History*, Columbia University Press, New York.

Scott, Joan W. (1988b) 'Deconstructing Equality-Versus-Difference or, the Uses of Poststructuralist Theory of Feminism', *Feminist Studies*, 14 (1), 33–50.

Showstack Sassoon, Anne (ed.) (1987) *Women and the State – The Shifting Boundaries of Public and Private*, Hutchinson, London.

Sigurardóttir, Erla (ed.) (1992) *Työn vaativuus palkkaperusteeksi*, Nord 19, Pohjoismaiden ministerineuvosto.

Sihvo, Tuire and Uusitalo, Hannu (1995) 'Economic Crisis and Support for the Welfare State in Finland 1975–1993', *Acta Sociologica*, 38 (3), 251–62.

Silius, Harriet (1992) *Den kringgärdade kvinnligheten*, Åbo Academy Press, Åbo.

Simmel, Georg (1984) *On Women, Sexuality and Love*, Yale University Press, New Haven, Conn.

Simonen, Leila (1991) *Feminist Social Policy in Finland: Contradictions of Municipal Homemaking*, Avebury, Aldershot.

Simpson, Richard L. and Simpson, Ida Harper (eds) (1988) *Research in the Sociology of Work – A Research Annual*, High Tech Work Vol. 4, JAI Press, London.

210   *References*

Sinkkonen, Sirkka and Haavio-Mannila, Elina (1980) 'Naisliikkeen heijastuminen kansanedustajien lainsäädäntötoiminnassa: Mies- ja naiskansanedustajien 1907–1977 valtiopäivillä tekemien aloitteiden vertailu', *Politiikka*, 22 (2), 101–17.

Smith, Dorothy (1987) *The Everyday World as Problematic: A Feminist Sociology*, Northeastern University Press, Boston.

Smith, Dorothy E. (1990a) *The Conceptual Practices of Power. A Feminist Sociology of Knowledge*, Northeastern University Press, Boston.

Smith, Dorothy E. (1990b) *Texts, Facts and Femininity – Exploring the Relations of Ruling*, Routledge, London.

Sorrentino, Constance (1990) 'The Changing Family in International Perspective', *Monthly Labour Review*, March, 41–58.

Sosioekonomisen aseman luokitus (1989) Tilastokeskus, Käsikirjoja 17, Helsinki.

Spender, Dale (1993) 'Electronic Scholarship – Perform or Perish?', in Taylor, H.J., Kramarae, C. and Ebben, M. (eds), 28–43.

Steinberg, Ronnie (1992) 'Gendered Instructions – Cultural Lag and Gender Bias in the Hay System of Job Evaluation', *Work and Occupations*, 19 (4), 387–423.

Strandell, Harriet (1984) 'Kolmen naissukupolven kokemuksia työstä ja perheestä', in Haavio-Mannila, Elina, Jallinoja, Riitta and Strandell, Harriet, 203–94.

Suchman, Lucy A. (1994) 'Located Accountability – Aspects of a Practice of Technology Production', in Eberhart, T. and Wächter, C. (eds), 124–31.

Sulkunen, Irma (1990) 'The Mobilisation of Women and the Birth of Civil Society', in Manninen, M. and Setälä, P. (eds), 42–54.

Suomalainen perhe (1994) Väestö 1994:5, Tilastokeskus, Helsinki.

Sørensen, Bjørg-Aase (1982) 'Ansvarsrationalitet: Om mal-middeltekning blant kvinner', in Holter, H. (ed.), 378–96.

Sørensen, Helene (1990) *Fysik og kemi undervisningen i folkskolen – set i pigeperspektiv*, Kemisk og Fysisk Institut, Danmarks Lærerhøgskole, København.

Sørensen, Rønnaug (1992) 'Det går på verdigheten løs!', in Brantsæter, M.C. and Widerberg, K. (eds), 51–75.

Tancred, Peta (1995) 'Women's Work – A Challenge to the Sociology of Work', *Gender, Work, and Organization*, 2 (1), 11–20.

Taylor, H. Jeanie, Kramarae, Cheris and Ebben, Maureen (eds) (1993) *Women, Information Technology and Scholarship*, Center for Advanced Study, Urbana, Illinois.

Therborn, Göran (1995) *European Modernity and Beyond: The Trajectory of European Societies 1945–2000*, Sage Publications, London–Thousand Oaks, Calif.–New Delhi.

Tijdens, Kea (1994) 'Behind the Screens – The Foreseen and Unforeseen Impact of Computerization on Female Office Workers' Jobs', in Eberhart, T. and Wächter, C. (eds), 132–9.

Tijdens, Kea, Jennings, Mary, Wagner, Ina and Weggelaar, Margaret (eds) (1989) *Women, Work and Computerization: Forming New Alliances*, North-Holland, Amsterdam.

Tikkanen, Märta (1986) *Punahilkka*, WSOY, Juva.

Truckenbrod, Joan (1993) 'Women and the Social Construction of the Computing Culture – Evolving New Forms of Computing', *AI & Society*, 7 (4), 345–57.

Työvoimatilasto 1992 (1993) Työmarkkinat 1993:17, Tilastokeskus, Helsinki.

Tyyskä, Vappu (1995) *The Women's Movement and the Welfare State: Child Care Policy in Canada and Finland, 1960–1990*. Suomalaisen tiedeakatemian toimituksia B 277, Helsinki.

Ungerson, Clare (ed.) (1990a) *Gender and Caring – Work and Welfare in Britain and Scandinavia*, Harvester Wheatsheaf, New York.

Ungerson, Clare (1990b) 'The Language of Care: Crossing the Boundaries', in Ungerson, C. (ed.), 8–33.

United Nations (1987) *Recommendations for the 1990 Censuses of Population and Housing in the ECE Region*, Statistical Standards and Studies No. 40, New York.

United Nations (1995) *Platform for Action: Report of the Main Committee*, Fourth World Conference on Women, Beijing, China, 4–15 September.

US Merit Systems Protection Board (1981) *Sexual Harassment in the Federal Workplace – Is it a Problem?*, US Government Printing Office, Washington, DC.

Varsa, Hannele (ed.) (1993a) *Shaping Structural Change in Finland – The Role of Women*, Equality Publications Series B: Report 2, Ministry of Social Affairs and Health, Helsinki.

Varsa, Hannele (1993b) *Sukupuolinen häirintä ja ahdistelu työelämässä – näkymättömälle nimi*, Tasa-arvojulkaisuja sarja A: Tutkimuksia 1, Sosiaali- ja terveysministeriö, Helsinki.

Vedel, Gitte (1984) *Just Pick up a Telephone! Remote Office Work in Sweden*, The Copenhagen School of Economics and Business Administration, Information Systems Research Group, Copenhagen.

Vehviläinen, Marja (1991) *Social Construction of Information Systems – An Office Worker's Standpoint*, University of Tampere, Tampere (unpublished).

Vehviläinen, Marja (1994a) 'Living through the Boundaries of Information Systems Expertise – A Work History of a Finnish Woman Systems Developer', in Adam, A. et al. (eds), 107–20.

Vehviläinen, Marja (1994b) 'Reading Computing Professionals' Codes of Ethics – A Standpoint of Finnish Office Workers', in Gunnarsson, E. and Trojer, L. (eds), 145–61.

Vehviläinen, Marja (1994c) 'Women Defining Their Information Technology – Struggles for Textual Subjectivity in Office Workers' Study Circle', *European Journal of Women's Studies*, 1 (1), 71–91.

Waerness, Kari (1984) 'The Rationality of Caring', *Economic and Industrial Democracy*, 5 (2), 185–211.

Wagner, Ina (1994) 'Hard Times, The Politics of Women's Work in Computerised Environments', in Adam, A. et al. (eds), 23–34.

Wajcman, Judy (1991) *Feminism Confronts Technology*, Polity Press, Cambridge.

Walby, Sylvia (1986) *Patriarchy at Work – Patriarchal and Capitalist Relations in Employment*, Polity Press, Cambridge.

Walby, Sylvia (1990) *Theorizing Patriarchy*, Oxford, Blackwell.

Webster, Juliet (1993) 'From the Word Processor to the Micro – Gender Issues in the Development of Information Technology in the Office', in Green, E., Owen, J. and Pain, D. (eds), 111–23.

Webster, Juliet (1994) 'Gender and Technology at Work – 15 Years On', in Adam, A. et al. (eds), 311–24.

West, Candace and Zimmerman, Don H. (1987) 'Doing Gender', *Gender & Society*, 1 (2), 125–51.

Whyte, Judith (1986) *Girls into Science and Technology – The Story of a Project*, Routledge & Kegan Paul, London.

Widerberg, Karin (1992) 'Vi og dem – et spørsmål om metode?', in Brantsæter, M.C. and Widerberg, K. (eds), 44–51.

Wilkinson, F. (ed.) (1981) *The Dynamics of Labour Market Segmentation*, Academic Press, London.

Wise, Sue and Stanley, Liz (1987) *Georgie Porgie – Sexual Harassment in Everyday Life*, Pandora, London.

Wittig, Michele A. and Lowe, Rosemary H. (1989) 'Comparable Worth Theory and Policy', *Journal of Social Issues*, 45 (4), 1–21.

Wittig, Michele A. and Turner, Gillian (1988) 'Implementing Comparable Worth – Some Measurement and Conceptual Issues in Job Evaluation', in Kelly, R.M. and Bayes, J. (eds), 143–8.

Witz, Anne and Savage, Mike (1992) 'The gender of organisations', in Savage, Mike and Witz, Anne (eds), 3–62.

Women and Men in the Nordic Countries: Facts and Figures 1994 (1994) Nord 1994:3, Nordic Council of Ministers, Copenhagen.

Zeitlin, Maurice (ed.) (1980) *Political Power and Social Theory*, Vol. 1, JAI Press, Greenwich, Conn.

Zuboff, Shoshana (1988) *In the Age of the Smart Machine: The Future of Work and Power*, Basic Books, New York.

Index

213

GENDERED PRACTICES IN WORKING LIFE

This book is to be returned on
or before the date stamped below

UNIVERSITY OF PLYMOUTH

PLYMOUTH LIBRARY

Tel: (01752) 232323
This book is subject to recall if required by another reader
Books may be renewed by phone
CHARGES WILL BE MADE FOR OVERDUE BOOKS